Mastering SQL Server™ 2000 Security

Mastering SQL Server™ 2000 Security

Mike Young
Curtis W.Young

Gearhead Press™

Wiley Publishing, Inc.

Publisher: Robert Ipsen
Editor: Ben Ryan
Consulting Editor: Donis Marshall
Managing Editor: Angela Smith
New Media Editor: Brian Snapp
Text Design & Composition: Wiley Composition Services

Designations used by companies to distinguish their products are often claimed as trademarks. In all instances where Wiley Publishing, Inc., is aware of a claim, the product names appear in initial capital or all capital letters. Readers, however, should contact the appropriate companies for more complete information regarding trademarks and registration.

This book is printed on acid-free paper. ∞

This publication is designed to provide accurate and authoritative information in regard to the subject matter covered. It is sold with the understanding that the publisher is not engaged in professional services. If professional advice or other expert assistance is required, the services of a competent professional person should be sought.

The Gearhead Press trademark is the exclusive property of Gearhead Group Corporation.

Library of Congress Cataloging-in-Publication Data:

ISBN: 0-471-21970-3

Wiley also publishes its books in a variety of electronic formats. Some content that appears in print may not be available in electronic versions. For more information about Wiley products, visit our web site at www.wiley.com.
Printed in the United States of America.

10 9 8 7 6 5 4 3 2 1

A Note from Gearhead Press

Gearhead Press is dedicated to publishing technical books for experienced Information Technology professionals—network engineers, developers, system administrators, and others—who need to update their skills, learn how to use technology more effectively, or simply want a quality reference to the latest technology. Gearhead Press emerged from my experience with professional trainers of engineers and developers: people who truly understand first-hand the needs of working professionals. Gearhead Press authors are the crème de la crème of industry trainers, working at the companies that define the technology revolution. For this reason, Gearhead Press authors are regularly in the trenches with the developers and engineers that have changed the world through innovative products. Drawing from this experience in IT training, our books deliver superior technical content with a unique perspective that is based on real-world experience.

Now, as an imprint of Wiley Publishing, Inc., Gearhead Press will continue to bring you, the reader, the level of quality that Wiley has delivered consistently for nearly 200 years.

Thank you.

Donis Marshall
Founder, Gearhead Press
Consulting Editor, Wiley Publishing, Inc.

Gearhead Press Books in Print

(For complete information about current and upcoming titles, go to www .wiley.com/compbooks)

Books in the Gearhead Press *Point to Point* Series
Migrating to Microsoft Exchange 2000 by Stan Reimer
ISBN: 0-471-06116-6

Installing and Configuring Web Servers Using Apache by Melanie Hoag
ISBN: 0-471-07155-2

VoiceXML: 10 Projects to Voice Enable Your Website by Mark Miller
ISBN: 0-471-20737-3

Books in the Gearhead Press *In the Trenches* Series
Windows 2000 Automated Deployment by Ted Malone and Rolly Perraux
ISBN: 0-471-06114-X

Robust Linux: Assuring High Availability by Iain Campbell
ISBN: 0-471-07040-8

Programming Directory Services for Windows 2000 by Donis Marshall
ISBN: 0-471-15216-1

Programming ADO.NET by Richard Hundhausen and Steven Borg
ISBN: 0-471-20187-1

Designing .NET Web Services Using ADO.NET and XML by Richard Hundhausen and Steven Borg
ISBN: 0-471-20186-3

Making Win32 Applications Mobile: Porting to Windows CE by Nancy Nicolaisen
ISBN: 0-471-21618-6

Programming Windows CE Wireless Applications by Barry Shilmover and Derek Ball
ISBN: 0-471-21469-8

Mastering SQL Server 2002 Security by Mike Young and Curtis Young
ISBN: 0-471-21970-3

Microsoft.NET Security Programming by Donis Marshall
ISBN: 0-471-22285-2

Contents

Acknowledgments

This book was only made possible by the dedication and patience of several individuals. First has been the work of J.W. Olsen as editor. Jerry has been very patient and informative as we struggled to learn the nuances of writing and publishing this book. He has also made up for our lack of writing skills to help us create a book worthy of publishing. We would also like to acknowledge and thank the entire staff at Gearhead Press and Wiley Publishing, Inc., particularly Donis Marshall, for giving us the support necessary to get this book off the ground.

Finally and most importantly, we want to acknowledge the employees of Softouch, who have had to put up with our constant discussions pertaining to this publication. Without their support and ability to fill in where necessary, this book would never have become a reality.

Introduction

Over the past several years I have developed an interest in security and the protection of data. Several tools and books are available that introduce security, but there is no comprehensive SQL Server security manual. This book is written out of a desire to see that type of a reference available to all administrators and developers of SQL Server.

As a reader of this book, your feedback is highly useful. If you have any suggestions or have had personal experiences that are not addressed by this book, I would appreciate your comments to help ensure that I can include them in an updated version. Any comments or suggestions can be sent to Mike@softouchtraining.com.

Throughout this book you will be introduced to the security concerns related to SQL Server. In working with the product over the years, I have come to realize that managing security is as much about what you can't do as it is about what you can do. You need to know the features and the limitations of the product. Through an understanding of the limitations, you can account for these items in some other manner. SQL Server security, if designed and implemented correctly, is easy to manage and troubleshoot.

Overview of This Book and Technology

Microsoft SQL Server 2000 is continuing to grow in market share. Microsoft has positioned it as a robust, fast, easy-to-use relational database management system. Because SQL Server is easy to install and configure, several third-party software development companies have chosen it as their back-end database. Because of this growth in market share, many organizations have the need to support SQL Server. Security is a constant area of concern.

Many organizations have made the decision to use SQL Server as their primary database management system. Organizations that have made this choice need to design a security strategy that can be applied somewhat consistently throughout their organization. It is also imperative that all SQL Server administrators and developers be on the same page pertaining to security implementation. Increased communication can help decrease troubleshooting time and frustration related to SQL Server security. A solid security design coupled with effective communication will result in less overhead of administration of SQL Server. This book has been written to lay out the design issues involved with SQL Server. You can take the suggestions and combine them with your internal political structure to create a solution that works for you.

Many other organizations have to support SQL Server even though it is not the primary database management system. This occurs when you purchase or develop an application that requires SQL Server as the database. Often, the security in this described environment is more complicated. This is because the application you purchased has already made most of the security decisions for you. It is your responsibility to support the application and troubleshoot the security concerns as they arise. This book provides information for individuals who have to occasionally support SQL Server.

As the market for SQL Server continues to grow, so do the requirements for educated individuals. As organizations move more data to SQL Server, the security concerns become increasingly important. In past versions many organizations have hesitated to store mission-critical data in SQL Server. Because Microsoft has overcome most of the scalability and robustness concerns, many organizations are overcoming their hesitations. As more mission-critical data is ported to SQL Server, an added emphasis should be placed on understanding SQL Server security. Then the understanding needs to be applied and supported.

As a consultant I have spent many hours with organizations trying to outline a consistent security design for SQL Server. I have yet to find a complete resource on the security considerations and configuration for SQL Server. I have written this book to provide that reference.

How This Book Is Organized

This book is organized in a modular format. It does not necessarily need to be read in the order in which it is presented. The book is divided into parts to categorize the main subjects. The book is written in five parts, which consist of the following items:

Part I: System Security Design. This part provides an overview of the book as well as an introduction into the security design of SQL Server. SQL Server security can be easy to implement and support, but it depends on a solid design. Many organizations fail to create a security design and the applications that are implemented do not follow a consistent security strategy. Inconsistent security approaches increase the overhead related to administering SQL Server security. This part outlines the necessary requirements for a solid security design and approach to SQL Server.

Part II: Security Management Fundamentals. This part introduces the basics of SQL Server security. The main topics covered include initial installation security issues, creating and managing logins, and managing object permissions. For experienced SQL Server users, this section is a review. This section introduces SQL Server security to those who are not proficient with the basic security parameters.

Part III: Application Development Security Concerns. This section is primarily for application developers. It outlines the application security design issues. Many applications are designed and created before security is considered. This part outlines the application security design issues and then moves to security considerations for the application developer. This includes a description of how to implement various security options from the front-end application. This part also introduces the security concerns related to multitier development.

Part IV: Data Management Security. After the design and initial configuration are out of the way, many of the day-to-day security issues are tackled in this part. This part of the book is beneficial to administrators who support SQL Server on a daily basis. This part focuses on the SQL Server Agent service and its security considerations. This part also addresses replication, data transformation services (DTS), distributed data security, and Analysis Server. Each of these facets of SQL Server has its own security considerations.

Part V: Managing Current SQL Server Activity. This final part of the book first focuses on your options for managing the current connections to SQL Server. The main item of concern in this part of the book is auditing. The SQL Server options for creating and managing an audit policy are described. This part also includes information about managing connections from the Internet.

The rest of this section identifies the chapters that make up this book. Chapter 4, "Establishing Login Security," is key to a large portion of the book. You will need to understand the role of logins and connections to perform most of the security suggestions throughout the remaining chapters. Additionally, Chapter 9, "Introducing the SQL Server Agent Service," is very important. The SQL Server Agent service and its associated security concerns are the core of many of the troubleshooting areas related to SQL Server security. It is strongly recommended that you become familiar with the information provided in these two chapters.

Chapter 1: Introducing SQL Server Security. This chapter introduces the chapters that are to follow. After reading this chapter, you should have an idea of the information contained in the rest of the book.

Chapter 2: Designing a Successful Security Model. This chapter may be the most important one of the book. A solid security design is key to keeping SQL Server administrative costs down. This chapter outlines the role of development, test, and production servers. Along with the server strategies, you will be introduced to several security fundamentals, such as creating all objects with an ownership of DBO. These fundamentals should be discussed and determined before the applications are deployed and running. Security should be part of the application design. The information in this chapter should be used to create an organization model for SQL Server security. This information should then be made available to all administrators and developers of SQL Server. It is important that all SQL administrative staff work from the same security goals and design.

Chapter 3: Exploring Initial Security Parameters. This chapter outlines the security necessary for installing and configuring SQL Server. It also describes the tools supplied with SQL Server and the security parameters for each of them.

Chapter 4: Establishing Login Security.   The primary goal of this chapter is to outline the purpose of a login in the security model of SQL Server. You are introduced to the various options for creating logins and how these logins relate to database users and roles. This chapter is key in laying the foundation for most of the chapters that are to come. This chapter describes the differences between Windows Authentication and SQL Server Authentication. This fundamental security principle is used and referenced throughout the book.

Chapter 5: Managing Object Security.   The permission architecture of SQL Server is described in this chapter. After reading this chapter, you will understand the implementation of permissions in SQL Server. You are introduced to the GRANT, REVOKE, and DENY permissions.

Chapter 6: Designing Application Security.   This is an important chapter if you are designing applications. You can take the suggestions provided and implement secure application architecture with SQL Server. An emphasis of this chapter is the role of stored procedures in security. This chapter also introduces application roles and describes how they can be used to isolate your application from other applications to increase the security infrastructure of SQL Server.

Chapter 7: Implementing Front-End Application Security.   This chapter details the security options when creating the front-end application. When creating an application that connects to SQL Server, the security credentials that are used for the connection are key. This chapter details your options for making that connection. Examples are provided of trusted and standard connections to SQL Server.

Chapter 8:   Understanding Microsoft's Enterprise Development Strategy. Interest in Microsoft's Enterprise Development strategy has grown over the last couple of years. This chapter first describes the strategy and then addresses the security concerns related to multitier development. This chapter is beneficial to developers who are charged with developing applications that need to scale with the organization.

Chapter 9: Introducing the SQL Server Agent Service.   In this key chapter, many of the security concerns related to SQL Server are associated with SQL Server Agent Service. This chapter describes the role of that service. The interaction with Exchange Server for e-mail is detailed. A good portion of this chapter describes the role of replication in SQL Server. The security considerations with SQL Server replication are defined along with preferred methods of configuration. This chapter is a must for all SQL Server administrators.

Chapter 10: Managing Distributed Data Security.   The need for distributing data continues to grow. This chapter introduces linked server, log shipping, and Federated Database Servers. All of these features can be used to interact with data stored on multiple servers. As you look for a distributed data strategy, you can use this chapter to identify the feature that you should be using to decide the best strategy. As you implement any one of these features, security becomes an immediate concern. When you are dealing with data that is spread across multiple databases, consistency becomes a key component. If the security models of the databases involved differ, the troubleshooting of failed actions increases in complexity. The intricacies of each server or database must be taken into account when deciding on a solution.

Chapter 11: Managing Data Transformation Services.   Data Transformation Services (DTS) have grown to be one of the most useful features of SQL Server. These services are used to move data from one location to another as well as perform administrative tasks in SQL Server, such as backing up the database or sending an e-mail notification. Because DTS is so vast, the security options within the DTS packages can become very complex. This chapter outlines the security options within a DTS package. This chapter is a must for any administrator or developer who is trying to transfer or transform data using DTS. After reading this chapter, you will have tools to securely set up DTS packages and troubleshoot security-related issues in DTS.

Chapter 12: Exploring Analysis Services.   Analysis Services are shipped with SQL Server, but are installed and configured as a separate application. Because they are isolated, they have a completely separate security model. In fact, the security model used for Analysis Services is not related to the SQL Server security model. If you implement the Analysis Services, this chapter will help identify your security considerations. It is suggested that you understand the security concerns before you install and configure Analysis Server to ensure you have a secure data model.

Chapter 13: Managing Current Connections.   This chapter first outlines the role of the transaction log in SQL Server security. This chapter identifies the things you *can't* accomplish with this product. This is important to appropriately set expectations and determine whether you need a third-party product to assist with security administration. This chapter also identifies your options available from the Current Activity Window of SQL Server. You will learn how to look at the current connections and kill the connections if you wish.

Chapter 14: Creating an Audit Policy.   This chapter is highly critical for many organizations. You will need to feel comfortable with your internal auditing requirements to fully understand this chapter. The purpose of this chapter is to present several options for auditing. These options range from the very basic to the more complex. You should only implement the level of auditing that you require for tracking purposes. Every additional level of auditing could decrease performance. This chapter is very beneficial for organizations that have specific auditing concerns and requirements.

Chapter 15: Managing Internet Security.   Recently, there has been an increased push to make data available over the Internet. With firewalls, proxy servers, and Secure Socket Layer (SSL) available, the connection over the Internet is somewhat more complex than a local connection. This chapter outlines the issues related to connections over firewalls and proxy servers. This chapter also outlines the process of configuring your SQL Server for SSL. Additionally, the code for making the connections from several current technologies (ASP.NET and JDBC) is provided.

Appendix A: XML for SQL Server 2000.   This appendix outlines the role of XML in the storage and retrieval of data with SQL Server 2000. It is provided as an extension to Chapter 15, "Managing Internet Security." You will be introduced to the purpose for XML storage and retrieval in SQL Server and the configuration of integration of SQL Server and Internet Information Server to support XML.

Appendix B: Third-Party SQL Server Security Management Tools. SQL Server ships with most of the tools you will need to manage the security of SQL Server, but this appendix introduces a couple of additional tools you may want to consider. The first is an auditing tool, which can decrease the overhead of creating an audit policy. The second type of tool is a log analyzer. This section of the appendix is used to extend Chapter 13, "Managing Current Connections." The transaction log of a SQL Server database can't be viewed without a third-party utility. If you need to undo (rollback) a transaction that has already been written to the log, you have to perform a database restore, which can result in a significant amount of lost data. A log analyzer allows you to look at your transaction log files (active or backed up) and roll back individual transactions. This feature allows for security management after the work has already been committed to the transaction log.

Appendix C: Answers to Review Questions. Each chapter of this book has a set of review questions to test your knowledge of the information provided. This appendix is a reference point to check your answers.

Who Should Read This Book

This book is a combination of administration and programming concerns. Security in SQL Server is a responsibility of the administrator as well as the developer. One of the primary concerns of this book is communication between the two sides of the fence. Oftentimes, security issues arise because of poor communication between the two parties. This book is a must for all database administrators. As a DBA, security is a primary responsibility, and this book provides the background necessary for a DBA to function in the security administration role. The DBA should read the entire book and be thoroughly familiar with the security aspects of all chapters.

Additionally; this book is a good read for a SQL Server developer. The developer should understand the organizational security model as well as the connection and security information necessary to work within the model. It is also beneficial for every developer to understand the security administration of the DBA. It is through this understanding that effective communication can be achieved. Part III, "Application Development Security Concerns," is the key section of the book for developers. The other sections are beneficial from an introductory standpoint.

Before reading this book, you as the reader should be somewhat comfortable with the basic administrative tasks of SQL Server. You should be comfortable using both Enterprise Manager and Query Analyzer. If you are reading this book for the development section, you should have a good understanding of your development tool. The examples in this book primarily use VB.NET and ASP.NET. If you use another tool, you will need to be comfortable with its syntax. The book moves from the basic topics to the more complex, so an understanding of the SQL Server security model is not required before reading this book.

This book is the complete handbook for security management with SQL Server 2000. After reading it, you will feel confident about accomplishing the security tasks required of you as they relate to SQL Server. This book provides a foundation that, when applied with your organizational standards and requirements, can decrease administrative overhead of SQL Server. Security is a large concern for many organizations; use this book to make it manageable.

Tools You Will Need

To effectively perform the tasks for the examples in this book, you should have access to a SQL Server. You will also need to have access to Analysis Server to complete the exercises for Chapter 12, "Exploring Analysis Services Security." If you don't have access to Analysis Server, Chapter 12 is the only chapter you will not be able to fully complete. Additionally you should have the following client applications installed on your machine:

VB.NET. The examples provided are specific to VB.NET. If you have an older version of Visual Basic on your machine, most of the exercises will work exactly the same. If you don't have a version of Visual Basic, you may not be able to perform the code examples supplied through the development chapters. You will be limited to reading the code that is supplied.

SQL Server Enterprise Manager. Most of the step-by-step procedures of the book are performed from Enterprise Manager. You should have some limited experience with Enterprise Manager.

SQL Server Query Analyzer. Every step-by-step procedure has a way to perform the action using Transact-SQL. You can perform the action from Query Analyzer. To complete all of the exercises from Query Analyzer, you should have a solid background with Transact-SQL.

SQL Server Books Online. Throughout this book, many technologies are introduced. They are often introduced for the purpose of getting to the security concerns. SQL Server Books Online is referenced throughout the book to remind you that you can get more information about a given topic

Lumigent Log Explorer. This tool is needed for Appendix B, "Third-Party SQL Server Security Management Tools." As mentioned in the appendix, this tool can be downloaded as a free trial version from www.lumigent.com. This tool is used to view the Transaction Log Files of a SQL Server database.

OmniAudit.   OmniAudit is also needed for Appendix B, "Third-Party SQL Server Security Management Tools." This is a tool used to simplify the auditing process of SQL Server. Krell Technologies developed this product. A trial version can be downloaded at www.krell-software.com.

The Remaining SQL Server client tools.   The Client Network Utility and Server Network Utility are used a couple of times throughout the book. They are installed by default when you install other SQL Server tools: Enterprise Manager and Query Analyzer.

Optionally, you could have a JAVA development tool to do the couple of code examples for JDBC. This is a very limited portion of the book.

Summary

This book provides a solid foundation for you to base your SQL Server security infrastructure. You should evaluate the needs of your organization and compare them with the options and strategies supplied by this book. This will allow you to create a security infrastructure that is securely controlled, easy to administer, and quick to troubleshoot. The goal of this book is to decrease your administration related to security and help make your job, as a DBA or a developer, a little easier.

About the Authors

Mike Young is the co-founder of Softouch Inc. Mike has spent the last several years teaching, consulting, and developing training materials about Microsoft products. Mike has spent the majority of his time over the years supporting and consulting about Microsoft SQL Server. He has a background in database administration and is concerned that his clients meet their expectations for the product. Mike's primary areas of expertise are Data Transformation Services (DTS), Analysis Server, and all areas related to security.

Curtis W. Young is the other co-founder of Softouch Inc. Curtis has a deep love for training and education. Curtis' background is on the programming side. He has taught and consulted regarding Visual Basic, Visual Interdev, Visual C++, and Java. Curtis has spent a significant amount of time designing and developing applications that use SQL Server as the back-end database. He receives the most satisfaction from providing systems solutions to business obstacles.

CHAPTER

Introducing SQL Server Security

Microsoft SQL Server has continued to grow in market share over the last several years. Many factors have contributed to this growth. Software development companies have chosen Microsoft SQL Server for their data storage, SQL Server is easy install and to maintain, and SQL Server integrates seamlessly with Internet applications. Consequently, organizations are using SQL Server 2000, and in many cases this results in database administrators supporting SQL Server systems before they have a good understanding of the product and its feature set.

SQL Server Security is easily misunderstood and often implemented inefficiently. This chapter introduces the main topics that are addressed throughout the rest of the book. After reading it, you will understand the core components of SQL Server security. This chapter addresses the following topics:

- Security overview
- Installation security
- Application security
- Distributed data management
- Auditing

Security Overview

The administration of security for Microsoft SQL Server, if designed correctly, should be low maintenance. As with most aspects of a solid database, system design is the key. Security management will be minimal if ample time is spent in the design phase. The design phase is typically used to design the database and the application architecture before the application is developed.

Security should be a primary consideration in the overall design, but often security is an afterthought. As a result the cost of maintenance related to security administration can increase. Effective database design is the key to successful application deployment and maintenance.

Many existing systems are purchased from an outside vendor, inherited from another developer or development team, or created before security was completely understood. When security is an afterthought, it can easily become overwhelming and a point of frustration for any database administrator (DBA).

This book answers the questions you may have developed while supporting the SQL Server security model; it is designed to give you a better understanding of your SQL Server system security. Although security may affect every aspect of your system or application, it is necessary to break security down into four main areas as follows:

1. Analyzing requirements

2. Providing access to SQL Server

3. Accessing the databases on a SQL Server instance

4. Providing permissions to objects in a SQL Server database

Once these areas are accounted for, it is essential to document your security fundamentals. Documentation will give you as a DBA a point of reference and help ensure that everyone is on the same page. The document should be detailed in nature and should outline the goal of your database system as it relates to each of these four areas.

Requirements Analysis

The first key to designing a security solution is understanding your organizational business needs. You need to be clear on the following items to implement security effectively:

- The critical nature of the data
- The auditing requirements that exist
- Who will administer the server

These issues are discussed separately in the sections that follow.

The Critical Nature of the Data

Different databases may have completely different security expectations. It is important to answer a couple of questions related to the database and its business requirement related to its data. First, what user access is required for the data? Second, how much data can you afford to lose?

What User Access Is Required for the Data?

In addressing the first question you can determine the level of complexity of your security design and permissions management. It is important to evaluate the cost of administration versus security requirements. The cost of security implementation and administration increases as the security requirements increase. The recommendations made by this book may be more complex than required by your business process. First analyze the data access requirements. You should proceed to SQL Server security design only after you are clear on the requirements of the client's access to your data.

How Much Data Can You Afford to Lose?

Obviously, nobody wants to lose any data, but the amount of data that you can afford to lose varies per application. You must analyze how mission-critical the data is. Is it acceptable to back up the data every evening and if data loss occurs during the day restore to the previous day? In some cases the answer is yes, while in other cases the answer is no. You need to determine how much data you can afford to lose. After this question is answered, you then know how stringent your security design has to be. As the amount of data you can afford to lose decreases, your permissions management and security design become more complex and critical. Details of application security design will be addressed in Chapter 6, "Designing Application Security."

Auditing Requirements

It may be necessary to track certain events within SQL Server or the application that is accessing SQL Server. When analyzing requirements, it is necessary to determine which events must be audited. As these events are chosen, it is generally a good idea to categorize them by priority. At a minimum you should separate the auditing requirements that must be met for the application to be deployed versus the events that it would be nice to audit. After the events are categorized, it is then possible to determine which auditing requirements must be accounted for in system design and which events can be discarded if the design becomes too complex or the cost of administration becomes too great.

Determining the auditing requirements is a combination of understanding SQL Server and understanding the business policies surrounding the application at hand. Through an understanding of SQL Server you will know the system-related events that should be accounted for. To complete the process of determining the audit requirements, it is also necessary to outline the business requirements that affect the application. For instance, internal audit procedures may define some standards for minimum event auditing. It is important to be clear on the events that need to be audited before the remaining portion of security and system design continues. If they are not accounted for, audit requirements could come back to haunt you. After the application is designed and implemented, it may be much more difficult to implement auditing strategies because many of the auditing strategies affect the overall database design. Auditing will be addressed fully in Chapter 14, "Creating an Audit Policy."

Who Will Administer the Server?

It is normal for a single organization to have multiple instances of SQL Server installed. Some of these instances may reside on the same physical server, while others may be installed on separate machines. Determining who has the responsibility for server administration is critical to creating a security infrastructure. Chapter 2, "Designing a Successful Security Model," addresses the roles of different servers (development, test, and production) and the administrative access to each.

It is generally a good idea to minimize the number of system administrators for any single instance of SQL Server. Typically, as the number of system administrators decreases, the individual accountability goes up. Not only is it easier to track who is responsible for a given action; tracking makes it more likely that the action will be accomplished. It is important to document the individuals who will be administering each server. This documentation should then be distributed throughout the organization. Every person in the organization who is affected by SQL Server should be clear about who is responsible for administration. This awareness will result in increased efficiency of support and a decreased risk of operational failure.

Be clear on who will perform what actions and when these actions will be performed.

Business politics should be considered. Is database administration the role of the application developer or of the members of the IT support staff? In reality, the database administrator is somewhere in the middle. The DBA should be an individual who understands Windows 2000 and SQL Server 2000 from an administrative standpoint. This individual should also be knowledgeable in Transact-SQL and the schematics of the databases implemented. The more knowledge the DBA has about the applications implemented, the easier troubleshooting database problems will be.

After the lines of accountability are drawn, document the results of the decision. Make the document available to anyone who needs to interact with SQL Server. When everyone within the organization is on the same mental security page, security management is simplified.

Access to SQL Server

A DBA can allow access to SQL Server through Windows Authentication or SQL Server Authentication. A user's access to SQL Server is provided through a login. The login is either granted from an existing Windows account (Windows Authentication) or created as a SQL Server login with no link to an operating system account. Both alternatives are discussed in the sections that follow.

Your ability to support each of these security alternatives for authentication is determined by the security mode you choose. The supported modes in Microsoft SQL Server 2000 are Windows Authentication mode and Mixed mode. Windows Authentication mode allows only Windows Authentication, while Mixed mode supports both levels of authentication. Microsoft SQL Server 2000 does not support a SQL Server-only mode. This doesn't mean, however, that all Windows users will have access to SQL Server. Chapter 4, "Establishing Login Security," explains more about each of these security modes. Chapter 4 also gives suggestions on implementing a security model, which does not include any Windows logins. The default mode on installation of a SQL Server instance is Windows Authentication. The mode can be changed during installation or anytime thereafter.

Windows Authentication

Windows Authentication is generally preferred because it provides an optimal level of integration with Windows 2000. User and group accounts from Windows are granted or denied access to SQL Server. Windows 2000 authenticates the user when the user logs on to the network. Because the password is authenticated at network login, SQL Server does not need to know or verify the password of a user. Windows Authentication provides the following advantages over SQL Server Authentication:

- Windows Authentication can grant group accounts access to SQL Server, thus minimizing the overhead of login administration.
- Users are authenticated by Windows 2000, resulting in a secure authentication over the network.
- Users could be able to use the same user credentials for network and database access.
- Audited events can be tracked to a network user.

SQL Server Authentication

SQL Server Authentication is preferred in the following scenarios:

- The user is not logging in to a Windows domain.
- The Windows domain is unavailable.
- Your network does not have a Windows 2000 domain.
- It is not feasible to manage all Internet users on the Windows domain. You prefer to manage them separately from your normal Windows domain administration.
- An application is acquired from a vendor that requires SQL Server Authentication.

NOTE When an application is purchased from a vendor, a security mode is already chosen. Before making any changes to the security mode, consult with the vendor to find out if there will be any consequences if you do so. These consequences could include invalid connection parameters for database access, failed audit policies, and violation of support contracts.

When creating a SQL login, the DBA must supply both a username and a password for each individual who needs access to SQL Server. These credentials are managed in SQL Server and have no ties to the operating system user account. When the user accesses SQL Server, the username and password are sent in clear text (unless both the client and the server are implementing secure sockets layer, SSL) across the network. By default the SQL logins do not have any restrictions on passwords and have no password policies in place.

Accessing Databases on a SQL Server 2000 Instance

After you have created a means for connectivity to SQL Server, it is necessary to devise the strategy by which logins will access the databases on your server. Each SQL Server instance will have multiple databases. The following system databases exist on each instance of SQL Server:

- The master database contains all server-level configuration. All logins, references to databases, and server configuration are stored in this database. Regardless of the data in any individual database, this database is the most critical to your system's functioning properly.

- The MSDB database stores all information related to SQL Server Automation. All scheduled jobs, system alerts, and operators designed to notify users of events are stored in this database. Losing this database will not prevent access to the database; it will just stop all automated processes.

- The model database is used as a template for all newly created databases. It is minimal in size, and any objects you want included in all future databases should be added here.

- The TempDB contains all temporary tables and stored procedures. It is also used to fill other temporary storage needs such as work tables needed by SQL Server.

- Pubs and Northwind are sample databases that are used to test SQL Server. They are not critical to the system.

In addition to these databases, you have the user databases needed for your organization's applications. Each database must have a user account for each individual accessing the database. This user account is the individual's identification while using the database. By default, the username on the database will match the login name on SQL Server. Although it is possible to have a database user with a name that is different from the login name, it is suggested that you keep the names consistent. This consistency can help reduce confusion with user and login administration.

Users can then be placed into roles at the database level. A role is similar to a group in Windows 2000. A role is a means of grouping a set of users to minimize the overhead of permissions management. As a DBA, you will need to determine the extent to which you plan on using roles. For instance, if you are granting Windows 2000 groups access to SQL Server, the users are already grouped and there may not be a huge need for roles. On the other hand, if you are using Mixed mode and most of the logins you create are SQL Server logins, you may be heavily dependent on roles to help with permissions management.

Additionally, SQL Server provides a set of predefined *fixed database roles*. These roles have a set of permissions that can't be altered. You should evaluate these roles to see if the set of permissions granted to a fixed role is applicable to your design. Predefined roles are a method of reducing the overhead of managing roles and permissions.

Permissions to Objects in a SQL Server Database

Permissions management can be a nightmare if your system is not designed correctly. The permissions architecture of SQL Server is different from that of most other database management systems. Many DBAs try to implement the permissions strategies they have learned from another system, which is not a good idea with SQL Server. Your permissions management should start at the time when the system and application are designed and should be planned from a Microsoft SQL Server perspective. A couple of issues are critical as permissions are implemented: First is object ownership, and second is object dependencies.

Object Ownership

Objects in SQL Server are the database pieces that work together to provide the functionality of a relational database management system. Typically, objects are created within a database, and the different database objects are used for different purposes. More information about each type of object can be found in SQL Server Books Online. Following are the database objects in SQL Server:

- Tables
- Views
- Stored procedures
- Indexes
- User-defined functions
- Rules
- Defaults
- User-defined data types

When an object is created within a SQL Server database it is given a four-part name. The name takes the following structure:

Server.database.owner.object

The server part of the name defaults to the current server. The database piece of the name defaults to the current database, and the owner defaults to the user who is creating the object. If the user is part of the system administrator (sysadmin) role, which is explained in detail in Chapter 4, "Establishing Login Security," the object owner will be the database owner (DBO). If the user is defined in any other context, the object owner will be the individual's database username. The final piece is the common name that represents the object. This is the piece that has no default value and must be supplied. This is the last part of the four-part name and is the piece that will be typically used when referring to the object.

It is imperative that all objects created within a database have the same owner. The owner should be the DBO user account. If object ownership is the same for all objects, SQL Server checks only the user permissions on the objects the user interacts with directly. SQL Server checks a referenced object's permissions only when the owner is different from the owner of the object that references it. If the DBO is the owner of the objects, then the name is automatically resolved for all users. Then the user does not have to specify the owner in the path to the object. If the owner is someone other than the DBO, the name is resolved only for that user. All other users will have to include the owner part of the object name when using the object. This is one of the best methods for tying down access to your database tables. Stored procedures can be created that insert, update, and delete data in your tables. As long as the owner of the Stored procedure and the table is the same, the user can be given execute permissions to the stored procedure without having any access permission to the table. If the DBO owns all objects, permissions management can be clean and easy. Chapter 5, "Managing Object Security," goes into more detail on this process of permissions management. Chapter 5 also gives examples of how to change object ownership if your database doesn't comply with these standards.

Object Dependencies

Many objects in a SQL Server database depend on other objects in the database. For instance, a view is a *select* statement that is retrieving data from another view or table. A stored procedure is a SQL statement that is performing some action on a table or view.

Different permissions can be granted to each type of object. In an optimal world, the tables in your database may not need to have any permission set on them. But as part of your database design, you should know the objects that your users have to interact with and the dependencies each of these objects has. This information should be diagrammed and initially reviewed to see where appropriate changes could be made.

Installation Security

One of the first areas of concern in installing SQL Server is security. What permissions do you need to install? Did I set SQL Server up right in the first place? Can I change any parameters now that I have it installed? These are common questions that a database administrator can ask related to security before or immediately after installation. In this section you are first introduced to the permissions required to perform the installation. The section then describes the security options that are available during the installation process. Finally, we describe the services that are added during the installation process.

Installation Permissions

Installing Microsoft SQL Server is not a difficult process. In fact many people perform the installation without really understanding the questions they are answering. It is possible to install multiple instances of SQL Server on a single machine. This capability is new to SQL Server 2000. Following is a list of reasons you may choose to install multiple instances of SQL Server on the same physical machine:

Separate services.   Each instance will run its own SQL Server and Agent services. Thus stopping the service on one instance will not affect the services of another instance.

Separate security.   Each instance maintains separate security parameters. An individual could be a system administrator for one instance and have no access to another.

Separate purposes.   Many organizations would like to have a test environment, to simulate production. This may not have occurred in the past due to the overhead of multiple servers. (More details on the configuration of development, test, and production servers will be addressed in Chapter 2, "Designing a Successful Security Model.")

Whether you are installing the first instance or an additional instance of SQL Server, you will need the same permissions. Local administrator permissions are required to install an instance of SQL Server on a machine. The SQL Server installation will add files to the hard drive, settings to the Registry, and services to Windows 2000. If you are not a local administrator, the process will fail very quickly.

NOTE If you are installing an additional instance on a machine that is already running SQL Server, you will have to stop all running instances of SQL Server, so it may not be feasible to perform subsequent installations during prime business hours.

Installation Parameters

A couple of the settings determined during installation affect the overall security of your system. It is essential that you understand the ramifications of these choices before you do the installation. All of the parameters can be changed at a later time, although doing so may require that some services be restarted. During installation two key pages will prompt you for security information.

The first screen related to security is shown in Figure 1.1. You are asked to supply a Windows user account that the SQL Server and SQL Agent services will use when the services start. This account is commonly referred to as the *service account*. The default account, used for the service account, is the account you are currently logged on with. You will want to change this to a *dedicated domain account* that is not your Windows login. If you allow your personal account to remain the default account, when you perform maintenance to your account (password change), you will be affecting SQL Server, and the services may not start correctly.

The account used here should be a domain account, and all instances of SQL Server should use the same userID. The account defined here will be used by these services when starting. This is the feature that allows the services to start and be fully functioning without the server being logged on. The security context of these accounts will also be used for much of the server-to-server authentication, which has to occur for processes such as replication multiserver jobs. More information about this account is addressed in Chapter 3, "Exploring Initial Security Parameters."

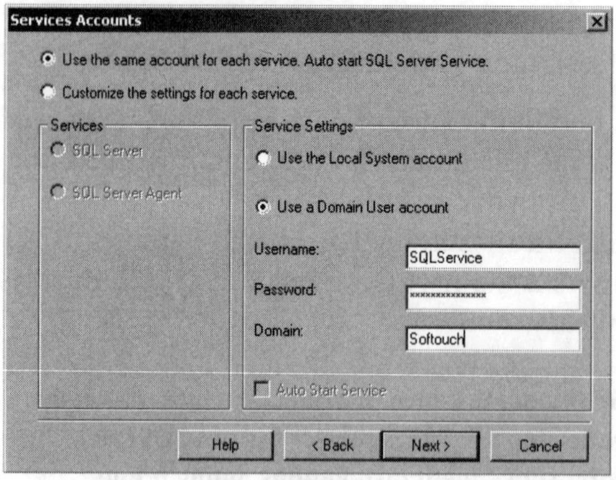

Figure 1.1 During installation, you are prompted for the SQL service account.

The second option of concern is related to authentication modes as shown in Figure 1.2. By default, Windows Authentication mode is selected. You can optionally change this to Mixed mode. In this screen you will notice a reference to the Server Authentication (SA) account. The SA account is a built-in account that has access to every function and option in SQL Server. When you select Mixed mode during the installation, you are prompted for a password for the SA account. If you want the password to be blank, you need to select the checkbox indicating you want a blank SA password. While choosing a blank password is convenient in a training lab or during initial testing, it should never be done in a production environment.

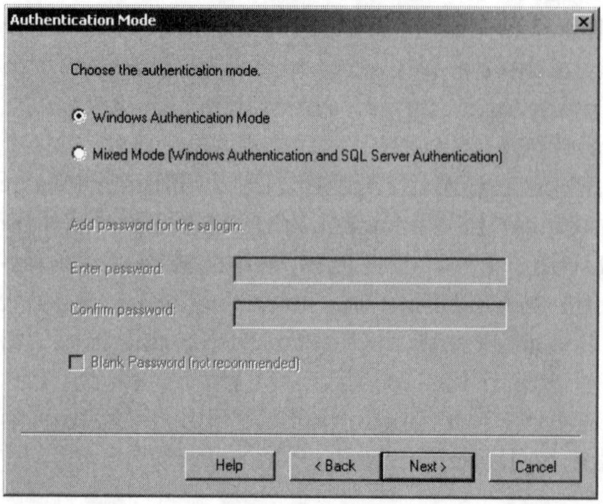

Figure 1.2 Authentication mode can be modified during installation.

Initial Services

After the installation is complete you will notice several services added to SQL Server. Although some of these services do not directly affect security, it is necessary to understand each of them in depth to understand the security analysis and recommendations of the coming chapters. The services added are as follows:

SQL Server Service (MSSQLServer).   The SQL Server service manages the databases owned by an instance of SQL Server. It is the component that processes all Transact-SQL statements sent from client applications. The SQL Server service allocates computer resources between multiple users. It also enforces business rules defined in stored procedures and triggers, ensures the consistency of the data, and prevents concurrency issues.

SQL Server Agent Service (SQLServerAgent).   The SQL Server Agent service handles the automation of administrative tasks. Jobs, operators, and alerts are components of the SQL Server Agent service that provide the automation features. The SQL Server Agent service will be explained more completely in Chapter 9, "Introducing the SQL Server Agent Service."

Microsoft Distributed Transaction Coordinator (MS DTC) Service. This service is a transaction manager that allows client applications to include several different sources of data in one transaction. It coordinates committing the distributed transaction across all the servers enlisted in the transaction.

Microsoft Search Service.   The Microsoft Search service provides a full-text query engine, enhancing the querying capabilities of the database to include proximity and full text searches that are not supported natively to ANSI-92 SQL. For more details on the Microsoft Search service, see the SQL Server Books Online.

When multiple instances of SQL Server are run on the same computer, each instance has its own SQL Server service and SQL Server Agent service. The service name for the default instance is MSSQLServer, and the service name for named instances is MSSQL$InstanceName. Likewise, the default instance names the SQL Server Agent Service SQLServerAgent; all subsequent instances are named SQLAgent$InstanceName.

Because each instance has its own services, each service has to be configured with a service account. The security of the service account has to be maintained for all instances and services of SQL Server. Note that you can decrease your overhead of managing multiple instances by ensuring that all of the services for each instance use the same domain account for the service account.

Application Security Overview

Users do not access Microsoft SQL Server directly; instead they use a front-end application created with data access mechanisms to access the data from SQL Server. This application could be a utility that comes with SQL Server, a third-party application that runs on SQL Server, or an in-house application. SQL Server can also be accessed through COM or Microsoft ActiveX components. As a developer, when you are designing the application, you need to take into account the following considerations as far as security is concerned:

- Interfacing with SQL Server
- Application security design
- Front-end application security parameters
- Three-tier architecture

Interfacing with SQL Server

Applications are developed to interface with SQL Server through a database application programming interface (API). A database API contains two parts:

- The language statements passed to the database. The language used with SQL Server is referred to as Transact-SQL. Transact-SQL supports all SQL-92 entry-level SQL statements and many additional SQL-92 features. It also supports the ODBC extensions to SQL-92 and other extensions specific to Transact-SQL. This is Microsoft's implementation of the Structured Query Language (SQL) for SQL Server.
- A set of functions or object-oriented interfaces used to send the language statements to the database server and process the results returned by the database server.

Application Programming Interfaces

Native API support defines the API function calls that are mapped directly to the network protocol sent to the database server. No translation to another API is needed. SQL Server provides native support for two classes of database APIs:

OLE DB.   SQL Server includes a native OLE DB provider. The provider supports applications written using OLE DB or other APIs that use OLE DB, such as ActiveX Data Objects (ADO).

ODBC.   SQL Server includes a native ODBC driver. The driver supports applications or components written using ODBC or other APIs that depend on ODBC, such as DAO, RDO, and the Microsoft Foundation Classes (MFC) database classes.

An example of nonnative support for an API would be a database that does not have an OLE DB provider but does have an ODBC driver, such as Informix. An OLE DB application could use the OLE DB provider for ODBC to connect to the Informix database through its ODBC driver. This provider maps the OLE DB API function calls from the application to ODBC function calls it sends to the ODBC driver. This allows you to use ADO, which is normally available through OLE DB, to access an ODBC data source. From the front end, developers can use the same data access methods regardless of the provider or driver that is available on their machine.

SQL Server also supports:

DB-Library.   DB-Library is an earlier API specific to SQL Server. SQL Server supports DB-Library applications written in either C or through a component known as VBSQL. Existing DB-Library applications developed against earlier versions of SQL Server can be run against SQL Server 2000, but the new features of SQL Server 2000 are not available to these applications.

Embedded SQL.   SQL Server includes a C precompiler for the Embedded SQL API. Embedded SQL applications use the DB-Library Dynamic Link Library (DLL) to access SQL Server.

The Microsoft OLE DB Provider for SQL Server, the SQL Server ODBC driver, and DB-Library are each implemented as a DLL that communicates to SQL Server through a component called a client Net-Library. Each of these providers is configured with connection information. It is through these providers that you supply security credentials from the front-end application to the database management system. It is possible through most of these providers to use the existing Windows credentials. In some cases, with certain ODBC drivers, you can't pass the Windows credentials and will have to use SQL Authentication.

Client Net-Libraries and Authentication

SQL Server 2000 clients use an enabled client Net-Library to communicate with a server Net-Library on a SQL Server 2000 instance. To support the desired network protocol, a matching pair of Net-Libraries must be active on the client and server computers. TCP/IP sockets and Named Pipes are the default client Net-Libraries for computers running Windows NT 4.0 or Windows 2000.

In most environments, you will not need to modify client Net-Library settings. On the client computer, use the SQL Server Client Network Utility to enable additional or different Net-Libraries, configure custom connection properties for each Net-Library, and specify the order in which the system will attempt to use each enabled Net-Library. More information on client and server Net-Libraries will be addressed in Chapter 7, "Implementing Front-End Application Security."

Application Design with Security in Mind

As the application is being designed, it is important to account for the current server security model. For instance, if Windows Authentication is the primary method for your organization to access SQL Server, it is not practical for you to write an application that is dependent on an SQL login to the server. The first step is being clear on the items stated in the preceding *Security Overview* section. As a developer, the system administration of the server, specifically security configuration, affects the method in which you should develop the application.

The next area to address is the interaction with the data stored in your database tables. If the ownership of all the objects is the same, SQL Server has to check permissions only on the objects with which the users are requesting interaction. If clients do not directly interact with your tables, the tables do not need to have any permissions set on them. Avoiding table-level permissions should be a goal of your application design. You can accomplish this by using the following logical database objects:

- Views
- Stored procedures
- Application roles

Views

A *view* is a virtual table whose contents are defined by a query. The query can use a single table, another view, or multiple tables as its data source.

Like a real table, a view consists of a set of named columns and rows of data. But a view does not exist as a stored set of data values in a database. The columns and rows displayed to the user can be restricted by the query used to access the data. The view does not contain any data itself; it is a look at the data that exists in your tables.

A view can act as a filter to the underlying data in your tables. Distributed queries can also be used to define views that use data from multiple heterogeneous sources. By acting as a filter, the view can restrict user access to a set of columns or rows in a table, which can be helpful in protecting sensitive data. Views should typically be used as a security mechanism for supporting ad hoc query environments.

Although views are a beneficial security measure, they degrade performance because they require running an additional query with each access of the data. Because the view is a query, it has to be executed each time the view is requested. If your environment is not an ad hoc query scenario, stored procedures will typically provide better performance and security options than views will.

Stored Procedures

When you use Transact-SQL statements, two methods are available for storing and executing the statements against the database server. You can store the statements locally and create application code that sends the statement to SQL Server and processes the results, or you can store the programs as a stored procedure in SQL Server. The applications you create will then execute the stored procedures to get the intended results.

Stored procedures in SQL Server are similar to procedures in other programming languages in that they can:

- Accept parameters from the user and return values as output parameters to the procedure or batch
- Contain programming statements that perform modifications against the database
- Call other procedures
- Return a status value indicating success or failure (and possibly the reason for failure)

You use the *execute* statement to run a stored procedure. Stored procedures provide the following benefits:

- They allow modular programming.
- You can create the procedure once, store it in the database, and execute it any number of times in your applications. Stored procedures can be created and modified independent of the source code.

- They allow faster execution.

- If the operation requires a large amount of Transact-SQL code or is performed repetitively, stored procedures can be faster than batches of Transact-SQL code. Stored procedures are parsed and optimized when they are first run, and an in-memory version of the procedure can be used after the procedure is executed the first time.

- They can be used as a security mechanism. Users can be granted permission to execute a stored procedure even if they do not have permission to execute the procedure's statements directly. As long as the object ownership is the same, users do not need to have permissions to the table a stored procedure is referencing.

Application Roles

You may want users to be restricted to accessing data only through a specific application without the ability to access data directly. This will close the door to their using Microsoft Access or Excel to access the data directly. As the Microsoft Office products continue to add features, direct access to SQL Server is becoming easier. You may not want users connecting to your data from an application such as Microsoft Access and Excel. If the users have permissions to the data, they will have the permission from all applications they use to connect to SQL Server. Application roles can be used to prevent a user from connecting to SQL Server using an application such as Access and executing a poorly written query, which will negatively affect the performance of the whole server.

SQL Server accommodates this situation through the use of application roles. Application roles have the following characteristics:

- Application roles contain no members. Users, Microsoft Windows NT groups, and roles cannot be added to application roles; the permissions of the application role are gained when the application role is activated for the user's connection through a specific application or applications. A user's association with an application role is due to being capable of running an application that activates the role, rather than being a member of the role.

- The application role is set by executing the *sp_setapprole* stored procedure, which is executed within the code of the application. Therefore the security context is limited only to the application and not to a specific user.

Front-End Application Security

A front-end application, or presentation layer, uses an API to send commands to a database:

- A C database API is a set of C functions an application calls to connect to a database and pass commands to the database.

- An object database API uses an object model consisting of objects, properties, and interfaces an application calls to connect to a database and pass commands to the database.

Commands sent to Microsoft SQL Server through the database API must comply with Transact-SQL. Transact-SQL complies with the entry level of the SQL-92 standard but also supports many more features of SQL-92, including some of the powerful extensions to the SQL-92 standard. The SQL Server OLE DB provider and SQL Server ODBC driver also support the ODBC SQL specification. For more information on ODBC and OLE DB, refer to Chapter 7, "Implementing Front-End Application Security."

It is important for the application developer to interact with the database in a manner that complies with organizational standards. The application needs to be designed around the server security architecture. For example, when possible, the developer should connect to the SQL Server using Windows Authentication. This will allow the entire system to take advantage of the advantages of Windows Authentication. The system administrator must understand the SQL Server security model. It is equally important that the application developer understand the security model. This will help ensure consistency throughout the organization.

Distributed Data Management

The need for centralizing and reusing data continues to increase. Many organizations are struggling with the task of finding efficient methods of reusing and centralizing data storage. However, distributing data is common. In many cases, organizations transfer the data to multiple servers and database platforms so the data can be accessed with other data that is related. It may make more sense, in certain cases, to leave the data in a single location and access it from multiple different locations. The data is centralized, but each application now accesses data that exists on multiple servers.

As an administrator you are walking a fine line as to what should be distributed to multiple locations and what should stay local for each application to come and get. This section describes the options you have for distributing data to multiple servers as well as the options available to access data that resides on another server. Both of these should be evaluated with your current data distribution needs in mind.

As data is distributed across multiple servers, a user or an application may interact with data from multiple data sources. Data may be distributed for a number of reasons, including:

- Getting data closer to the users who need it
- Integrating dissimilar systems (Oracle, Access, Sybase, and so forth)
- Separating transaction processing and analytical processing
- Developing transactions that are dependent on data from multiple sources

Microsoft SQL Server 2000 is the industry leader in providing distributed data solutions. SQL Server includes features to import and export data, replicate data, access data on another server, and analyze data in a summarized fashion. You can use as many of these features as required for your data solution.

As the solution you choose is implemented, a solid security approach is necessary to prevent an increased cost of administration. Because each of the solutions available for distributed data involves multiple servers, you need to account for the security model on each server involved in the strategy. If you know the current security settings for each server, you will be able to design a solution that meets your needs, and account for any possible permissions restrictions.

This section describes the following SQL Server features and their primary security concern:

- Data Transformation Services (DTS)
- Linked servers (support for distributed transactions)
- Replication
- Analysis services (separation of transaction and analytical processing)

Data Transformation Services

Microsoft Data Transformation Services (DTS) packages can be easily created to move data from one location to another. Two primary tools are provided to help with the creation of packages. First you are provided the import and export wizard. This is a very simple tool that will allow you,

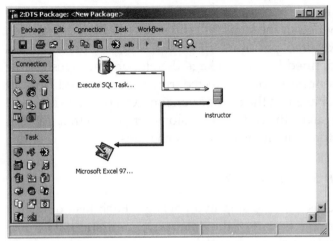

Figure 1.3   Data Transformation Services packages are displayed in the Data Transformation Services designer.

through a series of questions, to move data from one source to another destination. This is optimal when your needs are simple and you have a single source and destination. Your second tool for creating packages is the DTS designer. A sample package from the DTS designer is shown in Figure 1.3.

> **NOTE**   It is beneficial for many organizations to centralize data to assist with the decision-making process. Their existing data may be stored in a variety of formats and at differing sources. Data Transformation Services (DTS) provides a set of tools that lets you extract, transform, and consolidate data from multiple sources into single or multiple destinations. You can graphically build DTS packages or you can program a package with the DTS tools. You can also create custom data movement solutions tailored to the needs of your organization.

Packages

A DTS package is a collection of connections, tasks, transforms, and workflow constraints assembled together. This package can then be executed with a single command. The packages can be saved to Microsoft SQL Server, SQL Server 2000 Meta Data Services, a structured storage file, or a Microsoft Visual Basic file.

Each package contains one or more steps that are within a workflow. The workflow determines whether the steps will run sequentially or in parallel. The package when executed performs all of the connections and tasks within the workflow defined by the package developer. Packages can be modified, owner and user password protected, run as a scheduled job, and retrieved and modified based on the change version. As a package is edited and saved, SQL Server saves the different versions for you so that you can retrieve the version before you made a series of changes.

Data Transformation Services Task

A DTS task is executed as a single step in a package. Each task defines a work item to be performed as part of the data movement and data transformation process, or as a job to be executed.

Data Transformation Services supplies a number of tasks that are part of the DTS object model and can be accessed graphically through DTS designer. These tasks cover a wide variety of data copying, transformation, and notification situations. For example, DTS tasks can include the following:

Importing data.   Data can be imported from a text file or an OLE DB data source (for example, a Microsoft Access 2000 database) into SQL Server.

Transforming data.   The format or content of the data can be modified to meet the current database constraints and consistency requirements.

Copying database objects.   Database objects can be copied to and from other instances of SQL Server. Transferring indexes, views, logins, stored procedures, triggers, rules, defaults, constraints, and user-defined data types in addition to the data is possible with DTS. In addition, you can generate the scripts to copy the database objects.

Backing up the database.   The database can be backed up on completion or dropping and re-creating indexes.

Performing operating system tasks.   This can include .bat, .cmd, or .exe files.

Scripting files.   Scripting files can be used to interact with files, automate operating system tasks, or perform logical evaluation of data.

Data Transformation Services Security Concerns

Each task within a package has connection security requirements. For DTS to connect to the data sources and destinations it has to have security credentials supplied. Additionally as each package is saved it can be stored with an owner and/or a user password. The owner password will need to be supplied for the package to be modified. The user password is required for package execution.

In many cases packages will also be automated as a SQL job, and each job has an owner. The job owner will determine the security context in which the package is run. In general, it is easier to have all jobs owned by system administrators, although doing so may not be feasible in all cases. Chapter 9, "Introducing the SQL Server Agent Service," and Chapter 11, "Managing Data Transformation Services," cover this issue in much more detail.

All of these factors need to be evaluated as you use DTS to move data. It is essential that you are clear on the tasks that need to be performed. The design of your DTS packages is the most critical phase. Once you have a solid data transformation design, you should analyze the security at each step in the process. Security is often the piece that goes unaccounted for and can result in a failed package at production run time. Other security issues related to DTS will be addressed more thoroughly in Chapter 11, "Managing Data Transformation Services."

Linked Servers

Microsoft SQL Server 2000 supports distributed transactions through the Microsoft Distributed Transaction Coordinator (DTC) service. A *transaction* is defined as a unit of work that succeeds or fails as a whole. This can include multiple data manipulation statements (*insert, update,* and *delete*). A transaction will treat them as one unit and commit them as a whole or roll them back as a whole. You are guaranteed all of the steps are successful for the transaction to commit. A *distributed transaction* is then defined as a transaction where all of the statements are not run against the same server. The need for linked servers is increasing as organizations are striving to reuse as much data as possible. For example, it is common for many organizations to have data stored on another platform, as in a mainframe database. With linked servers you can connect to the database and access the data using Transact-SQL statements from SQL Server. You could have a single transaction that updates data on your SQL Server and your mainframe database.

Microsoft SQL Server 2000 allows for the creation of continuous links to other data sources for which you have a corresponding OLE DB database provider. After setting up a linked server through an OLE DB provider it is possible to do the following:

- Reference row sets from the OLE DB data sources in the from clause of a Transact-SQL statements.

- Create pass-through queries to allow the overhead for the *transact-sql* statement to run on the other data source

- Create distributed transactions to guarantee transactional consistency across multiple data sources

SQL Server 2000 supports OLE DB providers to set up linked servers to other instances of SQL Server or other databases such as:

- Sybase

- Access

- Oracle

- DB2

A user will typically execute a distributed transaction through a stored procedure or *transact-sql* statement that executes on one server. The server that is executing the statement will then connect through the linked server parameters to the other server on behalf of the user. The security context used to connect to the second server can take several different shapes. The two most common are impersonating the user and specifying a remote user. Impersonating the user passes the user's current login credentials to the other server for authentication. The account has to exist on both servers for this option to work. The remote server option allows the user's security context to be changed to a specific user on the other machine. The security options are shown in Figure 1.4.

NOTE Impersonating a user will not work with Windows Authentication unless Security Account Delegation has been set up. Security Account Delegation is addressed In Chapter 4, "Establishing Login Security."

Replication

Microsoft SQL Server replication is a method of copying and distributing data and objects from one database to another. The second step of the process is then synchronizing between the databases involved in replication for data consistency.

By using replication, you can distribute data to multiple locations with a low cost of administration. Replication can be used to enhance application performance, physically separate data based on a set of criteria, or help distribute the load of processing across multiple servers.

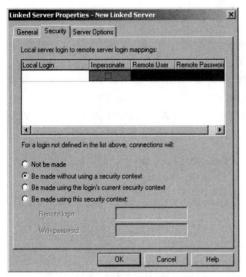

Figure 1.4   Linked server security options are mapped in this dialogue box.

Benefits of Replication

Replication offers various benefits depending on the type of replication implemented, but the common benefit of SQL Server 2000 replication is making the data available in close proximity to the users who need to access it. Other benefits include:

- Allowing multiple sites to keep copies of the same data is useful when multiple sites need to read the same data or need separate servers for reporting applications.

- If separating online analytical processing (OLTP) applications from read-intensive applications such as online analytical processing (OLAP) databases, data marts, or data warehouses is a primary need, you may want to consider OLAP services.

- Increasing read performance for the client.

- Using replication as part of a standby server strategy. Other choices for using SQL Server 2000 as a standby server include log shipping and failover clustering, which provide copies of data in case of server failure.

When to Use Replication

With organizations supporting diverse hardware and software applications in distributed environments, it may be beneficial to store data redundantly. With differing applications, replication should be used when data needs to be continuously updated from one source to another.

Replication is a solution for a distributed data environment when you need to:

- Copy and distribute data to one or more sites on a continuous basis. If the copy is only occasional you should consider DTS.

- Allow multiple users and sites to make changes and then merge the data modifications.

- Build Web applications where users can browse or add a large amount of data. You can have two servers, which users interact with, that replicate each other to create a single database for browsing.

Security Concerns with Replication

Replication can be a powerful tool in enhancing your distributed data strategy. But much like the other options for distributing data, security concerns related to replication need to be analyzed.

There are two primary concerns with replication security. First is the security context of the SQL Server Agent service. All servers involved in transactional replication should be using the same domain user for the SQL Server Agent service. This account should be a local administrator on each of the machines running SQL Server. It is possible to have service accounts that are not a member of the local administrators group. This may be appropriate in certain cases, but it will prevent some of the features of SQL Server from working correctly. To learn more about the required security level of the service accounts, refer to Chapter 3, "Exploring Initial Security Parameters."

The second prime concern is the strategy in which data is moved. Horizontal and vertical partitioning are used to help prevent unwanted data from being made available to users. For instance, the central database at headquarters may keep track of transactions for four different regions. This data is then replicated to a server at each of the regions. If the needs of the application require regional users to have access to only their corresponding regional data, it is not prudent to replicate all of the data to that region.

Only replicate the data that needs to be available to the user. Minimize the overhead of replication and permissions management of data by setting up replication to optimize the data that is transferred.

Analysis Services

Analysis Services is provided with SQL Server 2000 and is the upgrade to the SQL Server 7.0 OLAP services, the primary function of Analysis Services. In fact, some of the most significant enhancements provided with SQL Server 2000 are found in the Analysis Services. The feature set of this technology has been enhanced to also include data mining. Data mining provides tools for enhanced decision-based analysis.

The need for Analysis Services has been driven by the desire to separate transactional processing from analytical processing. In an environment that doesn't take advantage of OLAP, transactions are usually performed on the same database tables as the analytical querying (statistical analysis, reporting, aggregations for financial analysis, and so forth). This analytical querying, in many cases, is very resource intensive and affects the overall performance of the database server. Users who need to be modifying the content of the table suffer in transactional performance.

To avoid this, many organizations have developed strategies to separate the two. Implementing Analysis Services as a separation strategy increases the overhead of hardware and software needed for implementation, while increasing analytical and transactional performance. Choosing to separate the processes also introduces a new application and set of services, which can increase the cost of administration. The benefit is increased performance for both transaction and analytical processing. Also users will have access to a data mining model. If implemented correctly, the data mining features will open the door to decision-making analysis tools that will make everyone's life easier. In most cases the benefit is worth the cost. You will need to test the technology to make the best decision for your organization. More information about this strategy can be found in Chapter 12, "Exploring Analysis Services Security."

Online Analytical Processing   OLAP

Data warehouses and data marts are the data stores for the analysis data. They are used as a repository for the data that was separated from the transaction processing systems. *Online analytical processing (OLAP)* is the technology that enables client applications to efficiently access this data, typically for reporting and analysis purposes. It provides many benefits to users, for example:

Allowing for the creation of cubes.   The cubes are multidimensional data objects that allow the users to access a specific cell within the cube. The cell is an intersection point of multiple dimensions. Figure 1.5 displays a cube from a data mart.

Querying with the multidimensional expressions (MDX) language. This supports keywords that help the user or developer identify the cells to retrieve.

Precalculating frequently queried data.   This allows for quick retrieval for the user. Aggregations do not have to be performed at user run time.

Storing options to separate the OLAP cubes from the traditional relational format.   This format allows the data to be easily stored and retrieved in multidimensional format.

Data Mining

Data mining, an exciting feature introduced as part of Microsoft SQL Server 2000 Analysis Services, provides tools for decision analysis by discovering patterns and rules in data and using them for predictive analysis, using industry standard data mining algorithms.

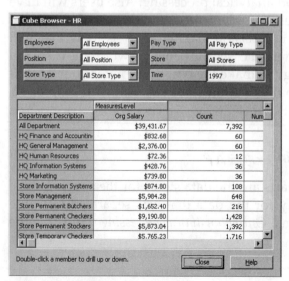

Figure 1.5 Analysis Manager displays cube data.

The primary mechanism for data mining is the data mining model, an abstract object that stores data mining information in a series of schema row sets. Data mining models are easily accessible with a variety of tools. You can use the Mining Model wizard to create data mining models, and you can use Data Mining Model Browser to display data mining model content in a graphical format. Data mining is explained in more detail in Chapter 12, "Exploring Analysis Services Security."

Analysis Services Security

Analysis Services security can be a confusing subject. Many things need to be taken into account when dealing with Analysis Services strategies. As with a relational database, the database administrator should have a solid security design before Analysis Services is implemented.

Because security related to Analysis Services is often misunderstood, the potential for security weaknesses is high. Some of the information stored in the multidimensional cubes could be critical to decision support analysis and should be treated with care. All of the security in Analysis Services is based on Windows Authentication, and the security model is very different from the normal SQL Server security model.

The first level of security concern is the user's authentication to the Analysis server. Roles can be created in the Analysis Manager (the primary administrative tool of Analysis Services). The roles are dependent on Windows 2000 or NT 4.0 user accounts. Authentication of these user accounts depends on the method with which the user is attempting to connect to the Analysis Server. Analysis Services supports both direct connections to the server (typically via Analysis Manager) or connections through the Pivot Table Service. The Pivot Table Service depends on HTTP, and therefore the authentication is based on Internet Information Server (IIS). The database administrator should be thoroughly comfortable with the current IIS authentication configuration. Internet Information Server authentication methods are addressed in much more detail in Chapter 12, "Exploring Analysis Services Security."

Because DTS is the core tool for maintenance of the OLAP data strategy, DTS security should also be thoroughly understood by the database administrator. More information on DTS security can be learned in Chapter 11, "Managing Data Transformation Services."

After users and groups are assigned to roles, permissions can be assigned to the role. The user gains access to the data based on the role or roles in which they are a member. Security can be defined at the database, cube, cell, and mining model levels. Additionally the database administrator can define both end-user and administrative security in the Analysis Manager tool.

Auditing

Auditing is a critical function to overall security analysis. Microsoft SQL Server has some built-in auditing functions, which can be taken advantage of. Your application should also be designed and created with auditing in mind. Some of the most successful audit trails are written into the front-end application that is accessing data from SQL Server. This section will be broken down into features provided within SQL Server for auditing and designing an audit trail within the application.

SQL Server Auditing

Microsoft SQL Server 2000 provides auditing as a way to trace and record activity that has taken place on each instance of SQL Server (for example, successful and failed logins). SQL Server 2000 also provides an interface, SQL Profiler, for managing audit records. Auditing can be enabled or modified only by members of the *sysadmin* fixed security role, and every modification of an audit is an auditable event.

There are two types of auditing:

- Default auditing provides some level of auditing but does not require the additional configuration and overhead of C2 auditing. It is presented as the auditing options within SQL Server. You don't need to do any configuration outside of Enterprise Manager and SQL Profiler. Default auditing is highly effective for managing logins and critical system events, but it lacks the details about each individual action that may be required by some applications. Additional auditing can be configured through C2 auditing or through the front-end application.

- C2 auditing requires specific procedures. The details for enabling and disabling C2 auditing will be described in Chapter 14, "Creating an Audit Policy." C2 auditing tracks C2 audit events and records them to a file in the \mssql\data directory for default instances of SQL Server 2000, or the \mssql$instancename\data directory for named instances of SQL Server 2000. If the file reaches a size limit of 200 megabytes (MB), C2 auditing will start a new file, close the old file, and write all new audit records to the new file. This process will continue until SQL Server is shut down or auditing is turned off.

In addition to the audit levels already mentioned, SQL Server also comes with SQL Profiler, which is a powerful assistant to auditing. *SQL Profiler* is a graphical SQL Server 2000 tool used to monitor (trace) selected SQL Server events and save the information to a table or file with a .trc filename extension for later analysis. For example, you can monitor stored procedures that are taking a long time to execute or events immediately preceding deadlocks. You can create traces and then replay them (in real time or step-by-step) on another computer running SQL Server (a test server) to debug performance and coding problems with Transact-SQL statements or stored procedures. Figure 1.6 is an example of an audit trace set up in SQL Profiler.

Audit logs can be used in SQL Profiler to automate the use of SQL Profiler auditing. Turning on SQL Profiler and tracing information can be costly in terms of the additional overhead of logging. Therefore SQL Profiler is generally suggested as a solid troubleshooting and auditing tool for server-level events. For individual actions on a single table, programmatically addressing auditing requirements within the application can usually reduce the audit trail overhead. Use SQL Profiler to audit the following events:

- End-user activity (all SQL commands, logout and login, and the enabling of application roles)

- DBA activity (grant, revoke, deny, and other security events)

- Security events (security statements, login, and user management)

- Utility events (backup/restore/bulk insert/BCP/DBCC commands

- Server events (shutdown, pause, and start)

- Audit events (add, modify, and stop audit)

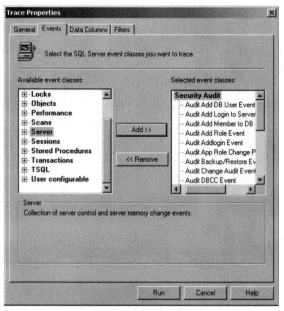

Figure 1.6 SQL Profiler audits SQL Server events.

Application Auditing

Auditing can additionally or alternatively be implemented within an individual application. Many third-party vendor applications extend the functionality of the auditing features of SQL Server by writing auditing procedures into the application. Application auditing requires that the application developer provide additional code to provide an audit trial. Typically, the additional auditing data is stored in the table structure of a SQL Server database.

In most cases application auditing is implemented first at the table level. In addition to the normal columns provided for a table, the developer would provide additional columns to store the userID of the individual performing modifications to the table. Every modification statement will then update the user information. Some applications use multiple columns to account for inserts, updates, and deletes separately. The front-end application will then usually provide an interface to view the information stored in the tables. The application administrators then easily have access to the user that performed the last modification statements.

When a user connects to a database and attempts to modify a data record, the developer can choose how the audit trail should be tracked. The changes can either overwrite the existing information with the username of the user who made the modification being stored, the old data could be moved to another SQL table that is used to store a history of changes, or the information about the change could be added to a text file on the operating system. This decision should be made based on the audit requirements of the application.

As with all auditing features, application auditing will take some overhead. Plan for some lost performance. This is an area where security requirements will affect the speed.

REVIEW QUESTIONS

1. Why is security critical to application design?

2. What are the advantages to Windows Authentication over SQL Server Authentication?

3. Why would you need to implement SQL logins?

4. What is the purpose of a role?

5. Who should own all database objects?

6. What are the advantages of using stored procedures?

7. Why would you use an application role?

8. What are Data Transformation Services (DTS)?

9. What are the primary concerns with replication security?

10. What is the SQL Profiler tool?

CHAPTER

Designing a Successful Security Model

Before you begin loading Windows 2000 and SQL Server, you should have a good idea how you want to design your SQL Server security system. By carefully designing your SQL Server security infrastructure, you can avoid spending costly administrative time troubleshooting or maintaining your security infrastructure. If you design your system efficiently and set up your infrastructure correctly, you will find that security is easy to maintain.

This chapter first outlines the role of the servers within your environment. The first section outlines the purpose of production, test, and development servers. Next the chapter breaks down two areas of concern related to the implementation of the servers within your network. The first area of concern is defining administrative roles. The chapter outlines the responsibilities of the DBA versus the responsibilities of the developer. These responsibilities have to be tied back to the production, test, and development server architecture. The second area of concern is the physical implementation, and this chapter first addresses different versions of Windows 2000 and SQL Server 2000. Along with the description of the product introduction, you will be given some decision-making criteria as to when to use one version over another. This discussion leads to issues related to deploying multiple instances of SQL Server on a single machine. Multiple instances on a single server can be used to isolate applications and help with security configuration.

Next the chapter describes the purpose of the application being deployed. This section compares an online transactional processsing (OLTP) system to a batch processing system and an online analytical processing (OLAP) system. The features of each type of system vary, and therefore your security design must reflect the system in use.

The chapter then moves into an evaluation of Windows clustering services and a specific description of configuring SQL Server 2000 in a clustered environment, which is the method of creating a fault-tolerant SQL Server solution. Although using a clustering service is not a direct reflection on your security configuration, it is certainly a method of securing the data that has been entered into your system. Clustering services can be used to protect your application data from hardware failures.

The chapter ends with a section on documentation. Documentation is key to successful deployment of SQL Server. All support staff, end users, and developers should have access to your security documentation. This documentation can then be used to make sure everyone is on the same page. By the end of this chapter you should have a clear set of documentation that defines the security infrastructure of your SQL Server model. This concise documentation is the key to making the architecture work for you. You will find it to be a valuable tool for training new employees, bringing contractors up to speed quickly, and refreshing your memory in the event that things get foggy or forgotten in the future.

Server Architecture

As an organization, you must first outline the number of servers you will be investing in SQL Server 2000 and how each of these servers should be configured. It is essential to describe the function of the various servers before you begin deploying applications. The names of the servers as well as the versions of the products they have installed should be planned out before the first server is set up.

It is also important that all information about the role of your servers be documented and readily available. As a new development team starts working with SQL Server, it is important to be able to hand team members documentation that details their development, test, and production machines. It is also beneficial to have an example of how current applications are working within the server architecture. Whenever you implement an application that doesn't fit into the organizational standards, you should explicitly document the exception.

In most cases, three levels of deployment and, therefore, three servers are suggested: the production server, the test server, and the development server. Although this may seem an expensive solution, it is best to ensure that all objects are created with the proper security context. The most important level to account for is that of the production server. This is the area where the work gets done and the applications get used.

It is also beneficial to have a test server. The test server should match the production server from a security configuration perspective. If test and production are set up with an identical security configuration, you decrease the chance of encountering security-related issues when you move the application from test to production.

if you also have a Dev server

The most important time in the life of an application is the stage at which it gets deployed to production. The last server level to account for is that of the development server. The development server is the server used by developers to create the databases and applications. The following sections further define the role of each of these servers as well as the role of the scripting options in SQL Server 2000.

The Production Server

Your production server is where the work gets done. An application should be fully developed and tested before it reaches this stage. This server should be set up with the logins necessary for the applications that are to be deployed. At this server the sysadmin role should contain only the database administrator (DBA) or team of administrators. It is not recommended that you set up database developers as system administrators on the production server. Although this may not be popular politically, it will probably promote system stability in the long run. On the production server it is best to decrease the number of individuals who are accountable for server tasks. As the number of individuals who are accountable decreases, the likelihood that the task will get accomplished increases. It is best to set up an environment that minimizes the amount of finger-pointing. When everyone is clear on the individuals who are responsible, the work tends to get done.

Applications can be deployed to production easily from the test server. Because the security models should be identical, the DBA can use any transformation option to move the data and application from the test server to the production server.

NOTE In some organizations, the developer of the application and the DBA are the same person. In these cases it is best to create separate accounts for development and administration, in order to prevent accidents.

Typically, your production server will be installed on Windows 2000 Server, Advanced Server, or Datacenter Server. You will then install either the Standard or Enterprise Edition of SQL Server 2000.

The Test Server

The test server should be set up to test the applications before they are deployed to production. This server should be set up with the same security settings as exist on the production server. The same individuals who are system administrators on the production server should be configured as system administrators on the test server. Job steps, as defined in Chapter 9, "Introducing the SQL Server Agent Service," run in the security context of the job owner, depending on whether that owner is a member of the system administrator role. The success of your scheduled tasks may depend on the test and production servers' maintaining identical security settings.

The same version of Windows 2000 and SQL Server 2000 should be installed on the test server and the production server. The machine doesn't need to have the same hardware specifications as the production server, unless you are planning on simulating load testing. In most cases the test server is used to verify functionality of the application and databases. All automated tasks and application functions should be examined at the test server before deployment to production.

NOTE If you use the different versions of SQL Server on the production and test servers, you may have different results when testing your applications. You should ensure that you use only the features that will be available on the production server.

The Development Server

The development server should be used for application and database development. This can be installed and configured as either a single server or it can be the Personal Edition installed on each of the developer's personal computers. In either case the developer will need to have more privileges than do users in test and production. If the developers are given system administrator role privileges on the development server, all of their objects will automatically be created for the DBO. This is the preferred method of creating objects. More information on object ownership issues can be found in Chapter 5, "Managing Object Security."

The development server can be the Developer Edition of SQL Server or the Personal Edition of SQL Server depending on your method of deployment. You should be careful to use the features that will be available on the production server. If you are using the Developer Edition of SQL Server for the development server, you will have access to all features of the Enterprise Edition of SQL Server. If your production server is only a Standard Edition of SQL Server, you should note the differences and use caution in your development. You would want to avoid features in the development server that are not available on the production server.

> **NOTE** If you will add developers to the sysadmin role on the development server, it will be beneficial to create an instance of SQL Server for each development team to help prevent the developers from making modifications that affect all other developers. More information on installing multiple instances of SQL Server can be found later in this chapter in the section *Multiple Instances of SQL Server*.

Scripts

You need a strategy for moving data between your three levels of deployment. A popular method of moving the objects is via Transact-SQL scripts. SQL Server has a built-in method for generating SQL scripts, which is beneficial if the developers are using Enterprise Manager to create their objects.

Issues can arise as you develop a strategy for moving your application databases from the development server to the test server. Many individuals like to use the transfer objects options that are available in Data Transformation Services (DTS). The problem with the transfer options is that they drop and recreate the objects. By itself that is not a bad thing. The problem comes when the developer runs the DTS wizard.

Keep in mind that the developer has more privileges on the development server than he or she does with the test server. When objects were created in development, they defaulted to the DBO because the developer was part of the sysadmin server role. When the developer creates objects on the test and production servers, the ownership defaults to the developers' userID. Now the permission structure and evaluation may be different, and the stored procedures and SQL statements that previously worked may be suspect. There are three solutions to this problem:

Have a system administrator on the test and production server run the DTS wizard to move the database. The sysadmin on the production server should be a sysadmin everywhere, and the ownership of all objects should end up at DBO. The downside to this option is the additional overhead to the DBA of working on the production server.

Let the developer run the wizard and change the object ownership after the objects have been transferred. This is done by executing the sp_change_object_owner stored procedure. More information about this stored procedure can be found in Chapter 5, "Managing Object Security." The same downside exists with this option as with the prior option. Some individual will have to execute the stored procedure to change the object ownership.

The developer can generate SQL scripts of the objects created. These scripts can then be given to a DBA on the test server to be executed. The administrative overhead of executing SQL scripts is minimal compared to the overhead to the DBA of pursuing the other two options.

Generating SQL scripts is a solid recommendation for several reasons. You can reap the following advantages by storing the SQL scripts for your objects:

- Objects can be recreated easily if they become deleted or inappropriately altered.

- The scripts can be used for training purposes. It is beneficial to have the scripts to supply to new users of SQL Server. In many cases, Enterprise Manager is so easy to use that the individuals using SQL Server don't know what is going on at the Transact-SQL level.

- Scripts can be used as a template for future objects. When you need to create objects that are similar to other objects you already have, you can edit the script and execute it.

- Objects can be easily created on another server. This is a solid method of moving database objects from the development server to the test server. Executing scripts is very fast compared to the execution of the object transfer options that are available in DTS.

Generating SQL Scripts is an easy process. You can generate SQL Scripts for any database by performing the following steps:

1. Open Enterprise Manager.

2. Click to expand your server group.

3. Click to expand your server.

4. Click to expand Databases.

5. Right-click the database you want to generate scripts for and and select All Tasks.

6. From All Tasks select Generate SQL Scripts. See Figure 2.1.

7. Click the Show All button to display the options for the database objects.

8. Select the database objects you want to appear in the script.

9. Click the Options tab to display your current options. This should appear as shown in Figure 2.2.

From the Options tab you can also choose the file format and the number of files to generate. If you choose International, which is the default, all of your objects will have the letter N in front of them. The N designates the unicode context and will not prevent the script from running.

NOTE When creating scripts, in most cases it is best to generate one file for all objects. If you create a separate file for each object, you will end up with several files to traverse to find your object. With one file, you can open the file in Query Analyzer, highlight the piece of script you want to execute, and execute the piece you want to run.

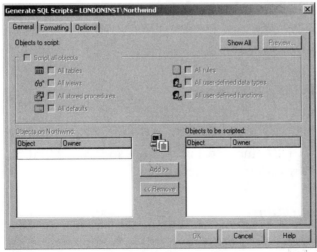

Figure 2.1 SQL Scripts can be generated for the creation of database objects.

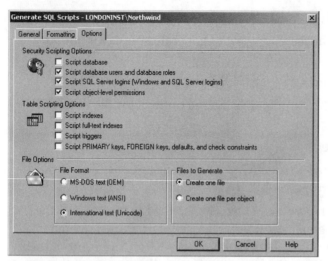

Figure 2.2 You can choose to include security information (logins, users, roles, and permissions) in your scripting options.

Administrative Roles

Every organization is different, but the following section outlines the basic functions of the database administrator and the developer. Who is accountable for the separate functions may vary in your organization, and your organization may not even implement many of the functions. In these cases you should not worry about the differing details. The most important part of this section is making sure that the items that need to get accomplished are accomplished.

Database Administrator Functions

This section introduces the duties that you might not be familiar with and offers suggestions on defining responsibilities for database configuration. Core responsibilities for a DBA include installation and configuration, security, operations, and service-level maintenance.

Installation and Configuration

The SQL Server DBA is often called upon to install new software on the server, to perform initial hardware and software configuration, or at least to participate in the process. The DBA should be involved in this process to guarantee that the system and the database are configured properly. Part of the DBA's job is to make sure that the system is configured to perform optimally with SQL Server. Following is a list of items that can be included in the installation and configuration of your system and database:

- The DBA must be involved not only with the installation of SQL Server but also with the installation of Microsoft Windows 2000 and other software components. Make sure that the proper options are set and that unnecessary components are not installed and configured. With the Windows 2000 installation, it is easy for unwanted components to be added unintentionally. Components such as Internet Information Server (IIS), Dynamic Host Configuration Protocol (DHCP) server, Message Queuing, and file and print services add a lot of overhead to the system even though these services might not be necessary.

- The DBA is responsible for the proper installation of SQL Server 2000. It is important to install SQL Server with the appropriate security parameters. The security settings can be changed after the installation, but not without incurring administrative overhead. It is best to get the installation correct the first time. The initial installation security parameters are addressed in more detail in Chapter 3, "Exploring Initial Security Parameters." After installation is complete, it is best to test the installation of both SQL Server and Windows 2000. If there are any problems with the current installation it is better to know up front. Reinstallation is much easier before the production databases and applications are deployed.

- It is generally the DBA's job to install and configure the production databases and applications. These databases should already be configured and tested on the test server. It is also the responsibility of the DBA to manage the test server. If the test server and production server are set up with the same security settings, all applications will have to be installed on the test server before they can be deployed to production.

- The configuration and stability of the production and test servers are the responsibility of the DBA. You will want to verify that the systems are set up with similar configuration and that the installations of Windows 2000 and SQL Server 2000 are in a stable state.

- Several server-level properties can be configured. These properties are the responsibility of the DBA. Following is a list of properties that could be configured at the server level:

- Memory configuration
- User connections
- Recovery interval
- Service startup accounts
- Processor usage

This list is just an example of the types of settings that can be configured. These options are available from Enterprise Manager or through the sp_configure stored procedure. To determine if any of the settings are appropriate for your server, refer to the SQL Server books online to find more information about all of the options available with sp_configure.

Security

Another responsibility of the SQL Server DBA is to monitor the security of the system and to report any problems. There are security experts, either at your company or with an outside firm, whom the DBA can call if necessary. The scope of access to your system determines the type and the amount of security that your database needs. A system that is accessed by only a few trusted employees and is not connected to the Internet obviously requires less security than a database that is accessed from the Internet. After you have determined the focus of your application and the user access needs of the database, it is much easier to define a security design.

The DBA is responsible for all SQL Server-level security configuration, including management of server roles and most system configuration. More information on server roles is available in Chapter 4, "Establishing Login Security."

Network Security

Network security includes the purchase, configuration, and deployment of network proxy servers and security gateways. Many companies sell this kind of hardware and software solution. The person in charge of network security for a company is responsible for investigating and choosing the right solution for that company. The subject of network security could fill a book by itself.

Within SQL Server, auditing and user management are the main security tasks that you as the DBA will be involved in. Network security is generally not the role of the DBA. It does, however, affect the DBA. All information that needs to pass through your firewall has to be coordinated with the network security administrator. Additionally, Windows Authentication is dependent on Active Directory users and groups, and as a DBA you will want to be familiar with the Active Directory infrastructure.

System Auditing

System auditing involves monitoring both the SQL Server error log and the Windows 2000 event log, as well as using SQL Server Profiler to monitor activity within SQL Server. The SQL Server log and the event log contain valuable information about SQL Server, Windows 2000, and security. You should monitor these logs closely for any signs of trouble. The DBA is the primary person responsible for system-level auditing.

Oftentimes, additional auditing strategies are written into the front-end application. If this is the case, application-specific auditing would generally fall under the developer's responsibilities. More information on auditing can be found in Chapter 14, "Creating an Audit Policy."

Operations

The most time-consuming activities of the SQL Server DBA are probably the day-to-day operational jobs. As the DBA, these thankless jobs will probably bore you at times, but remember that these are probably the most important activities for which you are responsible. The DBA is accountable for the uptime of the system, and tasks such as backup and restore are critical to that uptime.

Backup and Restore

Many consider the backup and restore operations to be the most crucial tasks that the DBA is charged with. These operations ensure that the database will survive a massive hardware failure, a virus, or some other anomaly that affects the stability of your data. If such a failure occurs, you must depend on the backup to return the database to service. The backup operation is consistent and straightforward, but you must repeat it frequently. To guarantee that the backups are good, you must also test and validate them regularly. By paying full attention to this activity, you can avoid mistakes and guarantee the safety of your system. This responsibility also includes a plan for disaster recovery.

User Management

Another day-to-day task is user management, which consists of managing SQL Server logins and database roles. This is an important duty of the DBA because everyone who wants to use the database must have authorized access. This access is granted by the DBA, usually after a human resources department approves the change.

Be sure to get approval before you grant access to each object within the database, and grant only as much access as the user needs. Avoid the temptation to grant blanket access to the database; the use of database roles is useful for granting specific access based on the needs of each department.

Permissions management is sometimes shared with the database developer. The developer is closer to the data and in many cases should be responsible for configuring the initial permission strategies.

Service-Level Maintenance

Ensuring that the system provides a particular level of service is an important task. The service level that your system must provide might be specified in a contractual service-level agreement (SLA). Even if it isn't, enabling the highest level of service possible is a responsibility and duty of the DBA. This task is accomplished by working for maximum uptime and by working for maximum performance via performance tuning, sizing, and capacity planning.

As the DBA you should constantly monitor the performance of the system and take note of any changes. If the system suddenly experiences higher response times, higher CPU usage, more context switches, and so forth, you might be seeing signs of an emerging problem. You need to monitor each system differently, and interpret the results of that monitoring differently as well. You must determine, based on your system, how to judge whether it is running well or not. If performance problems are indicated, you must troubleshoot those problems and develop solutions.

You must periodically monitor the system's resource usage and performance. By monitoring the system, you can expand the system before performance degrades.

Once the system capacity has been reached, expansion might be much more expensive in terms of both money and downtime. SQL Server offers several tools for monitoring the system; these tools are described here along with other monitoring tools:

System Monitor.   Used to monitor SQL Server and Windows 2000 resource usage. System Monitor is a Windows 2000 feature that is accessible through the Start menu.

SQL Server Enterprise Manager.   Provides both resource usage information and some limited performance information.

Third-party relational database management system monitors.
Provide a combination of monitoring and alerting capabilities for
relational database management systems (RDBMSs).

Network monitors. Used for occasional network monitoring; these
monitors include Microsoft Systems Management Server (SMS) and
third-party utilities.

User surveys. Used to gather information about how users feel about
the performance of the system. It is important to stay in touch with
the user community and determine whether users are satisfied. Too
often the only interaction between the DBA and user is when there's
a problem.

Tools for monitoring disk space usage. Include Microsoft Windows
Explorer and third-party monitoring tools. Some tools can monitor
Windows 2000 as well as SQL Server.

Database Developer Functions

The database developer functions can vary from organization to organza-
tion. In many cases the developer of the application and database also has
to fully support the application as the database administrator. The following suggestions are geared to those organizations that separate the roles.

The developer is first responsible for creating the database. In SQL
Server when you create the database you define the size of the database up front. This information should be coordinated with the DBA
to prevent taking too much drive space. The database layout is determined when the database is created. The layout includes the location
and size of both the data files and the transaction log files.

The primary purpose of SQL Server is to support business systems.
As a database developer you are required to develop or alter an
application that supports a business process. The developer is
responsible for designing and creating the application. When the
application is being designed, a primary function of the design
process is determining an application security design. More
information on application security design can be obtained in
Chapter 6, "Designing Application Security."

**As a developer you have chosen to use stored procedures or Transact-
SQL statements to access data in SQL Server.** You will need to

account for the users who need access to that data. Although the permissions may actually be configured by the DBA, it is the developer's job to get the appropriate information to the DBA. The developer knows the purpose of the application the best and needs to feel comfortable with the current security models used by the organization.

After the application is moved from the development server to the test server, you will need to sufficiently test the application to ensure that no surprises have unmasked themselves.   Because the development and test servers have different security models, it is possible for processes that worked in the development server to fail in the test server. You will want to make sure you iron out all the kinks before the application gets moved to production.

After the application is in production, things may change.   The purpose of the application could be altered, or the application may have new requirements that need to be tracked. It is the developer's job to take these changes and apply them on the development server. After they have been implemented in development you, as the developer, should then move them on to test and eventually to production. Your change management strategy should be implemented in a manner that will cause the least interruption to the production server. More information about change management is available in Chapter 6, "Designing Application Security."

Physical Design Requirements

This section looks at the physical design components of the implementation. It begins with a detailed look at the differences between various versions of Windows 2000 and SQL Server 2000 and moves on to outlining the reasons for deploying multiple instances of SQL Server 2000 on a single machine. It then describes the issues involved with determining the purpose for the server. Security concerns are different for OLAP application than for an OLTP application, which are discussed separately. The section will then outline the issues related to configuring clustering services and integrating SQL Server with clustering services.

Now that you have had a brief introduction to the types of applications available and the service-level requirements, you are ready to decide which software to install on your system. You can choose from four versions of Windows 2000 and multiple versions of SQL Server 2000. In this section, you will learn the differences between these versions and why you might select one over another.

Windows 2000 Versions

The four versions of Windows 2000 are designed to provide the appropriate software for the appropriate application. The features and functionality of Windows 2000 grow as you move from the Professional Edition on up to Datacenter Edition. The following sections describe the capabilities of each version. You should select the appropriate operating system for your needs.

Windows 2000 Professional is a desktop edition of Windows 2000.
Typically, a system running Windows 2000 Professional will take advantage of only the SQL Server 2000 client components. But if you need to run SQL Server on your computer, you can install the Personal Edition of SQL Server 2000. The Personal Edition permits only local access to the database; access from other systems is not permitted. Using Personal Edition can be beneficial for a developer who needs to travel and is not always connected to the server.

Windows 2000 Server is designed as a server operating system.
Installing Windows 2000 Server on a computer allows other systems to access resources on that computer. Windows 2000 Server supports SQL Server 2000 Standard Edition. Windows 2000 Server doesn't support systems with more than four CPUs and more than 4 gigabytes (GB) of memory. SQL Server 2000 allows remote clients to access the database as well. You will not have the option of installing clustering services on Windows 2000 Server. This operating system is appropriate when you don't plan on using the additional hardware, clustering services, or the Enterprise Edition of SQL Server 2000.

Windows 2000 Advanced Server is a more powerful server operating system than is Windows 2000 Server. As with systems that run Windows 2000 Server, systems that run Windows 2000 Advanced Server give other systems access to their system resources as well as SQL Server. In addition to having the capabilities of Windows 2000 Server, Windows 2000 Advanced Server supports up to eight CPUs and 8 GB of memory. You can also take advantage of Microsoft ClusteringServices (MCSs) for up to two nodes. Advanced Server also allows you to install the Enterprise Edition of SQL Server, which adds Federated Database Servers and Log Shipping as additional features. Federated Database Servers and Log Shipping will be addressed in more detail in Chapter 10, "Managing Distributed Data Security."

Datacenter is the most powerful edition of Windows 2000.   This version supports all of the components that the other editions of Windows 2000 do as well as up to 32 CPUs and 64 GB of memory. Windows 2000 Datacenter is available for purchase through server hardware vendors. Datacenter Server also extends the clustering services to support four nodes instead of two. More information on Microsoft Clustering Services (MSCS) is available later in this section. To take advantage of the additional CPUs and memory in SQL Server you must have the Enterprise Edition of SQL Server installed.

SQL Server Versions

In addition to the versions of Windows 2000 that you can choose from, there are several editions of SQL Server. It is fairly easy to choose a version based on the amount of memory you have and the number of CPUs that you need to use. The SQL Server 2000 client components consist of the network libraries and utilities needed to access a remote or local SQL Server system. These components are necessary for any system to access SQL Server, and they are identical regardless of which edition of SQL Server is installed.

Following are the editions of SQL Server:

The Personal Edition of SQL Server is designed for small databases that are accessed locally on a client system.   SQL Server 2000 Personal Edition does not allow other computers to gain access to the database. This feature can be beneficial for a developer who needs to store the data locally. With Personal Edition you don't have to have a network connection to have access to the data. You can create and test some objects before moving them to the test server.

SQL Server 2000 Standard Edition is one of the two server editions of SQL Server 2000.   Standard Edition functions the same way that Enterprise Edition (discussed next) does except that a maximum of four CPUs and 4 GB of memory can be accessed from the Standard Edition. Additionally the Standard Edition does not include support for clustering services, Federated Database Servers, and Log Shipping. If you need any of these services you will have to purchase the Enterprise Edition of SQL Server.

The Enterprise Edition of SQL Server supports all the features and functionality that the previously mentioned versions of Windows 2000 do. SQL Server 2000 Enterprise Edition requires Windows 2000 Advanced Server or Windows 2000 Datacenter. The Enterprise Edition of SQL Server is not limited in features. All of the SQL Server features are available. In addition, it supports clustering services, Federated Database Servers, and Log Shipping.

The Developer Edition of SQL Server is identical in functionality to the Enterprise Edition of SQL Server. The license for the Developer Edition limits access by a client for production purposes. This edition of SQL Server is beneficial for developers who need to centralize their data. In most cases, this is the best edition for developers because the features are identical to the features of the Enterprise Edition.

Multiple Instances of SQL Server

Multiple instances of SQL Server can be installed on a single server. In many organizations installing multiple instances of SQL Server on a single server is one of the best ways of isolating applications and guaranteeing a secure solution. During installation of SQL Server you will be prompted to designate the instance, as shown in Figure 2.3.

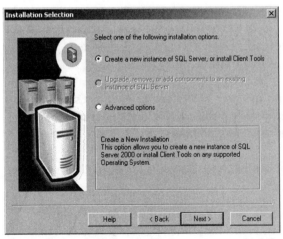

Figure 2.3 During the installation you are asked if you want to install a new instance of SQL Server.

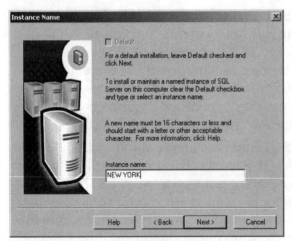

Figure 2.4 During the installation you are prompted for the name of the SQL Server instance.

If you choose to install another instance of SQL Server, you are then prompted to name the instance as shown in Figure 2.4. The name of the instance is appended to the name of the server to create the full name. For instance, if you installed an instance of SQL Server named NEW YORK on a computer named CHICAGO, the full name of the instance would be CHICAGO\NEWYORK. Additionally clients who access the instance must have Microsoft Data Access Components (MDAC) 2.6 installed, or the access to named instances will fail. Microsoft Data Access Components 2.6 enables the data access components to recognize the \ and include it in the path to the server instance. Microsoft Data Access Components is generally installed with a Microsoft Office installation.

NOTE When you install multiple instances of SQL Server you must stop the services of the instances that are already installed. It is best to perform the installation of subsequent instances during off hours.

By installing multiple instances of SQL Server you gain the following security and stability benefits:

Each instance has its own services.   If one application or instance fails, the failure will affect only that instance's own services. This setup isolates the application and helps prevent it from harming another application.

Each instance has its own sysadmin role.   The system administrators for each instance are defined separately. This distinction is very advantageous in a development environment, where database developers are given system administrator privileges to their instance. Defining the instances separately enables you to separate the developers and not let them affect each other's work.

Each instance has its own logins.   You can just add the logins that are appropriate for that instance. If the instance is supporting one application that needs only four logins, you have to create only the four logins.

NOTE Applications that have known stability problems should be run on their own instance of SQL Server, so that the problematic application doesn't affect the other applications.

Application Purpose

The next level of security design is understanding the purpose of the application. The application facilitates the use of SQL Server. Regardless of the type of application in use, you need to understand the purpose and role of the application. The next couple of sections outline the differences between OLTP, OLAP, and batch systems. In each of these sections you will learn about the security concerns related to the various systems' deployment.

Online Transaction Processing Systems

Online transaction processing (OLTP) systems are characterized by many users accessing and modifying data simultaneously. Users are waiting for a response from the server. Online transaction processing systems take a variety of forms and can include the following types of applications:

- Banking
- Order tracking
- Customer service
- Point-of-sales

All OLTP systems have one thing in common: The user is awaiting a response from the server. These systems are generally highly normalized and optimized for user input. With OLTP applications you should plan on using stored procedures for data modification to help your security infrastructure.

Online Analytical Processing Systems

Online analytical processing (OLAP) systems assist the user in analyzing data. These systems often make use of data that is not updatable by the user. The data is usually subject oriented and optimized to make possible speedy data retrieval. In an OLAP system, you are probably making use of data warehouse technology and should be comfortable with the functionality of the software. The following are examples of OLAP applications:

- Financial reporting and analysis packages
- Sales and marketing
- Performance monitoring packages
- Data warehousing
- Data mining

More information on Analysis Services security is found in Chapter 12, "Exploring Analysis Services Security."

Batch Processing Systems

Batch processing systems process offline jobs that do not have any end-user component. The system is charged with carrying out a set of tasks that is not related to the user or user activity. The security of the system is managed by the process itself. In many cases the batch process is scheduled as a Data Transformation Services (DTS) package and executed on a regular basis. If you are running batch processing systems, you will want to be comfortable with the security options available within DTS. More information on Microsoft DTS security can be found in Chapter 11, "Managing Data Transformation Services." The following tasks are typical jobs for a batch system:

Daily data refresh.   Some decision-support systems require data to be reloaded every night; batch processing systems often automate this task.

Data transformation.   This task is similar to data refresh, but the data is modified in some way by the transfer process.

Data cleansing.   This task accomplishes things such as removing duplicate accounts from the database.

Offline billing.   This task could consist of performing nightly billing of customers.

Batch processing systems are typically time dependent instead of user dependent. They generally have to complete a given job before a given time or before another process can occur.

Overview of Microsoft Clustering Services

Microsoft Windows 2000 Advanced Server and Datacenter Server operating systems enable organizations to deploy mission-critical business applications. Microsoft Clustering Services are key tools in making the system completely fault tolerant.

Clustering refers to linking multiple servers physically, via a shared network storage device, and programmatically through Windows 2000 services. The services are responsible for coordinating communication between the servers so they can perform common tasks. If any of the servers stop functioning, a process called *failover* automatically shifts that server's workload to another server to provide continuous service. The downtime is minimal and probably will be overcome before a user notifies you of the problem. In addition to failover, some forms of clustering also employ load balancing, which allows for the sharing of processing among servers.

Windows clustering technologies enable organizations to ensure the availability of critical applications while being able to scale those applications to meet increased demand.

Clustering Defined

A *cluster* is a group of computers that work together to run a common set of applications and provide the appearance of a single point of contact. To the user, all servers are one entity. The computers are physically connected by cables and programmatically connected by cluster software. These connections enable computers to use failover and load balancing, capabilities that are not possible with a standalone computer. Windows 2000 clustering technology provides the following advantages that can be used to promote the stability of your application:

High availability.   The cluster is designed to avoid a single point of failure. Applications can be distributed over more than one computer, achieving a degree of parallelism and failure recovery, and providing more availability.

Scalability.   You can increase the cluster's computing power by adding more computers.

Manageability.   To end users, applications, and the network, the cluster looks like a single-system, while it provides a single point of control to administrators. This single point of control can be remote.

Cluster Types

In the Windows 2000 Advanced Server and Datacenter Server operating systems, Microsoft introduces two clustering technologies, Clustering Services and Network Load Balancing, which can be used independently or in combination.The *Clustering service* is used to provide fault tolerance. This service is intended to provide failover support for applications such as SQL Server, Exchange Server, and file and print services. Clustering service supports two-node failover clusters in Windows 2000 Advanced Server and four-node clusters in Datacenter Server. The Cluster service is ideal for ensuring the availability of mission-critical applications.

The *Network Load Balancing (NLB) service* is used to balance the processing load for a set of servers. This service load-balances incoming Internet Protocol (IP) traffic across clusters of up to 32 nodes. Network Load Balancing enhances scalability of server-based applications such as Web servers, streaming media servers, and Terminal services. By acting as the load-balancing infrastructure and providing control information to management applications built on top of Windows Management Instrumentation (WMI), Network Load Balancing can seamlessly integrate into existing Web server farm infrastructures. Network Load Balancing also serves as an ideal load-balancing architecture for use with the upcoming Microsoft release of Application Center in distributed Web farm environments.

Windows Clustering and Network Load Balancing technologies can be used in conjunction to create highly scalable and available *n*-tier e-commerce sites. By deploying Network Load Balancing across a front-end Web server farm and clustering back-end line-of-business applications such as SQL Server databases, you can gain all the benefits of near-linear scalability with no server- or application-based single points of failure. Combined with industry-standard best practices for designing high-availability networking infrastructures, you can ensure your Windows 2000-based Internet-enabled business will be online all the time and can quickly scale to meet demand.

Clustering Service Advantages

Line-of-business applications are applications that are central to a company's operations and include systems such as SQL Server database, Exchange Server database, and file and print services. Clustering service in the Windows 2000 operating system ensures that these critical applications are online when they are needed by removing the physical server as a single point of failure.

In the event that a hardware or software failure occurs in either node, the applications currently running on that node (and you may run more than one) are then migrated by Clustering service to the surviving node and are restarted. Because Clustering service uses a shared-disk configuration with common bus architectures such as Small Computer Systems Interface (SCSI) and Fibre Channel, no data is lost during a failover.

The benefits of deploying the Windows 2000 operating system with Clustering service are as follows:

Clustering service reduces unplanned downtime.   Downtime caused by hardware or software failures can result in lost revenue, wasted IT staff work, and unhappy customers. Using Clustering service with a shared-disk solution on critical line-of-business applications can significantly reduce the amount of application downtime caused by unexpected failures.

Clustering service allows for the smooth deployment of upgrades. Clustering service is ideally suited for ensuring transparent upgrades of applications without inconveniencing your clients. By migrating your applications to one node, upgrading the first node, and then migrating them back, you can roll out hardware, software, and even operating system upgrades without taking the application offline.

Clustering service enables you to deploy applications that are mission critical.   Clustering service is supported by dozens of cluster-aware applications spanning a wide range of functions and vendors. Cluster-aware applications include databases such as Microsoft SQL Server 2000 and IBM DB2; messaging servers such as Microsoft Exchange Server 2000 and Lotus Domino; management tools such as NetIQ's AppManager; disaster recovery tools such as NSI Software's Double-Take 3.0; and Enterprise Resource Planning (ERP) applications including SAP, Baan, and PeopleSoft, and JD Edwards. You can now cluster such services as DHCP, WINS, SMTP, and NNTP.

> **Clustering service enables you to deploy applications on industry-standard hardware.**   Keep costs down by deploying Clustering service on standard PC server and storage hardware, avoiding costly and often proprietary alternative high-availability solutions. Most systems vendors including Dell, Compaq, IBM, Hewlett-Packard, Unisys, and Data General currently offer Cluster service solutions.

Clustering Modes

You can run SQL Server 2000 cluster support and MSCS in different modes. In active/passive mode, one server remains in standby mode, ready to take over in the event of a system failure on the primary server. In active/active mode, each server runs a different SQL Server database. In the event of a failure on either of the servers, the other server takes over. In this case, one server ends up running two databases. In this section, we'll examine the advantages and the disadvantages of using each of these modes.

An active/passive cluster uses the primary node to run the SQL Server application, and it uses the secondary node as a backup, or standby server. In this configuration, one server goes unused unless a failover occurs. It is to be hoped that this server will not be used very often. In fact, in many cases, the backup server is never used. Because the secondary server is not being used, it might be seen as a costly piece of equipment that is sitting idle. Because this server is not available to perform other functions, other equipment might have to be purchased to serve users, making the active/passive mode potentially expensive. With either the active/passive or the active/active solution, you will need to compare the cost of running and maintaining the additional server to the cost of potential downtime. How you perceive the expense involved is relative to the situation at hand. Although the active/passive mode can be expensive, it does have advantages. With the active/passive configuration, if the primary node fails, all the resources of the secondary node are available to take over the primary node's activity. With this configuration you will not notice a decrease in performance after the failover. You can configure the primary server to run at full capacity without worrying about potential loss of performance. This reliability can be important if you're running mission-critical applications that depend on a level throughput or user response time.

NOTE It is recommended that the secondary node and the primary node have identical hardware (that is, the same amount of RAM, the same type and number of CPUs, and so on). If the two nodes have identical hardware, you can be certain that the secondary system will perform at nearly the same rate as the primary system.

In an active/active cluster, each server can run applications while serving as a secondary server for another node. Each of the two or four servers acts both as a primary node for some applications and as a secondary node for the other server's applications. This is a more cost-effective configuration because no equipment is sitting idle. In this example both systems can actively respond to user requests. One disadvantage of the active/active configuration is that, in the event of a failure, the performance of the surviving node will be significantly reduced because it will bear an increased load. The surviving node will have to run not only the applications it was running originally but also the applications from the primary node. You need to evaluate your scenario to determine whether the performance hit is acceptable. If the performance hit is not acceptable, you will need to set up the Clustering service in an active/passive configuration.

SQL Server Cluster Configuration

After you have installed and configured MSCS, the next step is to configure SQL Server for clustering. SQL Server 2000 is cluster aware and is designed to make use of clustering. This section of the chapter will focus primarily on the different design issues for running SQL Server with the Clustering service.

Planning Your Deployment

The first step in planning a SQL Server cluster is determining the type of hardware to use and the mode of operation in which the cluster will run. You will have to choose whether your implementation of Clustering service for SQL Server will be active/active or active/passive.

Active/passive cluster configurations should consist of computers with identical hardware. Each of these machines should be capable of handling the workload of the databases. Because active/passive mode does not make use of the secondary system during normal operations, the performance of the SQL Server instance should remain constant. Users will not experience any performance change if the primary system fails over to an identical secondary system. With an active/passive cluster you have made the choice to invest in the additional hardware to guarantee the performance of the application. The only performance hit will be the time it takes for the failover process. In most cases the time should not exceed 90 seconds.

Active/active cluster configurations should consist of two systems, each of which is running a specific workload. The configuration and performance will also be the best if both systems are identical from a hardware standpoint. If a failure occurs, the surviving system will take over the workload of the failed system. That means that the load of both servers will be running on one server. If either of the two servers was at a high utilization rate before the failover, the failover process will most likely result in decreased performance. With active/active clustering you are typically choosing to have a fault-tolerant solution at the expense of performance. When the system performs a failover, the performance may be slower, but all of the data will be available to users. If you opt for the active/active cluster configuration, you should generally document the configuration of the cluster and inform users and other support staff that a failover will result in a decrease in performance.

The next step when you are configuring SQL Server for a cluster is to check and possibly change several SQL Server settings. The next three sections examine these three settings.

Setting the Recovery Time

In tuning SQL Server, previously you may have set the configuration parameter recovery interval to something other than the default value of 0. Changing this setting will increase the time between checkpoints and improve performance but will also increase recovery time. (The system must recover after it has failed over.) While this is appropriate in some cases, it is not appropriate when you are working with a clustered server. In a clustered system, the default value of 0, which specifies automatic configuration, should not be changed. Keeping the default at 0 may result in decreased performance due to the ongoing checkpoints, but the purpose of the Clustering service is fault tolerance. If you have not changed this setting, don't worry about it. The default of 0 is the suggested setting for SQL Server with the Clustering service. This default setting of 0 will cause a checkpoint and recover to occur about every minute. This will speed up the failover process and make the data available to users more quickly.

Configuring Min Server Memory

To create an active/passive cluster configuration, you might have to change one setting in SQL Server. If your secondary server is identical to the primary server, no change is necessary. If the secondary server has fewer resources than the primary server, you should set the SQL Server configuration parameter min server memory to 0. This setting instructs SQL Server to allocate memory based on available system resources, allowing for the dynamic allocation of memory. It is necessary for the system to control the memory when the two servers are not identical from a hardware standpoint.

In an active/active cluster configuration, you must set the SQL Server configuration parameter min server memory to 0. By doing so you enable the server to reconfigure the memory for each instance after the failover. If this setting is not configured at 0, the server instance that has failed over to the other server will not be allocated any memory, or the system will force everything the new instance does to the paging file, negatively affecting performance.

Installing SQL Server for Clustering

When installing SQL Server for clustering you should follow steps that are similar to those for a normal installation of SQL Server 2000. When you see the screen that asks you to identify whether the installation is for a local or remote server, you will have an option to select Virtual Server as shown in Figure 2.5.

The only other installation issue is your file paths. You will be prompted for the location of the program files and system database file path as shown in Figure 2.6. You will want to make sure that both of the paths are pointed to a drive located on the shared network storage device. By doing so you will ensure that the files are not kept local and that the failover process can be successful.

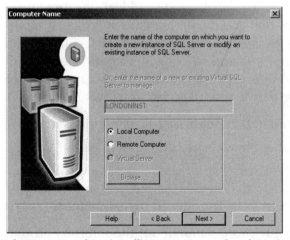

Figure 2.5 When installing SQL Server for clustering, you will need to install a virtual instance. In this case Virtual Server is grayed out because Cluster service was not configured first.

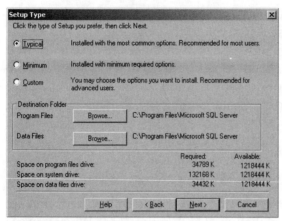

Figure 2.6   When installing a virtual instance of SQL Server you will want to store your files on the shared storage device.

Documentation

Documentation is the key to making this chapter work for you. You should have a clear picture of each of the items described in this chapter. The following suggestions for diagramming will help you get a clear picture of all the issues defined in this chapter and assist you in presenting them to others. If you don't document these items effectively, others may not grasp their context or meaning. After you have planned to address the previously defined issues, it is paramount that you document your analysis of the situation and the choices you have made for deployment. This documentation can serve as a reference point for you and others who need to interact with SQL Server. Based on the previous sections you will need a minimum of three sets of documentation to define your security strategy:

- You should have a document that defines your server architecture.
- You should have a document that clearly defines the roles of the developer and DBA within your organization.
- You should have a document that details the physical implementation issues that have already been introduced in this chapter.

The following sections provide more detail about the information that should be stored within each set of documentation.

Server Architecture

Your server architecture documentation should define your servers and the role they play within the organization, including details about the following items:

- The relationship of production, test, and development servers.
- The physical location of each of the servers.
- The system administrators of each of the servers.
- The number of instances of SQL Server installed on each server.
- The version of SQL Server and Windows 2000 Server installed on each machine.
- The level of testing required at the test server. Do you need to use benchmarking or load simulation software?
- The Personal Edition of SQL Server on developers' personal computers. You could either centralize your developers to a development server or you could give them their own desktop edition. Giving them their own instance of SQL Personal Edition increases the number of instances you have to support. On the other hand, it also enables the developer to travel and not have to be connected to the network.
- The method of moving objects from one server to another.
- The role that Transact-SQL scripts play in your installation and change management strategy.

Roles and Responsibilities

Although the documentation outlining roles and responsibilities may seem to be the most obvious of the three sets of documentation, it is probably the most critical. Regardless of how good a product SQL Server 2000 is, the success of your applications will depend on the people who implement and support your applications. Following is a list of questions that should be answered by the documentation that defines the roles and responsibilities within your organization:

- Who will design the application security model?
- Who will perform the server-level security and configuration (server roles and sp_configure options)?

- Who is responsible for user management at the database level?
- Who manages the object permissions?
- Who will develop the application?
- Who will deploy the application to test and production servers?
- Who supports application-related issues after the application has been deployed in production?
- Who is responsible for maintaining object ownership chains?

NOTE All of the items listed in the roles and responsibilities section are related to security, given the context of this book. But you should also consider expanding this document to deal with all issues of the application, including items such as backup and restore, server installation, and data transformation packages.

Physical Implementation

The last area of documentation related to security is physical implementation. Keep in mind that although this is the last level of documentation for designing your security system as a whole, each application should have its own security design, which should include some documentation as well. More information about application security design is found in Chapter 6, "Designing Application Security." There are several considerations for physical implementation:

- The versions of SQL Server and Windows 2000 should be documented.
- The number of instances of SQL Server should be well documented. There should be a diagram showing the number of instances on each server and the names of each of the servers and instances.
- The purpose of all applications and databases should be documented. All individuals who need to interact with the database should know the role of each database and application.
- The documentation should be clear on which systems are OLTP, OLAP, and batch processing systems as discussed in their respective sections earlier in this chapter.
- If clustering is used, the configuration should be documented and diagrammed.

NOTE The items referenced for physical implementation reference only security concerns. You should consider expanding your documentation to address other physical concerns such as the location of the transaction log and data file, backup strategies and tape solutions, and management of SQL services.

Best Practices

- The test and production server should match in security configuration to help prevent inconsistencies when the application goes live.

- The development server should allow developers to create all the objects they need for their applications.

- Use Transact-SQL scripts to move objects from development to test. Scripts are fast and, if they are executed by a system administrator, you will not lose your DBO object ownership.

- Define the roles of the DBA versus those of the developer. Everyone will appreciate knowing what each person is responsible for.

- Strive to decrease the lines of accountability. To help prevent finger-pointing when a problem occurs and help increase the chance that the task will be accomplished, make sure that your production and test servers have few system administrators.

- Choose versions of Windows 2000 and SQL Server 2000 appropriately. Use the same versions for test and production servers.

- Use multiple instances of SQL Server to assist in security management and to isolate applications.

- Know the purpose of each application and database. When appropriate, use tools such as DTS and Analysis Services to enhance your applications.

- Use Clustering services when the application is mission-critical. Clustering services are appropriate when the cost of potential downtime is greater than the cost of running and maintaining additional servers and network storage devices.

- *Document! Document! Document!* The key to making a security model last is documenting the decisions you have made. The documentation should be clear and concise.

REVIEW QUESTIONS

1. Why do you need a test server?

2. Why is it important that the test and production servers have a matching security configuration?

3. What is the purpose of the Clustering service?

4. As a DBA, why is it important to know the role of each database and application?

5. Why would you use multiple instances of SQL Server on a single server?

6. What is the difference between the Enterprise Edition of SQL Server and the Standard Edition of SQL Server?

7. Why is documentation of your security design so important?

CHAPTER 3

Exploring Initial Security Parameters

After planning for your deployment of SQL Server, you are ready to shift focus to the initial security concerns related to SQL Server installation. At this point, as discussed in Chapter 2, "Designing a Successful Security Model," you have determined the number of instances you will need to install. You also have a solid plan about the individuals who will administer each server. You will need to be comfortable with the security accounts you have chosen for your SQL Server and SQL Server Agent services. These services are the key to SQL Server working for you. Many of the features of SQL Server use the security context of these services when performing their functions.

This chapter addresses the security concerns related to the initial installation and configuration of the server. It also addresses the role of Enterprise Manager and Query Analyzer as tools for using and administering SQL Server. By the end of this chapter you should feel confident about using the security properties of these tools to define your connection to SQL Server.

First, this chapter outlines the purpose and creation of the service account. The security context of your service account is the key to several features, such as replication and email integration, working properly. Next, the chapter tackles the security requirements for the installation process. The chapter then moves to the files, folders, and Registry settings that are added to SQL Server by the installation. Finally, this chapter demonstrates the registration of a server instance with Enterprise Manager and SQL Query Analyzer. When an instance is registered with one of these tools, you will have to supply the security context (username and password) to be used when the connection is made to SQL Server.

SQL Services Account

Microsoft SQL Server and SQL Server Agent are started and run as Windows services. The security context in which these services run controls the security context of your server. Replication, email integration, scheduled tasks, and multiserver jobs all use the services' security context to perform their functions. The SQL services appear in the list of installed services along with all other Windows services in the Services dialogue box. The Services dialogue box is available from the Control Panel.

The two most important services to Microsoft SQL Server are the SQL Server service and the SQL Server Agent service. The *SQL Server service* handles all query processing and server configuration. The *SQL Server Agent service* manages all of the automated processes, which can include jobs, operators, alerts, and replication.

In addition to managing automated processes, the SQL Server Agent service account is used as the security context for executing the scheduled processes. If the account is not configured with the appropriate level of security, the jobs you schedule will not execute properly. The SQL Server Agent service account should be a local administrator for the machine on which SQL Server is installed. More information about the role of the SQL Server Agent service can be found in Chapter 9, "Introducing the SQL Server Agent Service."

For Microsoft SQL Server and SQL Server Agent to run as services in Windows, each service must be assigned a Windows user account to use when the service starts. This account is used so that the service can log on to the system. Typically, both SQL Server and SQL Server Agent are assigned the same user account. But it is possible to customize the settings for each service separately. You have two choices for configuring the service account: as a local system account or as a domain user account.

NOTE Microsoft Windows 9x does not support Windows services. The Personal Edition of SQL Server that runs on Windows 9x simulates the SQL Server and SQL Server Agent services. In these environments, you need not configure the user account for the service startup. You also must have the SQL Server open and running in order for the data to be accessed.

Using a Local System Account

A local system account can be configured to use at service startup and does not require the username or password to be configured by the DBA. A local system account does not have the network access required for most server-to-server activity. Using a local system account restricts an instance of SQL Server from interacting with other servers over the network for the purposes of replication, multiserver jobs, and email integration. Using the local system account as the SQL service account is generally not an option if you plan to use SQL Server replication, multiserver jobs, or email integration with SQL Server. If you choose to use the local system account as your service account, the features available to you will be limited.

Using a Domain User Account

A domain user account uses Windows Authentication—that is, the same username and password used to connect to the operating system is also used to connect to SQL Server. The domain user account is generally preferred because it does not limit your interaction with other servers. When you use a domain user account, the following items are available:

- Multiserver jobs.
- Replication.
- Backing up to network drives.
- JOIN statements that involve multiple server data sources.
- SQL Server Agent mail features and SQL Mail services. SQL Server Agent mail is used by the SQL Server Agent service and is the feature that is used to notify users of critical system alerts and the status of scheduled jobs. The SQL Mail service is integrated with the SQL Server service and allows the xp_sendmail stored procedure to be used to send email from Transact-SQL. Most email systems, including Microsoft Exchange, depend on the SQL services to be running with a domain user account as the security context.

NOTE All servers running SQL Server can share the same user account. If the account is created on a domain that all SQL Servers can access, all servers can be configured consistently. This is important when you are setting up replication. It is recommended that a Publisher and all its Subscribers share the same service account for the SQL Server Agent service. For more information on replication and the SQL Server Agent service, refer to Chapter 9, "Introducing the SQL Server Agent Service."

Requirements for Domain User Account

If the domain account you are using is a member of the local administrators group, the considerations mentioned in this section are already inherited. If you don't want the account to use a local administrator, you should evaluate the following considerations:

- The account must be able to access and change the SQL Server directory (\Program Files\Microsoft SQL Server\Mssql).

- The account must have access to read and change the .mdf, .ndf, and .ldf database files.

- The account must be assigned the Log On As a Service user right.

- The account must also be able to read and write Registry keys at and under the following:

  - HKEY_LOCAL_MACHINE\Software\Microsoft\ MSSQLServer—also for any additional named instance, HKEY_LOCAL_MACHINE\Software\Microsoft\Microsoft SQL Server)

  - HKEY_LOCAL_MACHINE\System\CurrentControlset\ Services\MSSQLServer—also for any named instance, HKEY_ LOCAL_MACHINE\System\CurrentControlset\Services\ MSSQL$Instancename

  - HKEY_LOCAL_MACHINE\Software\Microsoft\Windows NT\ CurrentVersion\Perflib

- The user account must be able to read and write corresponding Registry keys for these services: SQLAgent$InstanceName (for each named instance on the server), MSSearch, and MSDTC.

Additional permissions may be required to gain added functionality in SQL Server. Most of this additional functionality enables SQL Server to access and use services outside SQL Server. For example, you may want to configure integration with Exchange Server so that you have the option of using the xp_sendmail stored procedure to send email messages. Table 3.1 identifies the additional functionality options and the permission required to perform the additional action.

Table 3.1 Additional Functionality and Permissions Required with SQL Server Services

ADDITIONAL FUNCTIONALITY	PERMISSION REQUIRED
Use xp_sendmail to send email messages from your Transact-SQL code	The service account needs a mailbox that has permission to send messages.
Run xp_cmdshell to execute shell commands from your Transact-SQL code	The ct as Part of the Operating System and Replace a Process Level Token user rights need to be assigned to the service account. These user rights are assigned through Windows 2000.
Create CmdExec and ActiveScript job steps in a job owned by a non-sysadmin	The SQL Server Agent service account must be a local administrator.
Add and delete SQL Server objects in Windows 2000 Active Directory	SQL Server Agent service account must be a member of the local power users group.

NOTE It is generally easiest to add the service account to the local administrators group of the SQL Server. Doing so results in all permissions requirements being met. This may result in the account having access to some things that it doesn't need, but the administration will be much easier.

Changing User Accounts

After the service account has been defined, it is easy to change the password or assign the service to use another account. You can use either Enterprise Manager or the Services icon from the Control Panel to make the change. To change the SQL Server service user account or password at any time after installation, you should perform the following steps using Enterprise Manager:

1. Open Enterprise Manager.
2. Click to expand the server instance you want to manipulate.
3. Right-click the server instance and select Properties.
4. Select the Security tab, which leads to the dialogue box page shown in Figure 3.1.
5. Type the new username or new password.
6. You will be prompted to restart the service.

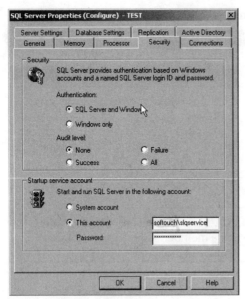

domain\id

Figure 3.1 Use the Security tab of the Server Properties dialogue box to change the service account used by a SQL Server service.

NOTE Changes to the service account used for the SQL Server service and the SQL Server Agent service require restarting the service. This process will take a couple of minutes and may affect connected users. It is best to either schedule this procedure during offline hours or to inform all users that the server will be down for a couple of minutes. You can use the current activity window in Enterprise Manager to send a message to a connected user. More information on the current activity window can be found in Chapter 13, "Managing Current Connections."

As noted, alternatively you can use the Services icon from the Control Panel to reconfigure the service account for one of the SQL Server services. This option is beneficial if you are having difficulties with Enterprise Manager and need to test the service to see if the service may be the cause of your problems. Often a stalled or misconfigured SQL Server service will cause Enterprise Manager to stop responding. Perform the following steps to modify service account information for the SQL Server service.

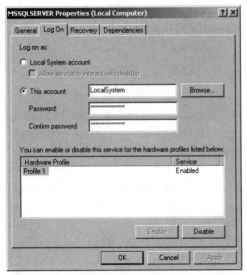

Figure 3.2 SQL Server services can be reconfigured from the Services option in the Control Panel using the MSSQLSERVER Properties dialogue box.

1. From the Control Panel, double-click on the Services icon.

2. Scroll down to the SQL Server service and double-click it to open the Service Properties dialogue box.

3. Click the Log On tab, which leads to the dialogue box page shown in Figure 3.2.

Change the account information as appropriate.

Installation Security

This section introduces the permissions required for performing a SQL Server installation. This section then identifies the files and folders that are added to your system during installation. This information is beneficial if you encounter errors related to missing or corrupted files. It is also useful if you have tried to perform the installation and it did not complete. SQL Server may be partially installed on your system, and the files and Registry keys may have to be cleaned up before you can try the installation again. The Rebuild Registry option is also described as a method for resetting your Windows Registry values.

Installation Permissions

It is necessary to determine the number of instances you will be installing on the server. Multiple instances and the decision to install multiple instances are described in more depth in Chapter 2, "Designing a Successful Security Model."

Whether you are installing the first instance or an additional instance, you need the same permissions. Local administrator permissions are required to install an instance of SQL Server on a machine. The SQL Server installation will add files to the hard drive, settings to the Registry, and services to Windows 2000. If you are not a local administrator, the process will fail quickly. You will receive an error message notifying you that you do not have the required permissions.

Locating Files and Folders and Rebuilding Registry Keys

During installation, you have the option of determining the path of the files that will be added to your system. Table 3.3 shows a list of default paths, which may vary if locations were changed during installation. Both program and data file locations can be changed, but the location of shared tools cannot be changed. The security to these files should be set automatically for you by the SQL Server installation process. It is not typically recommended that you change the permission settings to these files. You should control security through the SQL Server security model, which can be used to control who has access to various features of SQL Server.

> **NOTE** Do not delete any of the following directories or their contents: Binn, Data, Ftdata, HTML, or 1033. If you delete these directories, you may not be able to retrieve any lost functionality or data without uninstalling and reinstalling SQL Server 2000. Additionally, do not delete or modify any of the .htm files in the HTML directory. They are required for SQL Server Enterprise Manager and other tools to function properly.

Shared Files for All Instances of SQL Server 2000

Although each instance on a single machine maintains its own autonomy, some files are shared between instances of SQL Server. Table 3.2 introduces the files that are shared for all instances of SQL Server on a single machine.

Table 3.2 Installation Files That Are Shared on a Single Machine

LOCATION	DESCRIPTION
\Program Files\Microsoft SQL Server\ 80\Com	Dynamic-link libraries (DLLs) for the COM objects.
\Program Files\Microsoft SQL Server\ 80\Com\Binn\Resources\1033	Resource files (RLLs) used by the DLLs in this COM directory. (Note: 1033 is for U.S. English; localized versions use different directory numbers.)
\Program Files\Microsoft SQL Server\ 80\Tools\Binn	Client executable files.
\Program Files\Microsoft SQL Server\ 80\Tools\Books	SQL Server Books Online.
\Program Files\Microsoft SQL Server\ 80\Tools\DevTools\	Header files, library files, and sample files.
\Program Files\Microsoft SQL Server\ 80\Tools\Html	Microsoft Management Console (MMC) and SQL Server HTML files.
\Program Files\Microsoft SQL Server\ 80\Tools\Templates	SQL script templates to help you create objects in the database.

Program and Data Files for the Default Instance of SQL Server 2000

Each instance of SQL Server also has its own set of data files. Table 3.3 shows the locations of the program and data files for the default instance of SQL Server 2000. These are the default file locations, which can be changed during installation.

Table 3.3 Program Data Files for the Default Instance of SQL Server 2000

LOCATION	DESCRIPTION
\Program Files\Microsoft SQL Server\ Mssql\Backup	Default location for backup files
\Program Files\Microsoft SQL Server\ Mssql\Binn	Microsoft Windows NT server executable files and DLL files for extended stored procedures
\Program Files\Microsoft SQL Server\ Mssql\Binn\Resources\1033	Binn directory for resource files used by the DLLs

(continues)

Table 3.3   Program Data Files for the Default Instance of SQL Server 2000 *(Continued)*

LOCATION	DESCRIPTION
\Program Files\Microsoft SQL Server\ Mssql\Data	System and sample database files
\Program Files\Microsoft SQL Server\ Mssql\Ftdata	Full-text catalog files
\Program Files\Microsoft SQL Server\ Mssql\Install	Scripts run during setup and resulting output files
\Program Files\Microsoft SQL Server\ Mssql\Jobs	Storage location for temporary job output files
\Program Files\Microsoft SQL Server\ Mssql\Log	Error log files
\Program Files\Microsoft SQL Server\ Mssql\Repldata	Working directory for replication tasks
\Program Files\Microsoft SQL Server\ Mssql\Upgrade	Files used for version upgrade from SQL Server version 6.5 to SQL Server 2000

All subsequent instances of SQL Server have a similar path. The MSSQL folder is replaced with an MSSQL$*namedinstance* folder, where *named instance* is the name of the installed instance of SQL Server.

In addition to the files and folders that were referenced previously, following is a list of Registry keys that are added during a SQL Server installation:

- HKEY_LOCAL_MACHINE\Software\Microsoft\MSSQLServer
- HKEY_LOCAL_MACHINE\Software\Microsoft\Microsoft SQL Server
- HKEY_LOCAL_MACHINE\System\CurrentControlset\ Services\MSSQLServer
- HKEY_LOCAL_MACHINE\System\CurrentControlset\ Services\MSSQL$Instancename (for each named instance of SQL Server)
- HKEY_LOCAL_MACHINE\Software\Microsoft\Windows NT\ CurrentVersion\Perflib

It is possible to use the installation procedure to rebuild the SQL Server settings in the Registry. The Rebuild Registry option is available only through the installation process. Rebuilding the Registry is very beneficial if you feel that the Registry is corrupted or has been updated incorrectly. This procedure can also be used if the security settings to your Registry keys have been unsuccessfully changed. The Advanced Options Setup screen allows you to rebuild the Registry for a corrupted Microsoft SQL Server installation. This process fixes only the Registry; it does not fix data errors or rebuild the system databases.

NOTE To rebuild the Registry, you must enter setup information using the same choices that you entered during the initial installation. If you do not know or are unsure of this information, do not use this Registry rebuild process. Instead, to restore the Registry, uninstall and reinstall SQL Server.

Registering Servers

It is important to remember that Enterprise Manager and SQL Query Analyzer tools are *not* SQL Server. They are simply tools that enable you to connect to the server in order to perform some action involving the server and its databases. This is the reason that the tools need to be refreshed to reflect new changes you have made. When you provide the security credentials for your connection to SQL Server, you are supplying the credentials that Enterprise Manager or Query Analyzer should use when you request a connection to SQL Server. If you choose Windows Authentication, your current Windows logon credentials will be used for the connection.

When you begin using each of these tools, the server that you want to configure must be registered with the tool. During registration you provide the user account and other required and optional information that is used when you are connecting to the server. The security information you supply here is used as your security credentials while you are connected to SQL Server. You will be limited in functionality based on the security information you supply. The registration process is what keeps access to the server through the management tools secure. You must register a local or remote server before you can administer and manage it by using SQL Server Enterprise Manager. When you register a server, you must specify:

- The name of the server.
- The type of security used to log on to the server.
- Your login name and password, if appropriate. (You could alternatively use Windows Authentication. When you use Windows

Authentication, Windows 2000 Active Directory performs the authorization of your username and password.)

- The name of the group where you want the server to be listed after it is registered. The group is used to organize servers logically within Enterprise Manager. This feature is useful in large environments when you have to manage multiple servers. You can group the servers logically to keep them organized in your management interface. This grouping has no effect on the performance or stability of the server.

NOTE When you register a server in Enterprise Manager, the SQL Server service is automatically started and the status of the server is displayed.

When you run SQL Server Enterprise Manager for the first time, it automatically registers all instances of a local SQL Server. The registrations are set up with Windows Authentication as the connection property. If you are a member of the system administrator's server role, you will have access to all of the features of SQL Server. If you have one instance of SQL Server registered and then install more instances of SQL Server, only the original instance of SQL Server will be registered. Multiple instances of SQL Server can be registered after installation by performing the following steps:

1. From Enterprise Manager, right-click on a server or a server group and then click New SQL Server Registration. This starts the Server Registration Wizard.

NOTE If you selected the From Now on I Want to Perform This Task without Using a Wizard checkbox the last time you used the Register Server Wizard, SQL Server Enterprise Manager displays the Registered SQL Server Properties dialogue box. Otherwise the Server Registration Wizard will begin.

2. In the Server box, type the name of the instance you want to register.

3. Select either Use Windows Authentication or Use SQL Server Authentication. Windows Authentication will use your current Windows login credentials. The SQL Server Authentication requires a username and password. Click Next after making your selection.

4. In the Server Group list, click the server group where you want this registration to be placed.

NOTE If the server group you need does not exist yet, create it by clicking the Build (...) button and then completing the Server Groups dialogue box. Server groups are used to organize the server registrations within Enterprise Manager.

5. You have the option of selecting one or more of the following, as shown in Figure 3.3:

   ■ Select the Display SQL Server State in Console checkbox to turn on Service Polling.

   ■ Select the Show System Databases and System Objects checkbox to show all system databases and objects.

   ■ Select the Automatically Start SQL Server when Connecting checkbox to start an instance of SQL Server automatically.

When you connect to SQL Query Analyzer, you are not asked to register a server; you are just presented with a login screen. Similar to Enterprise Manager, you have the option to log in using Windows Authentication or SQL Server Authentication, as shown in Figure 3.4. After connecting to the server, you can use the Query Analyzer to type in your Transact-SQL statements.

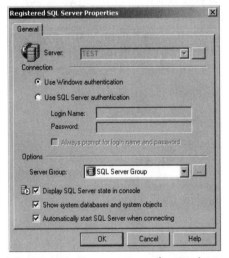

Figure 3.3 You can use the Registered SQL Server Properties wizard to determine whether to show your system databases in Enterprise Manager.

Figure 3.4   You must log in to the server before you can use SQL Query Analyzer.

Removing Registered Servers

Removing a registered server is easy. Remember, Enterprise Manager is just a tool to connect to SQL Server. When you remove a server from Enterprise Manager, you are not affecting the server. You are removing the object from your Enterprise Manager interface and disconnecting from SQL Server. When you remove the server object from Enterprise Manager, your connection and security settings of that server are removed. You are not physically removing the server and you don't affect anybody else who is connected to the server.

If you plan to re-register the server, you will need to supply your security and connection settings again. You can perform the following steps to remove a registered server running SQL Server.

1. From Enterprise Manager, click on SQL Server Group and then right-click the server you want to remove.

2. Click Delete SQL Server Registration as shown in Figure 3.5.

3. Confirm the deletion.

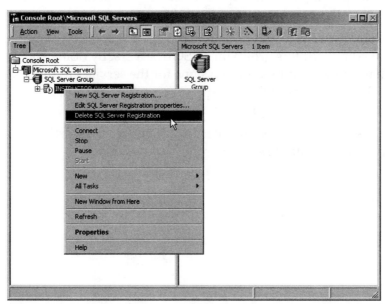

Figure 3.5 A registered server can be removed from Enterprise Manager.

Best Practices

- Create a domain account to use for your SQL services account. The local system account is very limited in network access.

- Use the same account for the SQL Server service and the SQL Server Agent service in order to decrease confusion and minimize the configuration of email integration.

- Use the same service account for all SQL Servers that need to interact with others. Doing so will help ensure that replication and other tasks will not fail in the future.

- Add the domain user account you are using for the service account to the local administrators group on all SQL Servers. By doing so you will have all the required permissions for the services to run properly. This is also easier than configuring each folder and Registry key with the appropriate security settings.

- Register the servers you need in Enterprise Manager. This makes it easy to administer multiple servers from your desktop.

REVIEW QUESTIONS

1. What is the purpose of the SQL Server Agent service?

2. What is a service account?

3. Why should you use a domain user account for your service account?

4. What is the purpose of a server group in Enterprise Manager?

5. What permissions are required in order to install a SQL Server instance?

6. Why would you want to create multiple instances of SQL Server on a single machine?

7. What is the purpose of the SQL Server service?

CHAPTER

Establishing Login Security

SQL Server 2000 must authenticate a user before the client is allowed to perform any activities within the database. This chapter introduces the various options for user authentication.

Initially you will learn about the authentication process to lay a foundation for the authentication methods that will be described later in the chapter. The authentication process defines the required steps for SQL Server user validation. The chapter then focuses on presenting the three choices for an authentication method: Windows Authentication, SQL Authentication, and Mixed mode. The authentication method is the configured security level for a SQL Server instance.

The first authentication method explained is Windows Authentication. Windows Authentication allows for the integration of Windows 2000 and SQL Server 2000 security. Under this mode of authentication, Windows 2000 users and groups can be granted access to SQL Server. The second authentication method described is SQL Authentication. SQL Authentication has some disadvantages to Windows Authentication, which are addressed later in the chapter; SQL Authentication can be used to provide greater flexibility for heterogeneous client application and Internet access.

The third authentication method, Mixed mode, is a combination of Windows Authentication and SQL Authentication. This configuration allows for the integration of Windows 2000 and SQL Server security or for the implementation of SQL logins that do not depend on Windows 2000.

After a client has successfully authenticated at SQL Server, the client can then connect to a database in the SQL Server instance. Each database has a set of users and roles, which define the individuals who have access to a particular database. This chapter discusses database users and roles and how to implement them effectively within your organization.

Introduction to the Authentication Process

A login account must be created for each user who needs to perform a database task in SQL Server 2000. It is the database administrator's (DBA's) responsibility to create and manage the logins to SQL server. A login is either a security account created in SQL Server or a link to a specific Windows 2000 user or group account. When users attempt to access SQL Server, they supply their login credentials and the SQL Server service authenticates them. The process for authenticating a user depends on the method of authentication chosen. The following will detail the two options available for processing a login attempt: Windows Authentication or SQL Authentication.

Windows Authentication

Windows Authentication is used to integrate Windows 2000 security with SQL Server security. With this authentication option the client can use the same account for logging into Windows 2000 and SQL Server 2000. Windows Authentication depends on the user first logging in successfully to the Windows 2000 domain. When a user connects to SQL Server using Windows Authentication, the connection is referred to as a *trusted connection*. The user presents an access token to SQL Server to represent the user's identity. SQL Server 2000 uses the access token and compares this against a list of users who have been granted access to SQL Server.

Authentication is slightly different for an Active Directory client than for a client that does not support Active Directory. Active Directory clients are authenticated through Kerberos, whereas non-Active Directory clients are authenticated with Microsoft Windows NT LAN Manager (NTLM). The difference between the two is described in the following sections.

Kerberos Authentication

Kerberos is the preferred authentication protocol for a Windows 2000 domain. If the client doesn't support Kerberos, then NTLM authentication is used. Kerberos defines the network authentication services for client access to domain resources. Kerberos has the ability to implement mutual authentication, meaning that the client and the network service must identify themselves to each other. SQL Server uses mutual authentication to authenticate the clients as well as the SQL services.

When the client supplies its network credentials, Windows 2000 locates an Active Directory domain controller. The Kerberos service then issues a ticket-granting ticket (TGT), which contains encrypted data that confirms the client's identity. This identity is then passed to the Key Distribution Center (KDC). When the client wants access to a service, the TGT is sent to the KDC, and the client is then granted a session ticket for the requested service at the server where the service is registered. The client can then pass the session ticket to the server service that is managing the resource and use the ticket to identify itself.

After a client has supplied its credentials to the server, the server service is then required to identify itself to the client. The server will respond to the client, in encrypted format, with a message identifying itself. Each session ticket has an expiration time. The default expiration time is determined by the KDC. The ticket can be reused for access to the resource until the ticket expires. The ticket will also have to be rebuilt if the client logs off the domain.

Mutual authentication with Kerberos requires that the client and the server authenticate each other. The Service Principal Name (SPN) must be configured for the SQL Server service. The SPN is used by SQL Server to authenticate. Without the SPN, SQL Server is limited in its support of Kerberos and mutual authentication. Configuring the SPN is detailed later in this chapter under the section *Impersonation and Delegation*.

Windows NT LAN Manager Authentication

Windows NT LAN Manager (NTLM) authentication is the same authentication mechanism that was used in NT 4.0. It is used in a Windows 2000 environment only when the client and/or server do not support Kerberos. Windows NT LAN Manager is not a method of mutual authentication. It is an encrypted process whereby the client is authenticated with the server. When the user logs into the domain, the user is granted an access token.

This access token is used to identify the user identification, group identities, and user rights associated with that user. The client can then use this access token as an identity when attempting to access network resources. The access token is sent to the server, where the resource resides. The security subsystem on the resource server compares the access token with the list of users and groups (ACL) that have access to the resource. The user is then either granted or denied access to the resource. With NTLM, the SPN does not need to be configured. The SPN is not required because the client authentication does not depend on the server identity. Windows NT LAN Manager does not support the Kerberos ticket, mutual authentication, or security account delegation. Without these three features, NTLM is not as secure an environment as Kerberos is.

The Authentication Process of a Windows Login

After the user has logged in to the domain using either Kerberos or NTLM, the client can request access to a specific SQL Server. The client sends identification to the server and, based on the server's list of users (which is stored in the sysxlogins table on the master database), the user is either granted or denied access to SQL Server. The advantages to Windows Authentication will be presented later in this chapter in the section *Comparing SQL Authentication and Windows Authentication*. The detailed steps of Windows Authentication are as follows:

1. When a user initially connects to SQL Server, the client requests a trusted connection with SQL Server.

2. The user passes the Kerberos ticket or access token to SQL Server. SQL server uses the ticket or the token to verify that the user has already been validated in Windows 2000.

3. If SQL Server finds the account in its list of users, the server accepts the connection. SQL Server doesn't need to evaluate the password because Windows 2000 has already authenticated the user.

SQL Authentication

When a Windows 2000 domain has not authenticated the user, the only other option for accessing SQL Server is through a SQL security account. This method of authentication is particularly beneficial if the user is connecting to SQL Server from the Internet or from a non-Windows network infrastructure. In such cases you would not want the user to have to log on to a Windows 2000 domain. The user can supply username and password credentials to SQL Server, bypassing Windows 2000 security. After the user passes login credentials to the server, SQL Server compares the username submitted against the list of SQL Server 2000 security accounts. If SQL Server finds the username in the sysxlogins table, the user is granted access to SQL Server. With SQL Server Authentication the username and password are supplied to the server in clear text format, unless both the client and the server are using secure sockets layer (SSL) encryption for the entire session. When SSL is used, the client and server must both obtain a certificate. Certificates and SSL are described in more detail in Chapter 15, "Managing Internet Security."

Without SSL, SQL Authentication results in an unsecured method of authentication. The steps for authenticating SQL accounts are as follows:

1. A user requests a nontrusted connection to SQL Server. The username and password are sent to the server.

2. The credentials are compared against the list of SQL users stored in the sysxlogins table. The username and password both have to be verified.

3. If the account doesn't exist, or the password is not validated, the login will fail and the user will be denied access.

Comparing Windows Authentication with SQL Authentication

Although Windows Authentication is the preferred method of accessing SQL Server, both Windows Authentication and SQL Authentication may be necessary in your business environment. The following sections will provide justification for implementing either authentication method.

The Advantages of Windows Authentication

Windows Authentication is the default method of establishing security. Windows Authentication also provides several security advantages to administrators for supporting users. Microsoft suggests implementing Windows Authentication whenever possible. Following is a list of advantages of Windows Authentication:

- When a user logs in to the Windows 2000 domain, the credentials are encrypted before being passed to the domain controller.

- An audit trail is easy to maintain. You will easily be able to identify who did what and when. You can track events back to a Windows user or group account.

- After the user is authenticated against the Windows domain, the password is never sent to SQL Server.

- All Kerberos tickets and access tokens are encrypted.

- Windows 2000 supports password policies to enforce password requirements. These policies can help you manage a secure environment.

- The user needs to know only one login ID. The Windows domain user account and the account needed for access to SQL Server are the same.

- Windows 2000 groups can be granted access to SQL Server. Granting this access can potentially decrease security maintenance.

- One username can be used for access to multiple SQL Servers.

Justification of SQL Authentication

SQL Authentication may still be required in many organizations. In fact, your organization may have one server that supports Windows Authentication only and another that allows SQL Authentication as well. This method of authentication is appropriate when it is not realistic for all users to log on to the Windows domain. SQL Authentication is commonly used for Internet applications, for authentication over non-Microsoft networks, and to support some third-party applications. SQL Authentication is configured by setting your SQL security level to Mixed mode. While in Mixed mode a DBA may have a combination of SQL Security accounts and Windows Authentication accounts accessing a single SQL Server. The Mixed mode method of authentication is also required to allow connection to a SQL server 2000 machine from Novell, Banyan, Apple, and Unix clients. SQL Authentication provides the following advantages:

- Windows 2000 does not have to authenticate the user. This is beneficial if you are in an environment that does not have a Windows domain.

- Many third-party applications do not support Windows Authentication. SQL Authentication gives you more flexibility when you are dealing with outside vendors.

- With SQL Authentication you can separate Windows security and SQL Server security. If you want to completely separate the security models, you have that option.

Configuring Authentication Modes

An authentication mode is the configured representation of the authentication methods we have previously described. During the installation of SQL Server, the administrator is prompted for the authentication mode. The default mode provided during the installation is Windows Authentication. Alternatively the administrator performing the installation can change to Mixed mode at the installation security selection screen. If the mode is changed to Mixed, the administrator must then supply a password for the SA account. The SA account is a system administrator and has access to all features, functions, services, and data stored on the SQL Server instance. The mode of authentication could also be changed any time after installation by using Enterprise Manager. To change the authentication mode after SQL Server is installed, perform the following steps:

1. Open SQL Enterprise Manager.

2. Right-click on the server you want to configure and select Properties.

3. Select the Security tab as shown in Figure 4.1.

4. Select the appropriate security mode.

5. Click OK. You will be prompted to start and stop the SQL Server Service.

6. After the service is restarted, your new security settings will be in place.

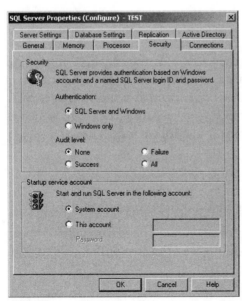

Figure 4.1   Set the SQL Server security level configuration with this dialogue box.

Because stopping the service is necessary for the new configuration to take effect, you should minimize the number of changes you make to security modes. When the service is stopped, all users connected to the server instance will be disconnected. The details about each authentication mode are described in the sections that follow.

NOTE When the SQL Server service is stopped and restarted, the memory used to cache procedures and data is flushed.

Windows Authentication Mode

While your system is in Windows Authentication mode, only Windows users can be given access to SQL Server. Each user who accesses SQL Server will be required to first log on to the Windows domain. The SA account is disabled in this mode, and SQL accounts cannot be created. The local administrators group will automatically be given access to SQL Server, and all other Windows users and groups will have to be granted or denied access manually. Using Windows Authentication mode gives all users access to the following domain features:

- Password expiration, security, and other password policies.
- Group management for access to SQL Server.
- Single account management. Passwords have to be maintained only at the domain level.

Mixed Mode Authentication

Mixed mode is a combination of Windows Authentication and SQL Authentication. Mixed mode is required if any access to SQL Server is through SQL accounts. SQL Server does not support a mode that is SQL only. Mixed mode enables the use of SQL Server Authentication, which is specifically helpful in supporting access to the following:

- Internet clients
- Non-Windows clients
- Third-party vendor applications that require a specific SQL login

Mixed mode also enables the SA account. While you are in Mixed mode, the Windows local administrators group is also granted full access to SQL

Server. While implementing Mixed mode you can still grant and deny access to Windows users and groups.

In some cases, it may be desirable to disable Windows Authentication. This is not one of the apparent configuration options, but the following steps can be taken to manage security through SQL logins only:

1. Configure the server to support Mixed mode authentication.
2. While logged in to SQL Server as SA, create a SQL login for all SQL system administrators.
3. Place these SQL logins in the sysadmin server role.
4. Remove the BUILTIN/Administrators account.
5. Create the SQL logins required for client access.

From this point on if you don't give Windows users or groups access to SQL Server, you will have effectively configured a SQL Authentication only mode. This option is not suggested in most cases and should be evaluated only when your current business policies require you to do so.

Encryption

Encryption is a method of protecting data by altering it into an unrecognizable format. In most cases encryption also increases processing overhead, and the security gains should be compared to the cost of performance. Microsoft SQL Server can encrypt some network traffic and objects that are stored locally, as discussed in the sections that follow.

Local Encryption

Passwords for SQL Server logins are stored in an encrypted format. Additionally certain Transact-SQL object definitions can be encrypted. Stored Procedure, Trigger, and View definition statements can be encrypted to prevent access to the source code. Object definitions are stored in the *syscomments* system table. When they are encrypted using the With Encryption option, the source code can't be opened.

NOTE When using the With Encryption option for creating stored procedures, views, and triggers, keep a copy of your original SQL. After an object is encrypted you can alter the object, but the source code cannot be viewed. An example of the With Encryption option is provided in Chapter 5, "Managing Object Security."

Network Encryption

Two levels of network encryption can be implemented. The first is encryption of passwords for Windows Authentication. With Windows Authentication the user does not have to send a password to SQL Server, and therefore encryption of the password is not an issue. When the user originally logs in to the domain, the password is encrypted using either Kerberos or NTLM authentication as described earlier in this chapter.

Alternatively, the entire session between the client and server can be encrypted using SSL. This kind of encryption, however, requires the use of certificates on both the client and the server machine. The detailed steps of implementing SSL are addressed in Chapter 15, "Managing Internet Security."

Impersonation and Delegation

Impersonation and delegation can be used to allow SQL Server to use the security credentials of the client when the server is accessing resources outside the local server. These features are also beneficial when you are performing the mutual authentication described previously in the section *Kerberos Authentication*. Impersonation and delegation are discussed in the sections that follow.

Impersonation

SQL can use the client's identity when the server is accessing resources on behalf of the client. An example of this is when one server is accessing another server through the linked server feature of SQL Server. The client accesses the first server to run a stored procedure or a SQL statement. The server then needs to connect, on behalf of the client, to the linked server that the statement references. When connecting to the other server it allows the SQL Server service to use the client's login credentials. The server impersonates the client's security context to allow authentication of the client's identity. This process ensures that resource access is limited to the client's own security context.

Delegation

Delegation allows a client to authenticate with one SQL Server. The identity that is established is retained and used for access to other SQL Servers, thus decreasing the overhead related to constant authentication. For example, user Softouch\Bill connects to a server named Chicago, which then connects to a server named New York. Server New York knows the client is Softouch\Bill. Delegation is supported only while all connected servers are running Windows 2000 and authenticating through Kerberos. Active Directory must be installed, and the client account, server settings, and SPN, as discussed in the following sections, must be configured.

Client Account Settings

In order to configure the client account settings, you will need to edit the properties of the user account that requires delegation. This editing should be accomplished through the Active Directory Users and Computers Management console. If the DBA is not also a system administrator in Windows, coordination with the Windows system administrator is essential. From Active Directory you will have to configure the following client account settings:

- The Account Is Trusted for Delegation setting must be configured on the account properties page for the user making the security request. Figure 4.2 illustrates the Properties page from the Active Directory Users and Computers Management console.

- You must ensure that the Account Is Sensitive and Cannot Be Delegated checkbox is not enabled. If it is configured, the delegation process will fail.

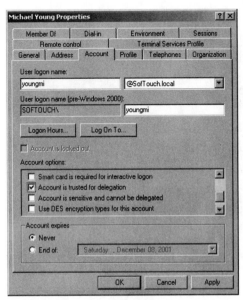

Figure 4.2 Use the Active Directory dialogue box to set up trusted user account delegation.

Server Settings

The following server settings, which allow the server to participate in the mutual authentication required for Kerberos, need to be configured at SQL Server:

- The Trust Computer for Delegation setting must be set as shown in Figure 4.3.
- TCP\IP must be installed and running.
- The SQL Server service must have an SPN assigned. Configuring the SPN is covered in the following section.

Service Principal Name

Prior to configuring security account delegation, the SQL Server instance must be configured to accept delegations. To use security account delegation, SQL Server 2000 must have a Service Principal Name (SPN). The SPN is created by a domain administrator and assigned to the SQL Server service account. Consequently, if the security account ever changes, the SPN

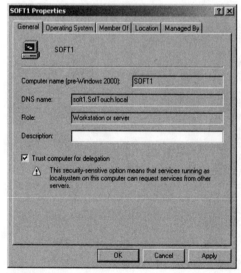

Figure 4.3   Server Account delegation must also be configured through Active Directory.

must be deleted and recreated. The SPN is used to prove that the SQL Server service is on at a particular socket address. Using the SetSPN utility, which is included in the Windows 2000 Resource Kit, the SPN can be created by typing the following:

```
Setspn -A MSSQLSvc/Host:Port serviceaccount
```

- *Host* is replaced with either the fully qualified domain name or the IP address.
- *Port* is the assigned port number for the SQL Server instance. The default instance is set to port 1433, which can be changed if necessary.

NOTE A *socket address* is the unique combination of IP address and port number.

- *Serviceaccount* is replaced with the account used to start up the SQL Server service.

NOTE If the SQL Server service is using the local system account for service login, an SPN is automatically registered each time the service starts and unregistered each time the service is shut down. The SPN needs to be assigned only if you are using a domain account for your SQL Server and SQL Server Agent service account.

Server Roles

Once the user is authenticated within SQL Server, the instance of SQL Server must determine what actions the client can perform on the system. The first area of evaluation is server configuration. Microsoft has provided several server-level roles, which grant server configuration permissions. Roles are similar to groups.

The next section details the importance of these server-wide configuration permissions. You'll be introduced to the various server roles that can be used to perform administrative functions on your SQL Server. Server roles can't be deleted, nor can the permissions assigned to these roles be changed. Table 4.1 identifies the server roles and their responsibilities.

Table 4.1 Server Roles

SERVER ROLE	EFFECTIVE PERMISSION
Sysadmin	Perform all actions on the server and its databases
Dbcreator	Create and manage databases
Diskadmin	Manage files on the hard disk
Processadmin	Stop, start, pause, and kill SQL Server processes
Serveradmin	Manage server configuration
Setupadmin	Server configuration, replication, and linked servers
Securityadmin	Configure and audit logins
Bulkadmin	Run Bulk Insert commands

Creating Login Accounts

A couple of built-in accounts exist: the SA account and the local Windows Administrators group. All client access beyond the built-in accounts must be added by the DBA.

You can create login accounts through three different methods. You can use the Create Login Wizard, SQL Enterprise Manager, or Transact-SQL. This book will give descriptive examples on the latter two. You will first be introduced to creating Windows 2000 Login accounts, and then you will see how to create SQL Login accounts. Each section provides the procedural steps required using both Enterprise Manager and Transact-SQL. The Create Login Wizard will not be demonstrated. The wizard is intuitive, and the other methods of creating logins define the underlying technology.

Built-In Accounts

SQL Server provides two default login accounts: SA and BUILTIN/ Administrators.

The SA account is a special account included with SQL Server that allows you to perform all actions against the database server. The SA account is enabled only while the server is configured in Mixed mode and is provided as a fail-safe. Typically this account should not be used. All system administrators should have their own account created on the SQL

Server instance. These accounts should then be added to the sysadmin server role, which is outlined in the following section. Using separate accounts for system administrators increases individual accountability by providing an audit trail. If all system administrators logged on and used the SA account, there would be no ability to track the individual who is making the system modifications. Use the SA account sparingly; additionally you should always have a complicated password assigned to the SA account. This account can't be deleted from the system and can be disabled only by choosing Windows Authentication mode.

The BUILTIN/Administrators account is the Windows group account that identifies the local administrators group. By default this account is given full access to all functions on the database server. This means all local administrators will have full access to SQL Server. You will need to determine if this is what you want. The BUILTIN/Administrators account can be removed and replaced with the appropriate set of administrators if necessary.

Creating Windows Login Accounts

Keep in mind that Windows Login accounts depend on a link to a current Windows user or group name. The user or group in Windows 2000 has to exist before the account can be granted access to SQL Server.

Windows Authentication Guidelines

Earlier in this chapter you were introduced to the advantages of using Windows Login Accounts. With that in mind you should also consider the following guidelines:

- The name of the login must include the Windows domain in which the account is stored.

- When granting Windows 2000 groups access to SQL Server, SQL Server will identify the group as one login account. Each user of the Windows group is not given a corresponding login account in SQL Server; each user will be identified by his or her group membership. This process allows simplified account management in SQL Server. If a user leaves the company, the user's Windows account can be disabled or deleted in Windows, and nothing may have to be done in SQL Server.

- When Windows groups are used for granting access to the server, SQL Server still maintains the identity of each user. The SQL Profiler utility or the USER_NAME function can be used to determine the Windows user identity.

- When an individual user or group account is deleted, Windows doesn't automatically delete the login in SQL Server. When a user account is removed from Windows first, it will also have to be removed from SQL Server.

- Logins have a limit of 128 characters, including the domain name as well as the username.

Managing Windows Authentication Logins

SQL Enterprise Manager can be used to grant Windows users access to SQL Server. Enterprise Manager provides a graphical interface that is helpful to many administrators. Although several methods are available for creating accounts, it is important that you find the method you are most comfortable with. One of the primary goals of security management is reducing the cost of administration as it relates to security. As you become more comfortable with one of the methods for creating logins your cost of security administration will decrease. To use Enterprise Manager to create SQL logins, take the following steps:

1. Open Enterprise Manager.
2. Click to expand the server instance you want to manage.
3. Click to expand the security configuration as shown in Figure 4.4.
4. Right-click on Logins and choose New Login from the pop-up menu that appears. The New Login dialogue box appears, as shown in Figure 4.5.
5. The default authentication type is Windows Authentication. Click the domain drop-down box and select your domain.
6. Type either the username or the group name in directly or use the ellipses to navigate through the list of domain users and groups.

It is possible for a Windows Account to be granted or denied access to SQL Server. A user has an individual user account and may exist in multiple Windows 2000 groups. Thus a user could be granted or denied access multiple times, creating a conflict of permissions. The Deny option supercedes the Grant option and therefore should be used sparingly. If a user is granted access to the server via a Windows user account and is denied access via a group to which he or she belongs, the Deny option will override the access that was granted. For instance, Steve has a login that is

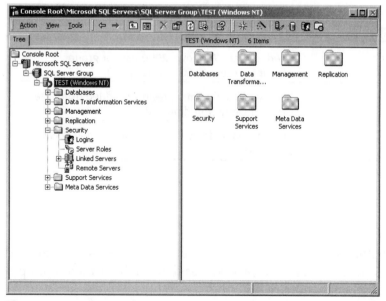

Figure 4.4 Use Enterprise Manager to manage and create logins to SQL Server.

granted from his Windows 2000 account. Steve also belongs to the Windows group named Sales, which has been denied access to SQL Server. Steve's effective permission is Deny. If you are not clear on who all the members of a Windows group are, be cautious with the Deny permission.

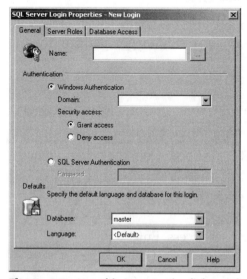

Figure 4.5 Use this New Login dialogue box to create both Windows and SQL Server logins.

Table 4.2 System Stored Procedures for Windows Authentication Login Management

STORED PROCEDURE	EFFECTIVE USE
sp_grantlogin	Used to grant Windows 2000 user or group accounts access to SQL Server 2000
sp_revokelogin	Removes a login entry previously added using the Grant or Deny stored procedure
sp_denylogin	Prevents a Windows user or group from accessing SQL Server

Windows Authentication logins can also be managed using Transact-SQL. Table 4.2 outlines the stored procedures that can be used to manipulate Windows Authentication logins.

Use the revoke option when you want to reverse a login that was either granted or denied access to SQL Server. Revoking a login can be performed in Enterprise Manager. Deleting an entry from the list of logins performs the Revoke statement for you.

The vast majority of your Windows Authentication management should be performed through Grant and Revoke actions.

Creating SQL Server Login Accounts

You can use Enterprise Manager to manage SQL Login accounts also. To create a SQL Authentication login in Enterprise Manager, perform the following steps:

1. Open Enterprise Manager.
2. Click to expand the server instance where you want to add the login.
3. Click to expand the security configuration option.
4. Right-click on Logins and select New Login from the pop-up menu that appears.
5. Select the bullet point to denote that this login is a SQL Server Authentication login.
6. A password is now required for user access. Enter a password.
7. Click OK.
8. You will be prompted to confirm the password. Confirm the password and close the new login screen.

Table 4.3 System Stored Procedures for SQL Server Login Management

STORED PROCEDURE	EFFECTIVE USE
sp_addlogin	Used to add a SQL login to SQL Server. This procedure requires the login name and password for the login.
sp_droplogin	Used to drop an existing SQL login.
sp_password	Used to change the login password.

As with Windows logins, SQL Server logins can be created using Transact-SQL. Table 4.3 identifies the stored procedures that are used to manage SQL Server logins.

The following considerations should be taken into account when you are creating SQL logins:

- SQL logins can be up to 128 characters in length and can't contain null values.

- SQL logins can contain letters, digits, and symbols. The only restricted character is the backslash.

SysxLogins System Table

The logins added through either Enterprise Manager or through Transact-SQL are stored in the sysxlogins table on the Master Database. This table can be viewed from Enterprise Manager or through a simple query. The system tables, by default, can't be edited directly. This can be enabled to allow the direct editing of the system tables, which could be necessary in some odd scenarios where a restore process has not been completely successful, or old scripts have been run against a new database server. In these strange scenarios, the login account may not appear to exist when viewed from Enterprise Manager, but when an attempt is made to add the account, the action fails because the account already exists. To enable system table updates, perform the following steps:

1. Open Enterprise Manager.
2. Right-click on the server instance you wish to modify.
3. Select Properties.

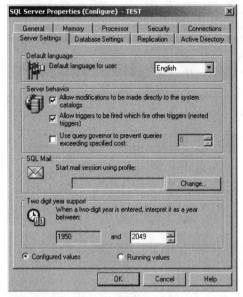

Figure 4.6   Use the SQL Server Properties dialogue box to update the SQL Server system tables.

4. Select the Server Settings tab as shown in Figure 4.6.

5. Click to enable the Allow Modifications to Be Made Directly to the System Catalogs.

6. Close out the Server Properties pages.

Database Access

Access to SQL Server 2000 does not by itself grant a user access to any of the databases in SQL Server 2000. In addition, except for membership in the sysadmin role, membership in a server role does not grant a database-specific permission. Database access rights must be specifically granted by a system administrator or by a member of an administrator role in the database. After the user has authenticated with SQL Server, the next step is to request access at the database level. The application the client is using requests access to a specific database on the server. The client's access to the database is determined by the person's user account and role membership for that database. The next several pages will detail the information needed to implement database users and roles.

Database Users

Specified clients can be granted user access to a database via their Windows 2000 or SQL Server 2000 security login account. A permitted database user is then granted permissions within the database through a database role, the public role, and specific grants of statement and object permissions.

Database users are automatically created for a login when the login is granted access to a database. The default name of each user is the same as the login name. Typically these names should not be changed. Differing login names and usernames can only result in confusion in security management. In Enterprise Manager, the following steps can be used to create a database user:

1. Open Enterprise Manager.
2. Click to expand the server instance you wish to add the user to.
3. Click to expand the security configuration container.
4. Click to expand the logins. This displays the list of logins on the server.
5. Right-click on the login you wish to configure and select Properties.
6. Select the Database Access tab as shown in Figure 4.7.
7. Click the Permit checkbox for the database where the user should be created. Notice that the user is created with the same name as the login, and the roles for the database appear in the lower window.
8. Click OK to close the Login Properties screen.

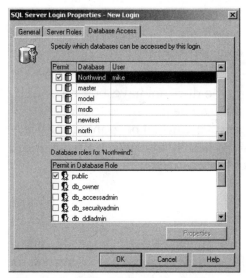

Figure 4.7 While adding a new login, you can grant access to a database from the SQL Server Login Properties dialogue box.

Table 4.4 System Stored Procedures for Database User Management

STORED PROCEDURE	EFFECTIVE USE
sp_grantdbaccess	Grants a login access to a database. This procedure adds the user object to the sysusers system table in the database in which the user is created.
sp_revokedbaccess	Removes a user from the database.
sp_change_users_login	Changes the login's link to the database user. This procedure is used to change the login's identity for a database.

Users and roles can be managed while the login is being created or anytime thereafter. Alternatively, you can also create and manage users from the users' configuration container located in the database they are to be created in.

As with most actions in SQL Server, the users can be manipulated with Transact-SQL. Table 4.4 defines the stored procedures that can be used to manipulate user access to a database.

A couple of database user accounts can be used for special purposes. They are defined as follows:

- The database owner (DBO) account specifies a user account as the owner of the database—as the one who can perform any activity with respect to the database. The DBO has full access to everything within the database. Every database has a DBO. By default the DBO will be granted to the user that created the database.

- The guest account is an authenticated user who has access to an instance of SQL Server 2000 (but who does not have a user account to access a particular database) and can be permitted to access a database as a guest user. The guest account can be granted specific permissions within the database (generally to read certain data). By default, a user database does not have a guest user account.

Database Roles

A *database role* is an object created within a database that can be used to group users. After users are grouped into roles, permissions can be managed at the role level and individual database users do not need to be given permissions. Every database comes with a set of fixed database roles.

NOTE When Windows 2000 groups are granted access to SQL Server, the group is given one login to SQL Server. When this login is given access to a database, one database user is created for the Windows 2000 group. Within Enterprise Manager you will see the entire group represented as a single item. Consequently, if you are granting Windows 2000 groups access to SQL Server, your users are grouped at the Windows 2000 level, and the administration of roles could be minimal. Roles are used within SQL Server to group the database users. When you have granted Windows groups access to SQL Server, you have already grouped the users.

Fixed database roles are built-in roles with a predefined purpose. Most of the permissions assigned to these roles are administrative in nature. The permissions given to a fixed database role, other than the public role, can't be changed. The *public role* includes all users of a database and does not have a fixed permission. The public role has a fixed membership instead of fixed permission. With fixed membership the database users who are members of the role cannot be changed. If the user is granted access to a database, the user is automatically a member of the public role. The membership can be managed for other fixed roles.

Public Role

All users of a database are automatically added to the public role. Users can't be removed from the public role. The following characteristics define the public role:

- Should be used for default permissions to the database.
- Is contained in every database.
- Has membership that cannot be managed. All users are members.
- Can't be deleted from any database.
- Is not granted permissions to any database with the exception of the system databases.

Other Fixed Roles

Fixed database roles are stored in the sysusers table of each database. They can be used to group users to provide database functionality. The

Table 4.5 Fixed Database Roles

ROLE	PURPOSE
db_owner	Perform any database activity
db_accessadmin	Add and drop users and roles
db_ddladmin	Manipulate database objects
db_securityadmin	Assign object and statement permissions
db_backupoperator	Perform database backups
db_datareader	Read data from any table in the database
db_datawriter	Insert, update, and delete data from any table in the database
db_denydatareader	Deny read access to all data in the database
db_denydatawriter	Deny insert, update, and delete for all data in the database

membership of these roles can be modified by any member of the db_owner role. Table 4.5 identifies the fixed database roles and their purposes.

Membership to fixed database roles can be modified by using Enterprise Manager or by executing the sp_addrolemember and sp_droprolemember stored procedures.

User-Defined Roles

User-defined roles can be created for group users who need to be able to perform the same database tasks. Permissions can be assigned to roles instead of to individual users. This will minimize the list of permissions for a given object and decrease the maintenance associated with permissions management. You should consider the use of user-defined roles if one of the following conditions exists:

- You are using SQL Authentication mode.
- The current Windows 2000 groups do not meet your database needs.
- Multiple Windows groups need the same access to the database.

Enterprise Manager can be used to create and modify user-defined roles. Take the following steps to create a role from Enterprise Manager:

1. Open Enterprise Manager.

2. Click to expand the server instance you want to modify.

3. Click to expand databases.

4. Click to expand the database where the role is to be created.

5. Right-click on Roles and select New Database Role.

6. Enter the name of the role you want to create. The default role type is Standard. Application roles are described in more depth in Chapter 6, "Designing Application Security."

7. In the Database Role Properties dialogue box, click on Add to add users to the role as shown in Figure 4.8.

8. When you are finished adding the appropriate number of users, click OK and exit the Database Role Properties dialogue box.

The sp_addrole and sp_droprole stored procedures are used to add and remove roles using Transact-SQL. Additionally, you can use the sp_addrolemember and sp_droprolemember stored procedures to modify the membership of your roles.

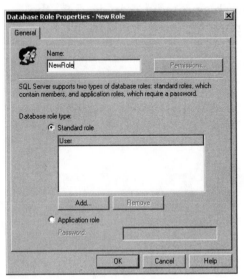

Figure 4.8   Add users to a database role using the Database Role Properties dialogue box.

Best Practices

- Use Windows Authentication whenever possible. Windows authentication increases security and performance while decreasing administrative maintenance.

- Use Mixed mode only when necessary. Mixed mode is appropriate when you do not want the client to log in to a Windows 2000 domain (such as with Internet applications, heterogeneous environments, and third-party vendor applications).

- Use Windows 2000 groups to grant access to SQL Server. Group access decreases the number of logins in SQL Server and eases the overhead of maintaining security.

- Use the public role to assign default permissions. Because all users are part of the public role, the public role can be used to set the default permissions on your database objects.

- Avoid the use of the SA account. All database administrators should have their own login and be added to the sysadmin server role. This allows for the most flexibility in administrative auditing.

- Create user-defined roles when Windows 2000 groups are either not available (SQL Authentication) or insufficient. Permission can be granted to the user-defined role. This procedure can decrease the overhead of permissions management.

REVIEW QUESTIONS

1. What are the advantages to Windows Authentication over SQL Authentication?

2. Why would you need to use SQL Authentication?

3. What is the difference between Kerberos and Windows NT LAN Manager (NTLM)?

4. What is impersonation?

5. What levels of encryption are available with SQL Server 2000?

6. What is the difference between the public role and the guest account?

7. Why should you avoid the use of the SA account?

8. Under what circumstances should you create user-defined roles?

CHAPTER 5

Managing Object Security

When a user connects to an instance of Microsoft SQL Server, the activities that individual can perform are determined by the permissions granted to the person's database user and roles. To interact with the database, the user must have permissions set on the database objects. This includes the right to change the schema (design) of the database and to interact with the data stored in the database tables. Each database consists of several objects, which can include tables, views, stored procedures, functions, rules, defaults, indexes, and triggers. These core objects and their organizational structure are referred to as the *database schema*. It is through these objects that users manipulate the information stored in the database. A user's permissions on the database tables, views, and stored procedures define the activities that the user can perform with SQL Server and those database objects.

NOTE It is important to make the management of permissions as easy as possible. If time is invested to set the permission structure up appropriately in the beginning, permissions administration should be minimal.

This chapter introduces the types of permissions that can be implemented in SQL Server, including a description of object, statement, and implied permissions. Then the chapter provides the steps required for implementing permissions, and addresses administration issues such as object ownership and object dependencies. Ownership in SQL Server is a critical issue. Ownership in SQL Server is different from that of many other database management systems, so it needs to be evaluated for efficient database administration. Finally, this chapter presents the reasoning and steps required for creating an object with a database owner (DBO) ownership.

Types of Permissions

Managing permissions within SQL Server is generally performed by the DBA, but some organizations require the DBA to support so many databases that the role may be partially distributed to the database developer. In these cases, the DBA should still be accountable for server-level permissions. The developer can then take over the individual object-level permissions. Regardless of the strategy you deploy, it is important that your strategy be well documented and understood by all individuals who have any support responsibilities for the database. If the security and permission design is solid and the information is documented thoroughly, the administrative overhead of permissions management is decreased. In many cases, the overhead of permissions management comes from a lack of understanding of either the security model or the current implementation. Appropriate design and documentation can help you to overcome these obstacles.

Permissions management in SQL Server 2000 includes the administration of the following three types of permissions, which are discussed separately in the following sections:

- Object permissions
- Statement permissions
- Implied permissions

Object Permissions

Object permissions are the set of permissions that allow the client to interact with the database objects. Therefore these permissions require the highest level of continuing attention. Most other permissions are established once or inherited based on a server role the user belongs to. Object-level permissions are managed by a DBA or developer and need to be monitored to ensure a secure database. It is important to have a strategy for implementing permissions before the database is created. The permissions you choose to use depend on the type of objects you deploy within your database. If your application takes advantage of stored procedures and views, the security infrastructure is different from that of an application that just uses database tables. The details of application security and suggestions for implementing a secure application are covered in more depth in Chapter 6, "Designing Application Security."

Object permissions are granted, revoked, or denied to a user or role. Table 5.1 identifies the object permissions that can be assigned to a user or role.

The following considerations should be kept in mind when you are establishing object permissions:

- Insert and Delete statements affect the entire row of a table and therefore can be applied only to tables and views. Both the Select and Update permissions can be applied to individual columns.

Table 5.1   Object Permissions

PERMISSION	FUNCTION	OBJECTS GRANTED TO
Select	Retrieve data for reading	Tables, columns, user-defined functions, and views
Insert	Add data to the table	Tables, columns, user-defined functions, and views
Update	Modify records that already exist in the table	Tables and views
Delete	Delete existing records from a table	Tables and views
Execute	Execute a precompiled statement	Stored procedures and user-defined functions
References	Create a Foreign Key constraint that references that table	Tables
All	Apply all available permissions to an object	All

NOTE Consider using views to restrict access to columns instead of individual column permissions. Avoiding table- and column-level permissions should be a primary goal of application security design. Application security is described in much more detail in Chapter 6, "Designing Application Security."

- Execute permissions can be applied to precompiled SQL statements (stored procedures and functions). Execute permission can be the most powerful permission used for security management. For example, a user can be given the ability to execute a stored procedure that inserts a new record into a table without having insert permission on the table. Execute permissions can be an effective means of restricting this type of insert that can occur. This strategy will be addressed later in the chapter in the section titled *Object Ownership Chains*.

- The References permission is required on an object that is referenced by a view or function using the WITH SCHEMABINDING clause. More can be read about the SCHEMABINDING clause in the SQL Server 2000 Books Online.

Statement Permissions

Statement permissions are used to manipulate the objects of the database. Statement permissions, when granted, allow for the modification of the database schema. This class of permissions is established at the database level and should be used in the context of appropriate object ownership rules. Object ownership rules will be detailed later in the section titled *Object Ownership Chains*. Statement permissions, such as CREATE VIEW, are applied to the statement and grant access to perform the statement regardless of the object in question. Statement permissions are further defined in Table 5.2.

Table 5.2   Statement Permissions

STATEMENT PERMISSION	FUNCTIONALLY PERMITS
Create Table	Used to CREATE, ALTER, and DROP tables.
Create View	Used to CREATE, ALTER, and DROP views.
Create Stored Procedure	Used to CREATE, ALTER, and DROP stored procedures.

Table 5.2 (Continued)

STATEMENT PERMISSION	FUNCTIONALLY PERMITS
Create Default	Used to CREATE, ALTER, and DROP default objects. When bound to a column, a default specifies a value to be inserted into the column to which the default is bound when no value is supplied during an INSERT statement.
Create Rule	Used to CREATE, ALTER, and DROP rules. A SQL Server rule is a conditional expression written in Transact-SQL that defines a data-integrity constraint. The rule is bound to a column to define the types of values that are accepted in the column.
Create Function	Used to CREATE, ALTER, and DROP user-defined functions. Functions accept input parameters to a user and then return a single value.
Backup Database	Used to perform a database or differential database backup.
Backup Log	Used to back up the transaction log.

All members of the sysadmin role have the ability to perform all of the statement permissions. Use explicit statement permissions only when you need to define additional logins that need to perform the functions listed in Table 5.2.

Statement permissions can be implemented through Enterprise Manager or with Transact-SQL. To set statement permissions for a database, use Enterprise Manager to perform the following steps:

1. Open Enterprise Manager.

2. Click to expand the server instance where the permissions should be set.

3. Click to expand databases.

4. Right-click the database you want to alter and select Properties.

5. Select the Permissions tab as shown in Figure 5.1.

Figure 5.1   Statement permissions are set on a database using the Permissions tab.

6. Click the checkbox to set the statement permission that is appropriate for your scenario. The green check mark grants the permission, the red *x* denies the permission, and the blank box revokes a previously set permission. The section in this chapter titled *Implementing Permissions* details the difference between each of these actions.

7. Click OK to close the Database Property dialogue box.

> **NOTE**   When possible, a member of the sysadmin role should create all objects. The objects, when created by a sysadmin, default to an ownership of DBO. As a result you can avoid having to address the issues discussed later in the chapter in the section *Object Ownership Chains*. The DBO should own all objects whenever possible, because then you can look forward to decreased security maintenance and increased statement execution performance.

The GRANT, REVOKE, and DENY Transact-SQL statements are used to modify statement permissions from a query tool. You can read more about these statements later in this chapter in the section *Implementing Permissions*.

Implied Permissions

Implied permissions are permissions granted through the membership of a role. For example, a member of the sysadmin fixed server can perform

Table 5.3 Permissions Associated with Fixed Server Roles

NAME	EFFECTIVE PERMISSIONS
sysadmin	All permissions on the server and its databases
serveradmin	Reconfigure, Shutdown, and some of the database consistency check (DBCC) commands
securityadmin	DENY, GRANT, and REVOKE statements
processadmin	Kill SQL Server processes
bulkadmin	Bulk Insert commands
dbcreator	CREATE, ALTER, BACKUP, and RESTORE databases
diskadmin	Given no statement permission; can run some system-stored procedures
setupadmin	Given no statement permission; can run some system-stored procedures to configure replication and linked servers

any action in SQL Server. Implied permissions are not modified; they are inherited from a set of predefined role-level permissions. Object owners also have implied permissions, which allow them to perform any activities on the object they own.

There are some Transact-SQL statements that cannot be granted as permissions; the ability to execute these statements requires membership in a fixed role that has implied permissions to execute these statements. For example, in order to execute the shutdown statement, the login user must be a member of the sysadmin or serveradmin server role. Fixed server roles and fixed database roles have a set of statement permissions that all members of the roles receive as implied permissions. Table 5.3 identifies the fixed server role permissions. Table 5.4 describes the implied permissions associated with the fixed database roles.

Table 5.4 Permissions Associated with Fixed Database Roles

DATABASE ROLE	EFFECTIVE PERMISSION
db_owner	Perform any action on the database
db_datareader	READTEXT and SELECT statements
db_datawriter	UPDATE, INSERT, DELETE, WRITETEXT, and UPDATETEXT

(continues)

Table 5.4   Permissions Associated with Fixed Database Roles *(Continued)*

DATABASE ROLE	EFFECTIVE PERMISSION
db_ddladmin	CREATE, DROP, and ALTER objects; Truncate Table statement
db_backupoperator	Backup Database, Checkpoint, and some DBCC statements
db_securityadmin	DENY, GRANT, and REVOKE statements
db_accessadmin	No statement permissions allowed; can run some system-stored procedures

The following statements do not require specific permission; therefore, membership to the public role automatically allows the use of these Transact-SQL commands:

- Begin Transaction
- Commit Transaction
- Rollback Transaction
- Save Transaction
- Raiserror
- Print
- Set

NOTE By default all logins that are granted access to a database become members of the public role.

Implementing Permissions

When permission is granted, revoked, or denied to a SQL Server user, the specified user is the only account affected by the permission. If permission is granted to a SQL Server role, the permission affects all users in the current database who are members of the role. Permissions are implemented with the GRANT, DENY, and REVOKE statements. These statements can be implemented within Enterprise Manager or through Query Analyzer using Transact-SQL. The permissions structure for a database is stored in the sysprotects system table. The following sections describe the purpose of each of these statements, how to implement the actions from Enterprise Manager and through Transact-SQL, and finally how to address permissions conflict issues.

Granting Permissions

The GRANT statement gives a user either a statement or object permission. The examples from this point on in this chapter will use object permissions. The GRANT statement is used to give a database user or role the ability to work with the data stored in a database.

For example, you may be inclined to grant SELECT object permission on the Payroll table to all members of the Personnel role, allowing all members of Personnel to view Payroll. Months later, you may overhear members of Personnel discussing management salaries, information not meant to be seen by all Personnel members. In this situation, grant SELECT access to Personnel for all columns in Payroll except the Salary column.

> **NOTE** Object permissions can be granted only to a user in the database where the object resides. If a database user needs permission to an object in another database, the user account must be created in the other database. If a database user is not given permission to a database object, the user will not have access to the object. System-stored procedures are the exception, because EXECUTE permissions are already granted to the *public* role. This EXECUTE permission gives every database user the ability to run system-stored procedures. However, after EXECUTE has been issued, the system-stored procedures check the user's role membership. Some of the system-stored procedures depend on fixed database role membership. If the user is not a member of the appropriate fixed server or database role that is necessary to run the stored procedure, the stored procedure will not continue.

Denying Permissions

Microsoft SQL Server 2000 allows Windows 2000 users and groups to be granted access to SQL Server. Additionally, SQL logins can be created and granted access to SQL Server. Any of these logins can then be given access to a database as a user and placed in one or more roles. The result is a hierarchical security system that allows permissions to be applied through several levels of roles and members. Several permission statements may affect a single individual through various group and role memberships. But there may be times when you want to limit the permissions of a user or role to prevent access to a particular statement or object. Denying permissions on a user account:

- Removes the permission if it was previously granted to the user or role

- Overrides any GRANT permission that is given to another role or user that is linked to this login

- Deactivates permission inherited from another role or user account in the database

- Ensures that the user will not gain access through some other role or user in the future

NOTE Use the DENY permission with caution. Your role memberships may become quite complicated, and by using the DENY statement, you may inadvertently lock out a user who requires access to the data.

You can DENY permissions to either a user or a role. If you have a user who is continually causing security problems, the DENY permission can be a method of ensuring that the user is locked out.

Revoking Permissions

The REVOKE permission removes a permission that has been previously granted or denied. Revoking permission is similar to denying permission in that both remove a granted permission. But although revoking permission removes a granted permission, it does not prevent the user, group, or role from inheriting a granted permission from a higher level. Therefore a REVOKE does not guarantee that an individual will not have access to the object. If the user belongs to another role that has the permission granted or if the user account is granted permission to the object, the individual can still access the object. Therefore, if you revoke permission for a user to view a table, you do not necessarily prevent the user from viewing the table.

The REVOKE statement removes a previously denied permission. GRANT and DENY statements add an entry to the sysprotects system table. Both of these two statements force a permission to an object. The REVOKE statement simply deletes a previous record from the sysprotects table. This helps manage the size of the system tables. The REVOKE statements neutralize the GRANT and DENY statements.

Permission Conflicts

A person within your organization may belong to multiple groups and therefore may be granted access to SQL Server through multiple logins. Each of these logins is managed separately in SQL Server. It is possible that each of these logins may be given access to the same database. So the end result is, a single person may have several user accounts and role memberships for a single database. Multiple logins increase the complexity of permissions management.

GRANT permissions are cumulative. For instance, user Mike belongs to a role *rUpdateCustomer* for the *tblCustomer* table. Mike is granted SELECT permission to the table and the *rUpdateCustomer* is granted INSERT and DELETE permission for the table. Mike's cumulative permission is SELECT, INSERT, and DELETE. The GRANT permissions are cumulative for Mike's multiple memberships. The issue is a little stickier when a DENY permission is added to the mix.

If there are permission conflicts between a group or role and its members, the most restrictive permission (DENY) takes precedence. DENY permissions always take precedence over the GRANT permission. Therefore use the DENY statement with caution. Using the DENY statement for a role or Windows 2000 groups may effectively restrict access from users who, through another user or role, should be able to access the data.

The REVOKE statement removes granted permissions, and the DENY statement can be used to prevent a user from gaining permissions through a GRANT to the person's user account. Use the REVOKE permission to remove unnecessary permission entries or to change access to the database. Most of the security statements should be GRANT or Revoke.

NOTE A GRANT permission takes precedence over a DENY permission only when the GRANT is applied to the same user or role as the original DENY. The entry in the sysprotects table is changed from a DENY to a GRANT and thus reverses the previous DENY action.

Setting Permissions

Enterprise Manager or the *sp_helprotect* system-stored procedure can be used to view the permissions on a database object or users. Enterprise Manager enables you to easily view all of the permissions that are set on an object. To view object permissions in Enterprise Manager, complete the following steps:

1. Open Enterprise Manager.

2. Click to expand the instance of SQL Server you want to configure.

3. Click to expand the database where your desired object resides.

4. Click to expand the type of object you want to configure (such as tables, views, or stored procedures).

5. Right-click on the object you want to view and select Object Properties.

6. Click on the Permissions button.

7. The currently set permissions will appear, as shown in Figure 5.2.

A granted permission appears as a green check mark. Denied permissions are represented as a red *x*. Revoked permissions remove previously granted or denied permissions and therefore appear as an empty box. Remember that a REVOKE permission granted to a user is different from denying a user permission.

Permission can easily be altered within Enterprise Manager. Simply click the checkbox corresponding to the user or role for which you want to alter permissions. Click until you reach your intended result.

Enterprise Manager is an excellent tool for viewing and altering object permissions. The graphical user interface (GUI) tool is easy to decipher. As with almost every action against SQL Server, permissions management can also be performed with a query tool, such as Query Analyzer. The next several sections detail the Transact-SQL commands used to manage object permission.

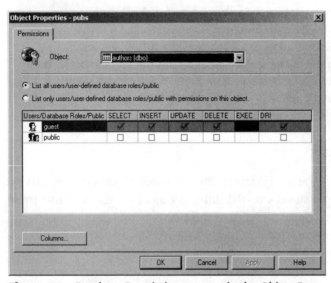

Figure 5.2   Database Permissions are set in the Object Properties dialogue box.

GRANT Permission

This first example uses multiple GRANT statements to help describe the GRANT permission in SQL Server. The users involved in the next several examples are not critical to the statement and have been provided solely to add practicality to the syntax. This first SQL statement grants Mike, Kenny, and the Sales group from the Softouch domain a couple of statement-level permissions.

```
GRANT CREATE DATABASE, CREATE TABLE


TO Mike, Kenny, [Softouch\Sales]
```

The second GRANT statement demonstrates object permissions for the users of the pubs database. This example shows the preferred ordering of permissions. First, SELECT permissions are granted to the Public role, which is the default level of access. Then specific permissions are granted to the users of the database, specifically the authors table.

```
USE pubs
GO
GRANT SELECT
ON authors
TO public
GO

GRANT INSERT, UPDATE, DELETE
ON authors
TO Mike, Kenny
GO
```

The following example demonstrates the granting of permission to a role instead of individual database users. In the example, Accounting is the name of a database role.

```
GRANT CREATE TABLE
TO Accounting
```

The next example demonstrates the AS option as well as the WITH GRANT OPTION keywords.

The user Kenny owns the Authors table. Kenny grants SELECT permissions, specified the WITH GRANT OPTION clause on Authors to the Accounting role. The user Andy, who is a member of the Accounting role, wants to grant SELECT permissions on the Authors table to the user Mike, who is not a member of the Accounting role.

Because the permission to give other users SELECT permissions to the Authors table was granted to the Accounting role and not Andy as an individual user, Andy cannot give permissions for the table based on the permissions granted through being a member of the Accounting role. Andy must use the AS clause to assume the GRANT permissions of the Accounting role.

```
GRANT SELECT
ON Authors
TO Accounting
WITH GRANT OPTION

/* User Andy */
GRANT SELECT
ON Authors
TO Mike
AS Accounting
```

DENY Permission

The DENY statement is similar in syntax to the GRANT statement. Following are examples of denying permission first to a user and then to the Accounting role. Only use the DENY statement when absolutely necessary. In most cases, when a removal of permission is required, the REVOKE statement is more appropriate.

```
DENY SELECT, INSERT, UPDATE, DELETE
ON authors
TO Mary, John, Tom

DENY CREATE TABLE
TO Accounting
```

REVOKE Permission

A revoked permission removes only a previously granted or denied permission. The same permission granted or denied at another level, such as a group or role containing the user, group, or role, still applies.

For example, if the Sales role is granted SELECT permissions on the Customer table and Mike (a member of the Sales role) is explicitly revoked SELECT permissions on the Customer table, he still can access the table because of his membership in the Sales role. The following examples demonstrate the REVOKE statement:

```
REVOKE CREATE TABLE
FROM Mike, [Softouch\Bill]
GO

REVOKE SELECT
ON Authors
TO Andy
```

Object Ownership Chains

Ownership of objects is a critical issue in SQL Server 2000. In many other database systems it is important to define ownership based on the user who created the object. In SQL Server, this is not the case. A database should have the same owner for all objects.

This section demonstrates the object ownership issues of SQL Server. You should strive to avoid multiple owners of objects within the same database.

Views and stored procedures provide a secondary method of giving users access to data and the ability to perform activities. They provide users with access to underlying items in the database and bypass the permissions defined directly for specific objects and statements. Views and stored procedures are dependent on the underlying objects they reference.

Views can depend on other views or tables. Procedures can depend on other procedures, views, or tables. These dependencies can be thought of as an ownership chain. Ownership chains only apply to SELECT, INSERT, UPDATE, and DELETE statements. It is possible to view an object's dependency by using Enterprise Manager or the *sp_depends* stored procedure. To view object dependencies from Enterprise Manager, perform the following steps:

1. Open Enterprise Manager.
2. Click to expand the instance of SQL Server you want to configure.
3. Click to expand the database where your desired object resides.
4. Click to expand the type of object you want to configure (such as tables, views, or stored procedures).
5. Right-click on the object you want to view and select All Tasks.
6. Select View Object Dependencies. The Object Dependencies dialogue box is shown in Figure 5.3.

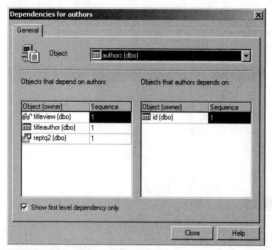

Figure 5.3   Object dependencies can be viewed using Enterprise Manager.

NOTE It is a good idea to verify all object dependencies before you delete an object. It is possible to drop objects that have other objects referencing them. This results in all dependency objects failing next time they are accessed.

Typically, the owner of a view also owns the underlying objects (other views or tables), and the owner of a stored procedure often owns all the referenced procedures, tables, and views. The owner of a view or a stored procedure should be the DBO account. It is recommended that all objects be created in the DBO owner context. This will prevent broken ownership chains.

The process of creating objects as DBO is described in the next section. Also, views and underlying objects are usually all in the same database, as are stored procedures and all the objects referenced. When temporary objects are created within a stored procedure, they are owned by the procedure owner and not by the user currently executing the procedure.

When a user accesses a view, SQL Server does not check permissions on any of the view's underlying objects if the objects and the view are all owned by the same user and if the view and all its underlying objects are in the same database. If the same user owns a stored procedure and all the views or tables it references, and if the procedure and objects are all in the same database, SQL Server checks only the permissions on the procedure. This permissions checking is a solid method of securing your tables. If all ownership is the same and the application and users interact with tables and views, then permission does not have to be defined at the table level. This strategy of application security will be addressed in more detail in Chapter 6, "Designing Application Security."

If the ownership chain of a procedure or view is broken (because not all the objects in the chain are owned by the same user), SQL Server checks permissions on each object in the chain whose next lower link is owned by a different user. In this way, SQL Server allows the owner of the original data to retain control over its accessibility. When SQL Server has to check permissions in this manner, performance of the statement is slightly slower. Additionally, the DBA needs to account for security at every object and not just the objects that users interact with.

Usually, a user who creates a view has to GRANT permissions only on that view. For example, Mike has created a view called *vwAuthors* on the Authors table, which he also owns. If Mike gives Andy permission to use *vwAuthors*, SQL Server allows Andy access to it without checking permissions on the Authors table.

A user who creates a view or stored procedure that depends on an object owned by another user must be aware that any permissions he or she grants depend on the permissions allowed by the other owner. For example, Andy creates a procedure called *spAuthorsUpdate*, which depends on Authors (also owned by Andy) and *spAuthorsInsert* (owned by Mike). These procedures in turn depend on other tables and views owned by Mike and Andy. Andy will now have to account for the permissions on every object that Mike owns. This can result in increased administrative overhead related to permissions management. When ownership chains are broken, the administrator typically has to set permissions on every object to avoid the confusion that comes with determining existing ownership chain violations. The next section outlines the necessary steps to creating objects under the ownership of DBO. If this procedure is followed with all objects within the database, then permissions management is limited to the objects that the applications and users have to interact with.

Database Owner Ownership Context

To avoid broken ownership chains, it is best to create all objects with the owner context set to DBO. This result will be increased performance and decreased administration of permissions.

When objects are being created, the ownership is defined by one of two things. The creator can either define the owner during the creation statement or the developer can allow the system to default to the owner it assumes should be used. The difference will be described in the next couple of sections.

Defining Ownership

When the developer is creating a database object, the developer can include the owner as part of the object name. The owner's name is appended to the beginning of the object name, and the object identifying name is separated from the owner by a dot ("."). This is accomplished as follows:

```
Create Table DBO.tblCustomers
     (CustID     Int Identity (100,5) Not Null,
      Lname      VarChar (25) Not Null,
      ...)
```

The object creator can use the DBO owner if the creator is either logged on as a sysadmin (which includes the SA account) or belongs to the *db_owner* database role. This method of creating a database object allows for clarity but does require that each object creator remember to define the owner with the object name.

Assumed Ownership

If the owner is not provided with the CREATE statement, SQL Server defaults to an owner. The default owner depends on the login context of the user. If the login is a member of the sysadmin role at the server level, the default owner for a created object is the DBO. If the user is working in any other context, SQL Server defaults to the current logged-on username. In this case, you may need to perform one of the following steps to make sure that all objects are created by the DBO:

Change the ownership after the object is created. The *sp_changeobjectowner* system-stored procedure can be used to change an object's owner to the DBO anytime after the object has been created. This stored procedure will have to be run for every object that is created by a user other than the DBO.

Use the sysadmin role for creating an object. This may require designing your infrastructure correctly in the first place. All database developers typically won't be system administrators on the production server. This requires the DBA of the production server to create the objects. For the more information on the design required to make this happen, see Chapter 2, "Designing a Successful Security Model."

NOTE It is generally a good idea to script object creation in the development environment. These scripts can then be given to the production DBA. These scripts can be used to make sure the object is created by DBO.

Best Practices

- Use the GRANT and REVOKE statements to set permissions. The DENY statement overrides all other permissions and should therefore be used sparingly.

- Use Enterprise Manager to view and set permissions. Enterprise Manager is an easy-to-use GUI tool.

- Use server roles to perform the actions defined by implied permissions rather than deal with each of these permissions.

- Avoid using the SA account. An individual login should be created for each administrator. This will increase accountability by providing a usable audit trail.

- View object dependencies before you drop an object. This may prevent other objects from failing later on.

- Avoid broken ownership chains, which result in slow performance and increased administration.

- Create all objects with a DBO ownership. This is best accomplished through the sysadmin role or by explicitly defining the object owner in the CREATE statement.

- Avoid the WITH GRANT OPTION. This option allows users that were granted a permission the ability to GRANT the same permission to others, which can make permission troubleshooting a nightmare.

REVIEW QUESTIONS

1. What is the difference between implied and object permissions?

2. Why is it best to avoid broken ownership chains?

3. How can you create an object with the owner being the DBO?

4. If an object was created with an owner other than the DBO, how can it be changed?

5. What is the difference between a REVOKE and a DENY?

6. Where are permissions stored in SQL Server?

7. What is the WITH GRANT OPTION? When is it appropriate?

8. When should you use the AS option?

Designing Application Security

Application development is the key tool for interacting with data stored in SQL Server. Although ad hoc query environments exist, most access of SQL Server data is done through a front-end application. As you design the application it is best to account for the security features you are going to incorporate within the application. For example, you will want to have a plan as to whether you will be using Windows Authentication or SQL Server Authentication for login access.

Many factors help to determine the appropriate methods of accessing data. In addition to your application access you will want to design security for the database you will be using. Many users are becoming more and more proficient with the Microsoft Office Suite, specifically Access and Excel. You will want to ensure that your application limits access to the data itself. If you are going to allow access from another front-end application, such as Excel, do you want this access to have the same permission as your application? This chapter answers these issues.

The chapter first addresses the issue of analyzing system requirements. Next it discusses protecting your tables, providing a detailed description of views and stored procedures as security objects. Then the chapter addresses data access strategies to secure front-end connectivity, describing the different design strategies based on the authentication method you have chosen. The authentication method is the key to creating a secure front-end application.

Finally the chapter moves to the issue of change management. You will want to have the change management infrastructure of your application planned before you deploy the application. It is necessary to understand the consequences of making changes to the application over time. This chapter introduces suggested means for applying changes to your application's database.

Analyzing System Requirements

The most important task in designing application security design is analyzing the requirements of the system. This also is often the most overlooked area of security. The requirements of your organization and the system you are about to design should be reflected in the security design of your application. For instance, if everyone in the organization needs to read the data within your system and that is all, your security design is quite easy. After you have a fair understanding of your current requirements, you can move on to other security issues.

In analyzing your current requirements, you should consider the following set of issues along within any other items that are specific to your organization:

- Auditing requirements.

- Access to data. Which users need access to which pieces of data?

- Number of users. This may affect your choice of authentication method and the level of security you write into your application.

- Limitations and requirements of your front-end development environment. Some development products don't support Windows Authentication as well as others do.

- User expectations. This is the most important area. You need to know what your users expect from the application.

Analyzing your current requirements is detailed in more depth in Chapter 2, "Designing a Successful Security Model."

Protecting Your Tables

With more users becoming proficient with products such as Excel, Access, and Crystal Reports, it is becoming easier for a power user to access data from your database. This is of particular concern if you are setting most of your permissions at the table level. Access and Excel have built-in features to link to SQL Server tables. This capability is beneficial in an ad hoc query environment, but it could be a nightmare for an application developer. It is important to develop a strategy to protect your tables.

The two database objects that are typically used to help with security are stored procedures and views. You can give permission to execute a stored procedure without giving access to the table referenced in the stored procedure. Keep in mind this type of permission is dependent on a consistent ownership chain. Ownership chains are discussed in more detail in Chapter 5, "Managing Object Security." If you design your application to execute stored procedures and query views instead of giving access to tables, you can control access to your data more effectively. In this scenario the tables do not have to be configured with any permission. You configure security on the objects the users interact with rather than on the tables. Stored procedures and views are described in more detail in the next couple of sections.

Stored Procedures

When scripts are executed, the commands within them are processed by SQL Server to display result sets, to administer SQL Server, and to manipulate data contained in a database. When the scripts are saved, they are stored in the file system and are commonly given a SQL extension. Alternatively, Transact-SQL scripts can be named and saved in SQL Server as stored procedures. You can then invoke stored procedures in a number of ways, such as through Query Analyzer, to process the Transact-SQL statements within them.

Stored procedures provide performance benefits, a programming framework, and security features that are unavailable to Transact-SQL commands sent to the server for processing. Performance is enhanced through storage that is local to the database, precompiling the code, and caching. A programming framework is provided through common programming constructs such as input and output parameters and procedure reuse.

Security features include encryption and privilege limits that keep users away from the underlying database structure while enabling them to run stored procedures that act on the database.

Performance

Every time Transact-SQL commands are sent to the server for processing, the server must determine whether the sender has appropriate permissions to execute the commands and whether the commands are valid. Once the permissions and the syntax are verified, SQL Server builds an execution plan to process the request.

A stored procedure is more efficient using Transact-SQL commands in part because the procedure is stored in SQL Server when it is created. Therefore the content in the procedure runs at the server when the stored procedure is executed. A complex Transact-SQL script contained in a stored procedure is called by a single Transact-SQL statement rather than by sending hundreds of commands over the network.

Before a stored procedure is created, the command syntax is checked for accuracy. If no errors are returned, the procedure's name is stored in the SysObjects table and the procedure's text is stored in the SysComments table. The first time the stored procedure is run, an execution plan is created and the stored procedure is compiled. Subsequent processing of the compiled stored procedure is faster, because SQL Server does not recheck command syntax, recreate an execution plan, or recompile the procedure. The cache is checked for an execution plan before a new plan is created.

Programming Framework

Once a stored procedure is created, you can call it whenever it is needed. This feature provides modularity and encourages the reuse of code. Code reuse increases the maintainability of a database by insulating the database from changing business practices. If business rules change in an organization, a stored procedure can be modified to comply with the new business rules. All applications that call the stored procedure will then comply with the new business rules without direct modification.

Like other programming languages, stored procedures can accept input parameters, return output parameters, provide execution feedback in the form of status codes and descriptive text, and call other procedures. For example, a stored procedure can return a status code to a calling procedure so that the calling procedure performs an operation based on the code received.

Software developers can write sophisticated programs in a language such as C++, and then a special type of stored procedure called an *extended stored procedure* can be used to invoke the program from within SQL Server.

A stored procedure should be written to complete a single task. The more generic the stored procedure is, the more useful it will be to many databases. For example, the built-in sp_rename stored procedure changes the name of a user-created object, such as a table, a column, or a user-defined data type in the current database. Thus, you can use sp_rename to rename a table in one database or a table column in another database.

Security

Another important feature of stored procedures is that they enhance security through isolation and encryption. Database users can be given permission to execute a stored procedure without being granted permissions to directly access the database objects on which the stored procedure operates. Additionally, a stored procedure can be encrypted when it is created or modified so that users are unable to read the Transact-SQL commands in the stored procedure. These security features insulate the database structure from the database user, further ensuring data integrity and database reliability.

Views

Views are generally used to focus, simplify, and customize each user's perception of the database. You can use a view as a security mechanism by allowing a user to access data through the view without granting the user permission to directly access the base tables that lie beneath the view. You can also use views to improve performance and to partition data when you are copying data to and from SQL Server 2000. This section will introduce views and the various functionalities they support.

A *view* acts as a filter on the underlying tables that are referenced in the view. The query that defines the view can be from one or more tables or from other views in the current database or other databases. You can also use distributed queries to define views that use data from multiple heterogeneous sources. The heterogeneous sources could include other database management systems such as Oracle or Access. This functionality is useful, for example, if you want to combine similarly structured data from different servers, each of which stores data for a different region of your organization.

A view can be thought of as either a virtual table or a stored query. The data that is accessible through a standard view is not stored in the database as a distinct object. What is stored in the database is a SELECT statement. The result set of the SELECT statement forms the virtual table returned by the view. A user can use this virtual table by referencing the view name in Transact-SQL statements in the same way that a table is referenced. You can use a view to perform any or all of the following functions:

- To restrict a user to specific rows in a table
- To restrict a user to specific columns
- To join columns from multiple tables so that they look like a single table
- To aggregate information instead of supplying details

NOTE For more information about the syntax necessary for creating stored procedures and views, refer to SQL Server Books Online.

Data Access Strategies

Your strategy for accessing data depends a great deal on the authentication method your application uses. An application can connect through Windows Authentication or SQL Server Authentication. More information about authentication methods is provided in Chapter 4, "Establishing Login Security." This section first describes the strategies for accessing data from an application if you use Windows Authentication and then describes your data access strategies if you use SQL Server Authentication. Finally, this section introduces the use of application roles, which can be an effective strategy for bypassing both of the mentioned authentication methods.

Windows Authentication

When using Windows Authentication, you need to be concerned about the login management in SQL Server first. Each user who uses your application needs a valid login to SQL Server. Granting a Windows 2000 user or group access to SQL Server creates this login. After the user is granted access to SQL Server, the database access and permission infrastructure is linked to the original login.

The second step of accountability is the login. First a Windows domain must authenticate the user. The user will be authenticated using either Kerberos or NTLM as described in Chapter 4, "Establishing Login Security."

After the user has authenticated with the domain, you can use the information to establish a connection between your application and SQL Server. When connecting, you need to supply a trusted connection to SQL Server. Examples of trusted connections are available in Chapter 7, "Implementing Front-End Application Security."

After the connection is made, the application can then send Transact-SQL commands directly to the server or can execute stored procedures. It is preferable to execute stored procedures to take advantage of the features that have already been described earlier in this chapter. By using stored procedures you can isolate the user application from the table. The user's login is established by the login to the Windows 2000 domain. This allows all applications that access the data to take advantage of the permissions that are set. If you configure permission at the table level, then all applications a user can use to connect to the table will have the same permission. If you use stored procedures, users could also execute them from another application. The difference between configuring permission at the table level and executing stored procedures is in the way the data is accessed. Since you write the stored procedures, you can define the contents and requirements for any data modification. When a user can connect directly to the table, the user has the ability to define his or her own context for data modification (ad-hoc modification queries).

SQL Server Authentication

Your application may need to access data from SQL Server by using SQL Server Authentication instead of Windows Authentication. An example would be cases where it is not feasible to have all users logging on to a Windows domain, as commonly occurs in Internet applications and applications that are written in heterogeneous environments.

When you are using SQL Server Authentication, it is important to plan for the weaknesses built into the process. If you recall from Chapter 4, "Establishing Login Security," SQL Server Authentication does not encrypt the username and password when it is sent back to SQL Server. Additionally, no password policies are enforced with SQL Server Authentication. As a consequence it is typically not recommended that you create a login for each user in SQL Server. You probably do not want each user sending clear text information to the server each time the user logs in. Your application should use a single SQL Server account to perform the necessary actions in SQL Server. This account should be created in SQL Server and should be granted access to the application database and given permission to perform all actions the application needs to perform.

The connection from your front-end application will use this account as credentials for accessing SQL Server. These credentials are entered into the code and compiled so that they are not easily viewable by anyone using the application.

The key to making this design work is then building the security into your application. User management and authentication should be written into the application. In many cases the data about the users and their passwords are stored in a table within the application database. The application users are not created as SQL Server users. The only SQL Server user is the user that is used within the compiled code to connect to the server.

The client is given a username and password to access the application. This account is not a valid SQL Server user, and therefore the client cannot use the account to access SQL Server tables from another application. The connection account has all the permission and privileges and is hidden from the users.

While this model is acceptable, it is not without its weaknesses. Because all connections to SQL Server are actually performed by the connection account, SQL Server will view all connections to the server as the same user. If you want to track the user who performed an action, you will have to write the auditing information into the application. This process is described in more detail in Chapter 14, "Creating an Audit Policy." Additionally all security administration is performed within the application and not within SQL Server. Thus the application will be limited in security to the abilities of the application.

Application Roles

The security system in Microsoft SQL Server is implemented at the lowest level: the database itself. This is the best method for controlling user activities regardless of the application used to communicate with SQL Server. But sometimes security controls must be customized to accommodate the special requirements of the application at hand, especially when you are dealing with large amounts of data or complicated logic models. In such cases you may want to isolate your application from all other applications. By implementing application roles you can also isolate the security within your application.

Additionally, you may want to restrict user access to data only through a specific application (for example, using SQL Query Analyzer or Microsoft Excel) or to prevent direct access to data. Restricting user access in this way prohibits users from connecting to an instance of SQL Server using an application such as SQL Query Analyzer and executing a poorly written query, which can negatively affect the performance of the whole server. By using application roles you can isolate an application from other applications, thus overcoming the weakness inherent in using only Windows Authentication. This way you can also manage your security within SQL Server and not be limited by the application developer. You are also thereby overcoming the primary weakness of using just SQL Server Authentication. In a sense, you get the best of both worlds.

Application roles are different in many aspects from standard database roles. Application roles should be used as an isolation mechanism and incorporated into your security design. They should not be grouped into the same category as other roles. Application roles have several characteristics that make them unique:

- Application roles contain no members. They are activated with the execution of a stored procedure, not with a username and password.

- Windows 2000 groups, users, database users, and database roles cannot be added to application roles; the security context is set by the application the user is interacting with.

- Application roles are inactive by default, and in order to be activated they require the execution of a stored procedure and a password.

- Permissions are granted to application roles similar to other roles.

- Application roles bypass standard permissions. The user's security context is defined by the application role, and therefore any permission that is granted to the user is ignored and the permission granted to the application role is used. This is an effective mechanism for isolating the application.

- Auditing is limited. All users of an application will appear as the application role and not by their own usernames. The result is increased troubleshooting and tracking efforts related to the database.

When the application role is activated by the application for a given connection, the connection loses all permissions applied to the login, user account, or other groups or database roles in all databases for the duration of the connection. The connection gains the permissions associated with the application role for the database in which the application role exists. Because application roles are applicable only to the database in which they exist, the connection can gain access to another database only through permissions granted to the guest user account in the other database. Therefore, if the guest user account does not exist in a database, the connection cannot gain access to that database. If the guest user account does exist in the database but permissions to access an object are not explicitly granted to the guest, the connection cannot access that object regardless of who created the object. The permissions the user gained from the application role remain in effect until the connection logs out of an instance of SQL Server.

To ensure that all the functions of the application can be performed, a connection must lose default permissions applied to the login and user account or other groups or database roles in all databases for the duration of the connection, and gain the permissions associated with the application role. For example, if a user is usually denied access to a table that the application must access, then the denied access should be revoked so that the user can use the application successfully. Application roles overcome any conflicts with a user's default permissions by temporarily suspending the user's default permissions and assigning the user only the permissions of the application role.

Application roles are granted, revoked, and denied permissions like any other database role. More information on setting permissions can be found in Chapter 5, "Managing Object Security."

Application roles enable the application, rather than SQL Server, to take over the responsibility of user authentication. Yet because SQL Server still must authenticate the application when it accesses databases, the application must provide a password, because there is no other way to authenticate an application. The password is sent to the server as a parameter of the sp_setapprole stored procedure. This system-stored procedure is executed by the client to set the application role security context and send the password for authentication.

If ad-hoc access to a database is not required, user groups do not need to be granted any permissions, because all permissions can be assigned by the applications they use to access the database. In such an environment, standardizing on one systemwide password assigned to an application role is possible, assuming access to the application code is secure.

There are several options for securing passwords without hard-coding them into applications. For example, an encrypted key stored in the Registry (or a SQL Server database), for which only the application has the decryption code, can be used. The application reads the key, decrypts it, and uses the value to set the application role. Using the Multiprotocol Net-Library, the network packet containing the password can also be encrypted. Additionally, the password can be encrypted before it is sent to an instance of SQL Server when the role is activated.

When an application user connects to an instance of SQL Server using Windows Authentication Mode, an application role can be used to set the permissions the Windows 2000 user has in a database when using the application. This method allows Windows NT 4.0 or Windows 2000 auditing of the user account and control over user permissions while someone uses the application to be easily maintained.

If SQL Server Authentication is used and auditing user access to the database is not required, it can be easier for the application to connect to an instance of SQL Server using a predefined SQL Server login. For example, an order entry application authenticates users running the application itself and then connects to an instance of SQL Server using the same OrderEntry login. All connections use the same login and relevant permissions are granted to this login.

As an example of application role usage, user Mike runs a sales application that requires SELECT, UPDATE, and INSERT permissions on the Products and Orders tables in order for the Northwind database to work, but he should not have any SELECT, INSERT, or UPDATE permissions when accessing the Products or Orders tables using SQL Query Analyzer or any other tool. To ensure these conditions, create one user database role that denies SELECT, INSERT, or UPDATE permissions on the Products and Orders tables, and add Mike as a member of that database role. Then create an application role in the Sales database with SELECT, INSERT, and UPDATE permissions on the Products and Orders tables. When the application runs, it provides the password to activate the application role by using the sp_setapprole stored procedure and gains the permissions to access the Products and Orders tables. If Mike tries to log in to an instance of SQL Server using any tool except the application, he will not be able to access the Products or Orders tables.

The first step of the process is creating the application role in SQL Server. The following steps outline the process of creating an application role from Enterprise Manager:

1. Open Enterprise Manager.

2. Expand a server group and then expand the server where the role should be created.

3. Expand Databases, and then expand the particular database (in our example we expand the Northwind database). The role is only available in the database in which you create it.

4. Right-click Roles and then click New Database Role. The New Role dialogue box will appear as shown in Figure 6.1.

5. In the Name text box, enter the name of the new application role. (For our example, we will call the role OrderEntry.)

6. In the Database Role Type region of the dialogue box click the Application Role radio button and then enter a password in the Password text box. After you select Application Role as the type of role, you no

Figure 6.1   The New Role dialogue box is used to create application roles.

longer have the option of adding members to the role. The Add option should appear grayed out as shown in Figure 6.1.

After the application role is created, it can be activated from the application. The activation is performed by executing the system stored procedure sp_setapprole. The syntax for the procedure is as follows:

```
sp_setapprole [@rolename =] 'role' ,
    [@password =] {Encrypt N 'password'} | 'password'
    [,[@encrypt =] 'encrypt_style']
```

Each of the arguments used to activate the application is described in more depth in the following list.

[@rolename =] *'role'*   @rolename is the name of the application role defined in the current database. The application role must exist in the database from which the stored procedure is being executed.

[@password =] {Encrypt N *'password'*} | *'password'*   @password is the password required to activate the application role. Each application role is given a password for security. The password is necessary because users are not added to the application role, so userIDs can't be used as a means of verifying the application role. The password

Table 6.1 Encryption Styles for Application Role Passwords

VALUE	DESCRIPTION
None	The password is not encrypted and is sent to SQL Server in plaintext format. This is the default if no other encryption style is specified.
ODBC	The password is encrypted using the ODBC Encrypt function. This can be specified only when the client is using ODBC or an OLE DB provider.

can be encrypted using the ODBC Encrypt function. When you are using the Encrypt function, the password must be converted to a Unicode string by preceding the password with *N*. More information on the ODBC Encrypt function can be found in SQL Server Books Online.

[@encrypt =] *'encrypt_style'*   @encrypt specifies that the encryption style used by @password. encrypt_style must be one of the values listed in Table 6.1.

NOTE More Information on clients using ODBC and OLE DB can be found In Chapter 7, "Implementing Front-End Application Security."

After an application role is activated with the sp_setapprole stored procedure, the role cannot be deactivated in the current database until the user disconnects from SQL Server. You can forcibly disconnect a user from the Current Activity window in Enterprise Manager. You should always inform the user about the disconnect before killing the user's session. More information about managing current connections is found in Chapter 13, "Managing Current Connections."

The sp_setapprole stored procedure can be executed only by direct Transact-SQL statements; it cannot be executed within another stored procedure or from within a user-defined transaction. Any user can execute the stored procedure as long as the user knows the correct password. The system is only as secure as the password that is chosen.

The following examples demonstrate the Transact-SQL statement necessary to activate the sp_setapprole stored procedure. The first example demonstrates the activation of the OrderEntry application role provided as an example earlier. The Transact-SQL statement will execute the stored procedure and send a password of *apple* to the server in plaintext format:

```
EXEC sp_setapprole 'OrderEntry', 'apple'
```

The second example is similar to the first. The difference is the demonstration of the ODBC Encrypt function. This example uses the OrderEntry application role and sends the same password of *apple*.

```
EXEC sp_setapprole 'OrderEntry', {Encrypt N 'apple'}, 'odbc'
```

Change Management

During application design it is also important to address change management strategies. Often system design or implementation goals change after the application has been deployed, causing the developer to have to alter the application to meet the new requirements.

Although it may be nice if changes never had to be made, the reality of application development is that changes have to occur with most applications. You will want to have a strategy to implement the changes with the least consequences to the server.

In many cases the individual who developed the database is not the same individual who administers the database. In fact, in many cases the developer does not have access to the production server for the purposes of connecting from Enterprise Manager to the database and performing the change. In most cases this is good. It is very difficult to support a system where all developers can connect at any time and perform changes. Changes should be coordinated through a single point to verify the necessity and structure of changes. The point of verification should be the DBA.

Alterations to the database should be done via Transact-SQL scripts and submitted to the DBA for approval and implementation. Making changes is more difficult after the database has been deployed and is running in production. Altering tables affects the schema of the application's database and can have consequences that affect your data. Altering stored procedures and views is less intrusive because it generally doesn't affect the underlying data. All of the alteration statements do, however, affect your security infrastructure. If you drop and recreate objects, the permissions associated with the objects will be dropped as well. It is best to write alteration scripts to perform the change.

Before writing an alteration script you should be familiar with the schema of the object that exists. For tables, the schema is the set of columns, data types, and constraints set on the table. This information can be viewed from Enterprise Manager by performing the following steps:

1. Open Enterprise Manager.
2. Expand a server group and then expand the server where the object exists.
3. Expand Databases and then expand the database where the table that you want to view exists.
4. Click to expand Tables.
5. Right-click on the table you want to view and choose Design Table. The design view of the table should appear as shown in Figure 6.2.

Stored procedures and views are a little different from tables. Their schema comprises the Transact-SQL statement that was used to create the object. They can also be viewed using Enterprise Manager as shown in the following steps:

1. Open Enterprise Manager.
2. Expand a server group and then expand the server where the object exists.
3. Expand Databases and then expand the database where the table exists that you want to view.

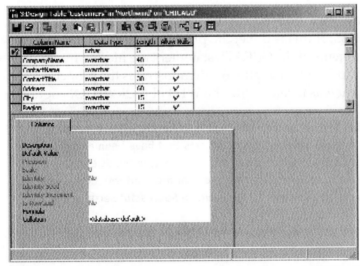

Figure 6.2 Enterprise Manager can be used to view and modify a table's schema.

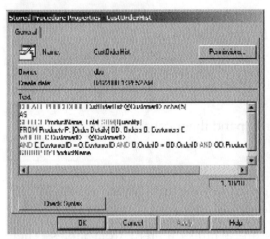

Figure 6.3   Enterprise Manager can be used to view the original statement used to create a stored procedure.

4. Click to expand either Stored Procedures or Views, as applicable.

5. Right-click on the object you want to view and choose Properties. The Transact-SQL statement should appear as shown in Figure 6.3.

NOTE The sp_helptext stored procedure can be used to view the original statement used to create a stored procedure or view.

Stored procedures and views can be created by using the WITH ENCRYPTION option. If this is done, the properties of the object will not be available. The contents of the CREATE statement are hidden from Enterprise Manager and sp_helptext. Figure 6.4 demonstrates the properties of a stored procedure that was created with the WITH ENCRYPTION option.

NOTE If you decide to use the WITH ENCRYPTION option when generating objects, keep your original scripts. Altering objects that have been encrypted is very difficult without the original code. You can generate the SQL scripts for the objects you create from Enterprise Manager. For more information about generating SQL scripts, see Chapter 2, "Designing a Successful Security Model."

The following sections demonstrate the ALTER statements required for changing tables, stored procedures, and views.

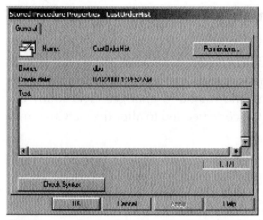

Figure 6.4 Objects that have been created with encryption hide the original Transact-SQL code.

ALTER TABLE Statement

The ALTER TABLE statement is helpful in that it allows you to change the schema of the table without affecting the permissions you have set. The ALTER TABLE statement can be used to accomplish any of the following tasks:

- Adding or deleting columns
- Modifying data types
- Adding constraints
- Disabling constraints

In the following example we see the Transact-SQL code being used to add a column to the Customer table. ALTER TABLE is used to add the Email column to the Customer table. This process is beneficial because all security settings for the table stay intact.

Note that the ALTER statements can be used for multiple functions and can get quite complex. Refer to SQL Server Books Online for more details about each of the ALTER statements.

```
ALTER TABLE Customer
Add Email     varchar(35) NULL
GO
```

ALTER PROCEDURE Statement

The ALTER PROCEDURE statement is used to alter stored procedures. When you use the ALTER PROCEDURE statement, the set permissions are not affected. When you are altering stored procedures you must rewrite the entire stored procedure including the intended changes. The following example illustrates the Transact-SQL code needed to alter the GetCustomer stored procedure:

```
ALTER PROCEDURE GetCustomer
@lname varchar(20)
@fname varchar(20)
AS
SELECT FName, LName, Address, City, State, Zip
FROM   Customer
WHERE  LName = '@lname'
AND    FName = '@fname'
GO
```

The only differences between CREATE PROCEDURE and ALTER PRO-CEDURE statements are in the Transact-SQL code. Altering a stored procedure is easier if you have the original Transact-SQL code. You can then easily make the alterations that are necessary and run the script.

ALTER VIEW Statement

You can alter views by using the Transact-SQL ALTER VIEW statement. The only differences between an ALTER VIEW and a CREATE VIEW statement are that ALTER VIEW will not fail if the object already exists and ALTER VIEW does not drop existing permissions. As with the ALTER PROCEDURE statement, the ALTER VIEW statement requires that you rewrite the entire statement. Following is an example of an ALTER VIEW statement on the CustName view.

```
ALTER VIEW CustName
AS
SELECT FName, LName
FROM Customer
GO
```

The ALTER VIEW statement can include the WITH ENCRYPTION and WITH CHECK OPTION syntax options. The WITH CHECK OPTION is used to verify that data inserted into the view also meets the criteria within the CREATE or ALTER VIEW statement. The following example creates a view that uses both the WITH ENCRYPTION and WITH CHECK OPTION options. Notice that the WITH ENCRYPTION option appears at the first of the statement, while the WITH CHECK OPTION appears at the end of the CREATE VIEW statement.

```
CREATE VIEW vwCustomer
WITH ENCRYPTION
AS
SELECT FirstName, LastName, Address, City, State, Zip
FROM Customer
WITH CHECK OPTION
```

Best Practices

- Know the requirements of the application. Be careful that you don't overdo the security configuration. In many cases the simpler the approach, the easier it will be to troubleshoot your application later.

- Use stored procedures and views to protect your tables. If all objects are owned by DBO, stored procedures and views should be used for security configuration.

- Use application roles to separate the application from the user context.

- Use the Encrypt function to hide the password across the network.

- Use Windows Authentication whenever possible. Windows Authentication is your best way to secure passwords and user access. It also provides support for group management and allows for auditing back to the Windows domain account.

- If you are using SQL Server Authentication, hide the connection account within compiled code. If the account used to connect to SQL Server is stored in compiled code it will be hidden from the users of the application.

- Use ALTER statements to make changes to your database. ALTER statements preserve the permissions set on your database objects. This change management strategy prevents your having to reapply permissions over and over again.

- Save your original CREATE scripts. If you have the scripts that you originally used to create the objects, altering them is just an editing process; otherwise you will have to write the entire statement again.

- Use the WITH ENCRYPTION option sparingly. This option encrypts your Transact-SQL code from everyone, including you. If you choose to use this option, make sure you save your original scripts.

- Generate SQL scripts for objects created in Enterprise Manager. When you create objects with Enterprise Manager, generate the Transact-SQL scripts to facilitate quick alterations later.

REVIEW QUESTIONS

1. What are the benefits of using stored procedures?

2. When should you use views?

3. What are the differences between application roles and standard data-base roles?

4. How do you invoke an application role?

5. Why is it important to use the ALTER statements?

6. What are the methods of viewing the original syntax used to create a stored procedure?

7. Why should all objects be owned by the DBO?

CHAPTER 7

Implementing Front-End Application Security

Among the primary concerns of database administration is the security level provided by the developers who create the front-end applications. The front-end application is often referred to as the *presentation layer*. The application that interfaces with the database defines the connection to the database server. The database is only as secure as the connection options that are used in the front-end application. Database administrators should generally be concerned with two related areas.

The first area of concern relates to the client tools supplied with SQL Server. Users who have the ability to install the client tools have access to both Enterprise Manager and SQL Query Analyzer. To prevent security violations from one of the client tools, you want to control the access each user has to the database. The client tools are interfaces that are created to manipulate both the configuration of SQL Server and its databases. A user can make significant changes to the database management system through the user-friendly client tools. The connection to SQL Server from the client tools is provided by the network libraries and is configured through the Client Network Utility and the Server Network Utility.

The second area of concern is the applications that will be used by the clients to perform activity against the database. These applications could either be a connection from a licensed product, like Microsoft Excel or Microsoft Access, or an application that is created by a developer to specifically interface with SQL Server. Typically the connections made through these applications to SQL Server are made via OLE DB or ODBC. The network library is included with the OLE DB provider or ODBC driver. Many of the security requirements are defined in the connection options through these interfaces. This chapter defines the security requirements for the OLE DB and ODBC drivers.

The chapter first addresses the management of clients who are using the client tools of SQL Server. This section includes an in-depth description of the Net-Libraries, Client Network Utility, and Server Network Utility. The chapter then moves to the management of clients that are connecting to SQL Server from an application. This section describes OLE DB and ODBC in more depth and introduces connection options from Active Data Objects (ADO.NET). The security requirements for the connections from ADO are presented, and examples are provided for securing your connections to SQL Server.

Managing Connections from the Client Tools

SQL Server ships with a set of client tools that can be installed on SQL Server as well as on any other machine running a Windows operating system. The client tools are often installed on multiple machines within the network to facilitate remote administration and development on SQL Server. For security purposes, you should install the client tools only on the computers where SQL Server administration and development are necessary. You want to avoid having the tools installed by users who don't need them.

The client tools use a network library and network protocol to connect to the server to perform the necessary actions. This section describes the relationship between the network library and the network protocol. This section then describes the network libraries that are available in SQL Server. Through these network libraries, you can configure security options such as Secure Sockets Layer (SSL) and an alternative port number for connectivity to SQL Server. Finally this section introduces the Client Network Utility and the Server Network Utility, which are used to configure the Net-Library that is used for the connection from the client tools to SQL Server.

Client Net-Libraries and Network Protocols

Microsoft SQL Server uses a dynamic-link library (DLL) called a Net-Library to communicate with a particular network protocol. A matching pair of Net-Libraries must be active on client and server computers to support the desired network protocol. For example, to enable a client application to communicate with a specific instance of SQL Server across TCP/IP, the client TCP/IP Sockets Net-Library (DBNETLIB.dll) must be configured to connect to that server on the client computer, and the server TCP/IP Sockets Net-Library (SSNETLIB.dll) must be listening on the server computer.

By themselves, a pair of Net-Libraries cannot support a client/server connection. Both the client and server also must be running a protocol stack supporting the Net-Libraries. For example, if the server TCP/IP Sockets Net-Library is listening on the server computer and the client TCP/IP Sockets Net-Library is configured to connect to that server on the client computer, the client can only connect to the server if a TCP/IP protocol stack is installed on both computers.

NOTE The Named Pipes and Multiprotocol Net-Libraries both support multiple network protocols (NW Link IPX/SPX, NetBEUI, and TCP/IP) and will select automatically any supported network protocol that is available. Using either of these Net-Libraries is useful if the client must connect to multiple servers running different network protocols and you do not want to create and manage configuration entries for each server-network protocol combination.

Net-Libraries

SQL Server supports the following Net-Libraries for the client connection to SQL Server:

- Named Pipes are used to create a virtual pipe between the client and server. The connection is based on shared memory addresses. Named Pipes supports multiple network protocols (NW Link IPX/SPX, NetBEUI, and TCP/IP.) Named Pipes connections are the least secure option.

- TCP/IP is used to create a socket connection from the client to the server. A socket is the combination of an IP Address and the SQL Server port number. The port number is used to identify the service within the TCP/IP protocol. If your connection is coming from the Internet, the port number is key in negotiating firewall security. The firewall has to be configured to allow passage of network packets that have identified the port defined by your SQL instance.

- Multiprotocol is used to create a connection based on remote procedure calls (RPC). Multiprotocol can be used with the same network protocols as Named Pipes and can be used to enforce data encryption over the network through Secure Sockets Layer (SSL.) More information on configuring SSL can be found in Chapter 15, "Managing Internet Security." Implementing SSL can be used to secure connection credentials as they are passed from the client to SQL Server.

- NWLink IPX/SPX is used for the connection to a machine running the IPX/SPX protocol. This is common in a Novell network.

- AppleTalk is used to connect via the AppleTalk protocol. This is beneficial in some Macintosh networks.

- Banyan VINES is used to connect to a Banyan VINES network.

NOTE Many Macintosh and Novell networks now run on TCP/IP. If this is the scenario, the NWLink and AppleTalk Net-Libraries do not have to be configured.

The client Net-Libraries are installed during SQL Server setup. You define which client Net-Libraries are used to connect to particular instances of SQL Server using the Client Network Utility. You can specify a default Net-Library for all connections and also define the use of specific Net-Libraries for connecting to specific instances of SQL Server. TCP/IP is the default protocol on clients running the Windows NT 4.0, Windows 2000, and the Windows 9x operating systems.

SQL Server can listen simultaneously on any combination of server Net-Libraries. Use SQL Server Network Library Configuration during or after the Setup program to choose the server Net-Libraries to be activated.

For computers running Windows NT 4.0 or Windows 2000, the default server Net-Libraries are TCP/IP sockets and Named Pipes. For computers running Windows 9x, the default server Net-Libraries are TCP/IP sockets.

When you install SQL Server client utilities on a workstation, SQL Server setup installs TCP/IP as the default client protocol. If most of the servers to which you will be connecting are not configured to support the current default client protocol, you can change the default to another protocol. The port number used for the instance is automatically defined. The first instance of SQL Server is assigned port 1433. The subsequent instances are assigned different port numbers. You will need to get this information passed to both the developers who are accessing SQL Server and your firewall administrator. The port number is used to guarantee a secure connection to SQL Server. The firewall should be configured to allow as few ports through as possible to decrease the chance of an attack from the Internet.

Client Network Utility

The Client Network Utility is used to manage the client Net-Libraries and define server alias names. It can also be used to set the default options used by DB-Library applications.

Most users will never need to use the Client Network Utility. The default settings are appropriate for most connections. To connect to SQL Server 2000, users can specify only the network name of the server on which SQL Server is running and, optionally, the name of the instance of SQL Server. The user will also have to supply security credentials. This can either be the user's current Windows account information or a SQL account.

In some cases, an instance of SQL Server may be configured to listen on an alternative network port number. This may be done to increase security. Many attacks on SQL Server 2000 from the Internet are focused on port 1433 because 1433 is the default port number. While changing this port number requires a small amount of administrative overhead, it may decrease the risk of attack. If the port number is changed, client applications connecting to that instance must explicitly specify the alternative port number. While applications could specify the alternative addresses on each connection request, it is easier to use the Client Network Utility to set up an alias specifying the alternative addresses. Applications can then specify the alias name in place of the server network name in their connection requests. The alias configuration and the port number configuration are performed from the Client Network Utility. You can alter the currently configured Net-Libraries by performing the following steps:

1. From the Microsoft SQL Server program group, click Client Network Utility to open the SQL Server Client Network Utility shown in Figure 7.1.

2. Click the General tab.

3. From the Disabled Protocols pick list, click the Net-Library you want to enable.

4. Click the Enable button. The Net-Library that you selected appears in the Enabled Protocols by Order pick list.

5. After you have configured the appropriate Net-Libraries, click OK to close the SQL Server Client Network Utility.

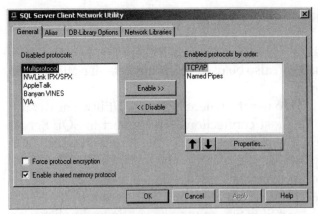

Figure 7.1 The SQL Server Client Network Utility configures the Net-Libraries with which the client can connect to SQL Server.

Server Network Utility

The Server Network Utility is used to manage the server Net-Libraries. This utility is used to specify the following list of information:

- The network protocol stacks on which an instance of SQL Server 2000 listens for client requests

- The sequence in which server Net-Libraries are considered when establishing connections from applications

- New network addresses that an instance of Microsoft SQL Server 2000 listens on

- Data encryption through Secure Sockets Layer (SSL) to ensure secure transmission of data

- The TCP port number that the SQL Server instance is listening on

Most administrators will never need to use the Server Network Utility. They will specify during setup the server Net-Libraries on which SQL Server listens. If you need to increase the default security, you can use this tool to change the port number of SQL Server and configure SSL. Both of these options can help prevent unwanted attacks against your server. After you have performed the installation, you can alter the Net-Libraries that the server is using by performing the following steps:

1. From the Microsoft SQL Server program group, click the Server Network Utility to open the SQL Server Network Utility shown in Figure 7.2.

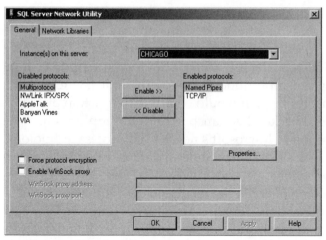

Figure 7.2   The SQL Server Network Utility configures the Net-Libraries on which SQL Server allows connections.

2. Select the SQL Server instance you want to configure by using the drop-down Instances on this Server Field pick list.

3. Click the Net-Library you would like to configure from the Disabled Protocols pick list.

4. Click the Enable button. The selection you made in the previous step appears in the Enabled Protocols pick list.

5. When you have completed the configuration, click OK to close the SQL Server Network Utility dialogue box.

NOTE The SQL Server Network utility is used to configure the port that SQL Server listens on and Secure Sockets Layer encryption. Both of these features facilitate secure communication over the Internet and through firewall infrastructures. For more information on configuring these features, refer to Chapter 15, "Managing Internet Security."

Application Connections

Discounting certain proprietary access protocols such as VBSQL, the Visual Basic interface to DB-Library, an application will most likely establish a connection with SQL Server through ODBC or OLE DB.

ODBC, or Open Database Connectivity, is a database-neutral application programming interface (API). In other words, an application can access the ODBC API and connect to different relational data sources simply by providing an appropriate ODBC database driver. Should you wish to change the database supporting the application, you would simply switch ODBC database drivers and the application would continue to function properly. The application's database backend is transparent to the application.

OLE DB is the foundation of Microsoft's newest data access technology, Universal Data Access. Like ODBC, it provides a database-neutral connection interface for applications. It was developed and introduced by Microsoft to permit access to not only the relational data sources accessible through ODBC but also to nonrelational data sources. The need for this extension was driven by intranet and Internet application data demands. In addition to OLE DB, the Universal Data Access platform also includes certain providers (similar in purpose to ODBC drivers) plus a programmer-friendly interface to OLE DB called Active Data Objects, or ADO.

Connection Security

Obviously if your SQL Server database data has any value, access to it must be secured. Setting up and maintaining security is the responsibility of the database administrator. Each user is granted or denied permission to various database objects. These permissions may range from a single field in a single table to the entire database. Generally, users should be granted permissions to only those database objects they require. This is most effectively accomplished by granting read and update access through views and stored procedures rather than by direct access to the underlying tables.

Whether an application is a user or reusable component, before the application, can gain access to SQL Server, it must be authenticated. This is accomplished by passing the user's login identification and password to the database server at the time the connection is requested. This information is typically part of the connection string the application uses to connect to a database. The login ID and the password must have been previously created by the system administrator so the database server can match the connection-string user information to the database server's data and thus authenticate the user.

The login ID can be hard coded in the application's connection string or it can be passed from the Windows operating system via a trusted network connection. A trusted network connection, not to be confused with a database connection, is established when users log on to their computer and are authenticated through a Windows domain. In essence, the operating system has already authenticated the user's access to the database server. This is referred to as *Integrated Security*.

Alternatively, the connection string may hard code a surrogate login ID and password that most likely is unknown to the user. All users accessing the application essentially log in as the same user. This presumes, of course, the application implements adequate front-end security measures to assure that only authorized users may access the database security through this surrogate login ID, and that the back-end database is not concerned about specific user activity.

Additionally, the application may display its own dialogue box to obtain the login ID and password directly from the user and incorporate it in the connection string. When a database client is not part of a trusted connection, this method permits specific user authentication when required. Additionally, it allows the application developer control over how the information is collected without subjecting the user or the developer to the default prompting behaviors of ODBC or OLE DB when login information is absent from the connection string.

Creating Connections with ODBC

As noted earlier, ODBC is a database-neutral interface that applications can use to access relational data sources. ODBC enables a database to become an integral part of an application. SQL statements can be incorporated into the application, allowing the application to read and update data from a database.

ODBC enables applications to access a variety of data sources, including a wide range of relational databases and local file-based data stores. ODBC supports applications in all Windows operating environments. An application can access any ODBC-compliant data source by selecting the appropriate ODBC driver for the specific data source. Also, many ODBC drivers can be configured as read-only, which can be a valuable security tool. If the user that is accessing your data only needs to read the data, a read-only ODBC driver can limit the user to read-only access to the data.

SQL Server programs that are written using the ODBC API communicate with SQL Server through C function calls. The SQL Server-specific versions of the ODBC functions are implemented in a SQL Server ODBC driver. The driver passes SQL statements to SQL Server and returns the results of the statements to the application. ODBC applications are also interoperable with drivers for heterogeneous data sources. Most ODBC drivers provide options for you to define the connection credentials for accessing the server. When accessing SQL Server, you have the option of using Windows Authentication.

Tools for developing C and C++ applications using the ODBC API are available in the Microsoft ODBC Software Development Kit (SDK). The ODBC SDK is part of the Microsoft Developer Network (MSDN) Professional subscription and can be downloaded from Microsoft's Web site at www.microsoft.com/data.

While C, C++, and Visual Basic applications can be written to call ODBC directly, Microsoft also provides several APIs that are wrapped in ODBC API. These APIs are simpler than accessing the ODBC API directly and offer improved integration with the respective programming languages that use them. These APIs, which are most often referred to as object models, are as follows:

Data Access Objects (DAO).   An object model functioning as a wrapper around Microsoft's JET Engine API. While it was designed primarily to access file-based databases such as Access, Paradox, FoxPro, and other ISAM file structures, DAO also permitted communication with ODBC data sources. In recent years, DAO has lost considerable ground to OLE DB (primarily) and RDO (see the following) as an ODBC interface.

Remote Data Objects (RDO).   A lightweight and programmer-friendly object model wrapping around the low-level, complex ODBC API.

Active Data Objects (ADO).   An API designed for interfacing with OLE DB, which permits indirect access to ODBC.

Most ODBC interfaces connect to databases using information maintained in an ODBC Data Source Name (DSN). The DSN must contain enough information to identify the type of database server, such as SQL Server, and the server's name or network identity. Optionally, other information, such as the database name or login ID and password, may be included. Once created and registered, the DSN information is stored in the Windows Registry for the application making the ODBC connection.

Creating a Data Source Name

To create a DSN, you open the ODBC applet in the Control Panel of Windows 95, Windows 98, or Windows NT. In Windows 2000 and Windows XP, you open Data Sources (ODBC) under Administrative Tools in the Control Panel. When the ODBC applet is opened, it starts the ODBC Data Source Administrator. As seen in Figure 7.3, you have the option of adding, removing, or configuring an ODBC DSN.

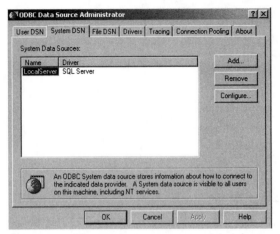

Figure 7.3 The ODBC Data Source Administrator dialogue box creates, removes, and configures ODBC Data Source Names (DSN).

Before creating the DSN, it is important to identify the three types of DSNs that can be created:

- A *User DSN* is created for a specific logged-in user on the current machine. This DSN and its related database connection are available only to that user.

- A *System DSN*, on the other hand, is available to all users on the current machine.

- A *File DSN* is more portable. All the connection information in this DSN is maintained in a file that can be easily distributed to the application machines that require access to the related database.

After you have decided on the type of DSN you want, you can add the DSN to the computer by performing the following steps:

1. Open Data Sources (ODBC) from the Administrative Tools program group.

2. Select the tab corresponding to the type of DSN you would like to create.

3. Click the Add button to open the Create New Data Source dialogue box as shown in Figure 7.4.

4. Select the desired SQL Server driver.

5. Click the Finish button to start the wizard for creating a SQL Server DSN.

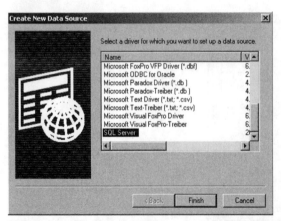

Figure 7.4 The Create New Data Source dialogue box lists all registered ODBC drivers on the current machine.

6. On the first screen of the wizard, specify the following information:

- The *Name box* provides the data source name used by an ODBC application when it requests a connection to the data source (example: *sqlPubs*). This name will be displayed in the ODBC Data Source Administrator dialogue box.
- The *Description box* is an optional description of the data source.
- The *Server box* is the name of all SQL Servers on your network. If you select a server name from the list, no further configuration is needed.

7. After you have supplied the appropriate connection information, click Finish to move to the security portion of the wizard shown in Figure 7.5.

8. On this second screen of the wizard, select among the following list of options:

With Windows NT Authentication Using the Network Login ID button. Specifies that the SQL Server ODBC driver request a secure (or trusted) connection to a SQL Server running on Windows NT or Windows 2000. When selected, SQL Server uses integrated login security to establish connections using this data source regardless of the current login security mode at the server. Any login ID or password supplied will be ignored. The SQL Server system administrator must have associated your Windows login with a SQL Server login ID.

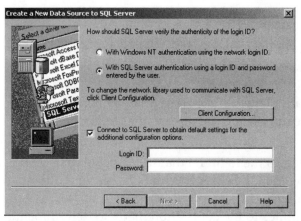

Figure 7.5   Create a New Data Source to SQL Server is the security screen for creating a SQL Server data source.

With SQL Server Authentication Using a Login ID and Password Entered by the User button.   Specifies that the SQL Server ODBC driver not request a secure (or trusted) connection to SQL Server. When selected, SQL Server uses standard login security to establish connections using this data source. You must specify a SQL Server login ID and password for all connection requests.

Client Configuration button.   Starts the Add New Network Library Configuration dialogue box of the SQL Server Client Configuration. If you specified a new name in the Server box on the first screen of the wizard, you may need to use this dialogue box to add a server alias configuration entry. That alias name must match the name you specified in the Server box on the first screen of the ODBC wizard.

NOTE Click Client Configuration if you want the connection to use a network library other than the client's default network library. Also, click Client Configuration if the actual network address of the server must be specified for a successful connection. For example, when using the TCP/IP Net-Library you may need to specify the port and socket address of the server, or if a SQL Server is listening on an alternative Named Pipe, you must specify the pipe name in the advanced entry.

Connect to SQL Server to Obtain Default Settings for the Additional Con-figuration Options checkbox.   When selected, the SQL Server driver obtains initial settings from SQL Server for the options on the screens of the wizard that follow. The SQL Server driver connects to the SQL Server named in the Server box on the first screen. When no server is named, the driver uses standard defaults as the initial settings for the options on the screens that follow in the wizard.

Login ID text box.   Specifies the login ID that the SQL Server driver uses when connecting to SQL Server if With SQL Server Authentication Using a Login ID and Password Entered by the User is selected. This only applies to the connection made to determine the server default settings; it does not apply to subsequent connections made using the data source after it has been created.

Password text box.   Specifies the password the SQL Server uses when connecting to SQL Server if With SQL Server Authentication Using a Login ID and Password Entered by the User is selected. This only applies to the connection made to determine the server default settings; it does not apply to subsequent connections made using the new data source.

NOTE Both the Login ID and Password text boxes are disabled if With Windows NT Authentication Using the Network Login ID *is* selected, or if Connect to SQL Server to Obtain Default Settings for the Additional Configuration Options *is not* selected.

9. Click Next to move to the next portion of the wizard. The SQL Service must be running and it must recognize the login ID and password provided. If you successfully connect to the server, you will see the screen in Figure 7.6. Otherwise, you will receive an error message prompting you for accurate information. This could include invalid login, connection, or driver information.

10. Click Next to accept the defaults for connection settings. The connection settings can be used to control the actions of a user for a given connection. You may want to view the SQL Server Books Online to learn more about them.

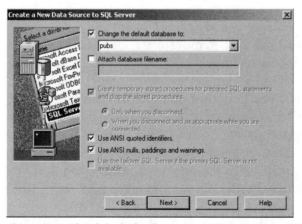

Figure 7.6   The default database screen for creating a SQL Server data source.

11. Click Finish to display Figure 7.7. Here, you can verify the setting you have made. Click on the Test Data Source button to to verify the setting you just created.

12. Click OK to create the DSN.

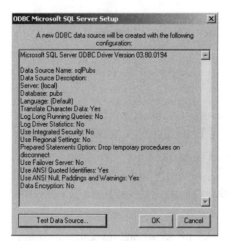

Figure 7.7   This screen displays your DSN configuration settings and allows you to test them.

Remote Data Objects

Prior to the introduction of OLE DB, Remote Data Objects (RDO) was Microsoft's flagship data access technology. While Active Data Objects (ADO) is now Microsoft's premier data access technology, RDO is still widely embedded in applications and continues to provide flexible and high-speed access to ODBC data sources. It was designed as a programmer-friendly interface wrapped tightly around the ODBC API. It did not require a database engine (DAO required the JET database engine) and consequently was lightweight. The RDO interface connected to underlying databases directly through the ODBC Driver Manager and the related ODBC driver.

Before you can reference the data in a remote database, you must establish a connection to the data source. There are a number of ways to establish connections with RDO, as described in this section. RDO does not *manage* connections for your application—it simply collects parameters necessary to call the appropriate functions to open and close a SQL Server connection. RDO does not cache connections or attempt to share them based on similar DSN entries. When you use the RDO Close method to close a connection, it is closed immediately.

When you are ready to open a connection, the options available to you are as follows:

- Use the RemoteData Control to establish a connection based on its properties and create an rdoConnection object as referenced by its Connection property.

- Declare an rdoConnection object and use the rdoEnvironment object's OpenConnection method.

- Create a stand-alone rdoConnection object using the Dim x As New syntax, set its properties, and use the EstablishConnection method.

- Use the EstablishConnection method on an existing rdoConnection object after having either created a stand-alone rdoConnection object or after having used the Close method on an existing rdoConnection object.

All of these techniques establish a physical link to a data source, generally using a DSN to specify the network location of the data source, the driver type, and a number of other parameters used to identify the user to the data source.

Creating Connections with OLE DB

OLE DB is an API that allows COM applications to access data from relational and nonrelational data sources. An application uses an OLE DB provider to access an OLE DB data source. An OLE DB provider is a COM component that accepts calls to the OLE DB API and interprets that request for the specific data source for which it was designed. The OLE DB provider for an OLE DB data source is functionally equivalent to an ODBC Driver for an ODBC source.

While several OLE DB providers were released with OLE DB, many potential OLE DB data sources do not have specific OLE DB providers. To ease the transition from ODBC to OLE DB, Microsoft provides an OLE DB provider for ODBC. While not as efficient as a native OLE DB provider, it does permit OLE DB access to any data source with a supporting ODBC driver.

SQL Server 2000 includes a native OLE DB Provider used by OLE DB applications to access the data in SQL Server. In SQL Server version 6.5 and earlier, OLE DB applications had to use the OLE DB Provider for ODBC layered over the SQL Server ODBC driver. While OLE DB applications can still use the OLE DB Provider for ODBC with the SQL Server ODBC driver, it is more efficient to use only the OLE DB Provider for SQL Server.

OLE DB as a low-level API is recommended for tools, utilities, or system-level development needing either top performance or access to SQL Server features not exposed through Active Data Objects (ADO)—the programmer-friendly interface to OLE DB. The core capabilities of the OLE DB specification provide the data access features needed by most applications and are easily accessible through ADO. However, those applications requiring certain provider-specific features of the OLE DB Provider for SQL Server must use the OLE DB API directly. Some of these features include:

- The interface to the SQL Server bulk-copy component
- The interface to get SQL Server-specific information from messages and errors
- Catalog information from the linked servers used in SQL Server distributed queries

OLE DB also supports the XML functionality of SQL Server 2000. This provides an easy migration path for Internet applications coded to use OLE DB to retrieve a rowset and then convert it into an XML document.

Most applications working with XML are written in ADO or use URLs, which are less complex than OLE DB.

ADO clients communicating with OLE DB need an OLE DB provider to query an SQL data source. For SQL Server, the following types of OLE DB providers can be used:

- Microsoft OLE DB Provider for SQL Server (SQLOLEDB), which maps OLE DB interfaces and methods over SQL Server data sources.

- Microsoft OLE DB Provider for ODBC (MSDASQL), which maps OLE DB interfaces and methods to ODBC APIs. OLE DB consumers connect to an instance of SQL Server using the SQL Server ODBC driver as an intermediary layer.

The native OLE DB provider, SQLOLEDB, is installed with SQL Server 2000 and is recommended when developing new applications. The OLE DB provider for ODBC—MSDASQL—is provided for backward compatibility.

Active Data Objects (ADO) is a data access interface used to communicate with OLE DB-compliant data sources, such as SQL Server. Data consumer applications can use ADO to connect to, retrieve, manipulate, and update data from an instance of SQL Server.

Architecturally, ADO is an application-level interface that uses OLE DB. Because ADO uses OLE DB as its foundation, it benefits from the data access infrastructure that OLE DB provides, yet it shields the application developer from the necessity of programming against the COM interfaces exposed by OLE DB. Developers can use ADO for general-purpose access programs in business and use the low-level OLE DB API for tool, utility, or system-level development.

Data sources in SQL Server are suited for access through ADO. Because SQL Server is OLE DB-compliant, you can use ADO to develop client applications, service providers, Web applications, and business objects that access data in SQL Server.

When working with Web-based applications, developers should consider using Microsoft's Remote Data Services (RDS). RDS is a Web-based technology that uses Internet Information Services (IIS) and special ActiveX controls to bind data from a SQL Server data source to data controls on a Web page. RDS is integrated with ADO technology. For more information about RDS, see the RDS documentation in the Microsoft Data Access Components (MDAC) SDK, located in the Platform SDK.

ADO can also be integrated with Active Data Objects (Multidimensional) (ADO MD), which you can use to browse a multidimensional schema, and query and retrieve the results of a cube; and Active Data Objects Extensions for Data Definition Language and Security (ADOX), which includes objects SQL Server database object creation and modification, and security.

Best Practices

- Only install the client tools for SQL Server on the computers where the user has to administer or develop using SQL Server. The client tools should not be available to all users.

- Use the Client and Server Network Utilities to configure the Net-Libraries with which the SQL Server connection can be made.

- Use the ADO to access OLE DB- and ODBC-compliant data sources. ADO, along with ADO.NET, represents Microsoft's latest data access technology and consequently is the technology receiving most of Microsoft's data access focus.

- When available, use native OLE DB providers rather than the OLE DB provider for ODBC.

- When using ODBC, whether directly through the ODBC API, RDO, or ADO, consider using DSN-less connections. They are typically easier to maintain and deploy.

REVIEW QUESTIONS

1. What security options can be supplied from the Server Network Library Utility?

2. Why would you ever have to configure the NWLink IPX/SPX Net-Library?

3. What is the advantage of using OLE DB rather than ODBC?

Implementing Microsoft's Enterprise Development Strategy

Distributed applications have been the focus of recent development, with software components running on every platform across the enterprise environment. Support for this distributed, and consequently tiered, development was a primary goal of Microsoft's Windows 2000 operating system. Its COM+ component services continued to extend and consolidate Microsoft's core component technology—Component Object Model (COM)—while enhancing the software developer's ability to create and deploy distributed components.

Microsoft's Enterprise Development Strategy enables organizations to build scalable applications that manage the information flow both within and outside an organization. The fundamental design goal of this strategy is to enable solutions to easily evolve with changing business needs through the ability to centrally manage these solutions and to ease their integration with existing systems and data.

The core of Microsoft's strategy is the integration of traditional client server application development and the Internet. This integration is accomplished through numerous COM+ related services and applications exposing features such as data access, transaction monitoring, message queuing, security, and directory services. Our ability to reuse and assemble existing components developed internally or by third parties manifests the power of COM+. This component-based approach enables developers to build, test, and maintain applications more efficiently.

However, as more developers embrace distributed application development and as the tools to build, test, and deploy these applications become more user-friendly and richer in functionality, security issues seem overwhelming. No longer are we able to simply implement security in the application's front end or at the point of data contact on a single database server. Our new distributed application model has numerous and varied front ends accessing sensitive components rich in functionality running on multiple computers across the network, which in turn are accessing remote data stores configured in ways to balance transaction demands with analysis requirements. As distributed applications begin to assemble their parts and pieces, the potential for security breaches seems to grow exponentially. The migration from protecting that one large "fat" client, or a solitary database server, to securing all the components distributed on numerous machines across the enterprise landscape, can be nightmarish and cause you to question your decision to undertake distributed application development.

Recognizing the inherent security problems in distributed applications and the vital role of security in most applications, Microsoft endowed COM+ with a set of security features that has the power and flexibility to secure an application's components. These components represent the middleware in the application and mediate security between an application's front end (typically requiring less security) and the database back end (typically requiring the most security). Developers working with network and system administrators can now implement security declaratively (defined with the components being used) or procedurally (through application code).

Properly used and understood, Microsoft's tools are a valuable aid in securing the new breed of applications being developed. To better understand the challenges and pitfalls of enterprise security management, we must have a solid, conceptual grasp of Microsoft's Enterprise Development Strategy and the technologies that support it.

This chapter first introduces the client/server architecture and terms, which more completely introduce the multitier architecture. The chapter then introduces the security considerations of the multitier model. Finally this chapter focuses on the implementation of security in the multitier environment.

Client/Server Architecture and Terms

Before discussing security problems and implementation strategies for distributed applications, we need to understand the main concepts and terms of client/server architectures. We first introduce those terms and concepts, which provide a foundation for the rest of the chapter. We discuss these concepts more thoroughly as we progress through the chapter.

The Client/Server Model

The classic definition of *client/server* describes physical deployment models where a client computer makes a request to a server computer, and the server computer responds to the request. This definition is often segmented into two implementations: a client/server computing model and a client/server request-response model.

The *client/server computing model* is defined as client applications running on a desktop or personal computer that access information on remote servers or host computers. This is most often implemented with desktop users accessing a remote database server. The client portion of the application, or the front end, is typically optimized for user interaction, whereas the server portion, or back end, provides centralized functionality for multiple users.

The *client/server request-response model* refers to one element of an application (client) making a request to another element of an application (server). This most often refers to a front-end client application or a component making a request of a server component. While it referred to a request-response relationship, often the server does not respond, but simply performs a service.

Services and Tiers

The client/server application architecture is based on a services model which views an application as a collection of discrete features or services. Additionally, and without regard to physical deployment, these services are conceptually placed in tiers, or layers. Both the services model and tiers are logical constructs to aid in the design of client/server applications.

A *service* is a unit of application logic accessed through a consistent interface that responds to requests for specific actions or information. The services an application performs are functionally classified into one of three types.

User services.   Typically, the visual user interface responsible for collecting information from and presenting information to the user.

Business services.   Application logic that ensures the way an organization conducts business is properly abstracted in the application. These "business rules" are typically at the core of an application's purpose.

Data services.   Application logic responsible for data integrity and the storage and retrieval of data.

Application tiers, or layers, represent those segments of the application that execute separately, and in some cases independently, from the other segments. For example, SQL Server as a service runs separately and independently of any client process making a request of it, even those clients executing on the same machine.

These tiers represent an abstraction of where the services of an application reside. Consequently, in a logical sense they mirror the application service types. The tiers are generally described as the presentation or user tier, business or middle tier, and the data tier. With this mirroring it would appear that the application's services would be in their respective tiers. This is not always the case. For example, it's not uncommon to have a stored procedure executing business logic in the data tier.

The first step in defining the application architecture is to select which tier or tiers can accommodate each of the application's services. The architectural mix of tiers and services is often classified as follows:

Desktop.   A nonclient/server architecture where all application services are consolidated in one tier, typically the presentation layer.

Two-tier.   Client/server architecture, typically including the presentation and data tiers. Business services are either consolidated in one of the tiers or shared between them.

Three-tier.   Client/server architecture, including all three tiers, each accommodating their respective application service.

N-tier.   An extension of the three-tier application where one or more of the tiers are separated into additional tiers, providing another layer of abstraction.

The goal of this step is to select the architecture most appropriate for the underlying business requirements. The three-tier (or n-tier) application architecture is generally most appropriate for enterprise-level applications.

Two-Tier Client/Server Architecture

Two-tier applications are the entry point in client/server application development. By using a database that runs as its own service, we can separate application data services from its user interface. In other words, the database, while still part of the application, is a process running in the data tier and is independent of the client's user interface, which remains in the presentation tier. These data services residing in the data tier are usually implemented as stored procedures.

While this separation of services between tiers is a logical one, two-tier client/server applications typically group presentation and application logic components on client machines, which in turn access a remote database server through a network connection. These applications work well in departmental-scale applications with a limited number of clients connected through a secure, fast network.

The advantage of two-tier applications over desktop applications is that the data and data services are centralized, which benefits an organization by:

- Sharing data
- Providing consistency in accessing data
- Reducing duplication
- Easing software maintenance

Figure 8.1 illustrates the logical design issues of a simple two-tier client/server architecture. While it's clear that the user services should be in the presentation tier and the data services in the data tier, it is not always clear where the business services should reside. Placing the business services in the presentation tier follows the "fat client" model, while placing them in the data tier favors the "thin client" model.

The fat client model favors implementing business services and some data services in the presentation tier. While these clients can be quite large, they take advantage of local client resources and tend to be very responsive.

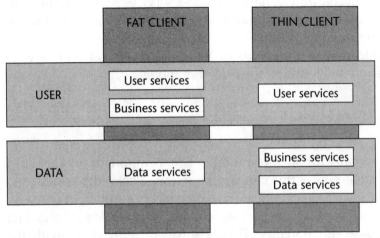

Figure 8.1 Two-tier client/server applications spread application user, business, and data services across two tiers, or layers.

Thin client development, however, strips all but the essential user services from the presentation tier and places them in the data tier. As a result, all application logic is consolidated in one place, simplifying application maintenance and deployment.

Three-Tier Client/Server Architecture

In three-tier architectures, all application services—user, business, and data—are conceptually separated into their respective tiers. Presentation elements manage user interaction and request application services by calling business-tier components. These components perform their business logic and in turn make requests of the data tier. This application design is more flexible than a two-tier design because clients can call server-based components as needed to complete a request, and components can call other components to improve code reuse.

Additionally, our underlying application model, with conceptual views of the definitions, rules, and relationships within our application structure, assures that our shared components are "loosely coupled," or independent units of functionality. This provides additional flexibility in maintaining and extending applications. As the business requirements evolve and increase in complexity, modifying and adding discrete components can be accomplished without disrupting other segments of the application.

Three-tier applications that are implemented using multiple servers across a network are referred to as *distributed applications*. Some services reside on client computers, typically user services, while business and data services generally reside on server computers that provide centralized, multiuser functionality. Figure 8.2 describes this general scenario. User services run on a client computer; shared business services represent the middle tier and run on a server computer; and shared data services are the third tier, also running on a database server.

Whereas application requirements dictate which application model to use, our discussion will focus on the three-tier model.

Application Infrastructure

In a three-tier application model, server components provide centralized, multiuser functionality for an application's client components or elements. The software that supports this concurrent access to shared business and data services is called the *application infrastructure,* or plumbing. For example, a relational database system such as SQL Server controls access to data and other database functionality. This is software that works with the

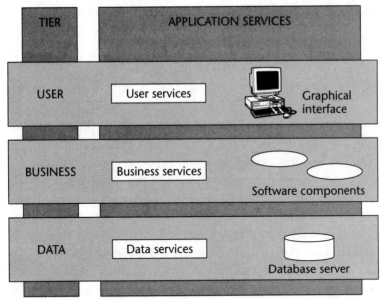

Figure 8.2 Three-tier client/server applications spread application user, business, and data services into corresponding tiers.

operating system to provide the centralized, multiuser functionality for most data services.

Additionally, COM+ supplies the application infrastructure that enables systems to interoperate efficiently with business logic shared by a large number of users. This reduces both the complexity and cost of building three-tier applications and enables developers to focus on the application's logic without worrying about the plumbing. This results in less complex, more rapid development.

COM+ overcomes the inherent problems of maintaining data integrity and system reliability in shared systems by:

- Managing processes, system threads, and other operating system resources to facilitate concurrent user access.

- Synchronizing access to shared data through connection pooling to maintain performance and conserve scarce server resources.

- Performing transaction monitoring to keep each user's actions isolated from the actions of others.

■ Implementing security so unauthorized users do not access the system.

Introduction to Security

Deciding where to enforce security in component-based applications can be difficult. As the parts and pieces of the application design fall into place, the issue of security can become complex. Where should security be implemented? Should security mechanisms be placed at the database or in the shared business components? Should the client application carry these mechanisms, or should they be implemented throughout the application?

One thing is certain. As the number and complexity of security mechanisms increase, application performance declines. Nevertheless, we must protect our data, and our business rules must be implemented and enforced. Additionally, each client's access to our application must be appropriate, with sufficient security checkpoints, to assure compliance with our organization's requirements.

Security in Two-Tier Applications

In a typical two-tier application model, users log on to the database directly. Each user has a separate login and that information resides in the database. The database is protected from unauthorized access because users must supply a valid login. In SQL Server these users can become members of roles, which facilitates easier management of permissions.

The two drawbacks to security in two-tier applications are reduced scalability and difficult integration. Since each user has a different login, each requires its own connection. The limited number of connections supportable by the database can be quickly used up causing *reduced scalability*. *Difficult integration* is the result of designing an application to incorporate the functionality of another, thus requiring additional security mechanisms to verify user credentials.

Security in Three-Tier Applications

As noted earlier, we place application business logic into a middle tier in three-tier applications. Rather than accessing databases directly, clients solicit components running in COM+ applications to perform data services. These COM+ components directly connect with the database and perform data services on the clients' behalf. Figure 8.3 illustrates the conceptual difference between data access in two-tier and three-tier applications.

Application security involves authorizing user access to specific components and interfaces in COM+ applications. Users are mapped to the COM+ application functionality they require through COM+ roles. Data security, on the other hand, involves authorizing the COM+ applications to access databases or other COM+ applications. Each COM+ application is assigned an identity or role that SQL Server or another COM+ application uses to authenticate the requester and, if appropriate, grant access.

The advantages to security in three-tier applications over two-tier applications are as follows

- Since all database access can be encapsulated in COM+ components, modifying data access logic is significantly simplified.

- Administration is reduced when setting up application access.

- Instead of thinking about end-user security in terms of database objects, we can use COM+ to think about security in terms of the roles that an individual plays in the organization.

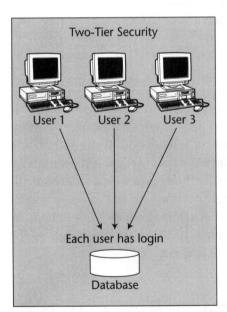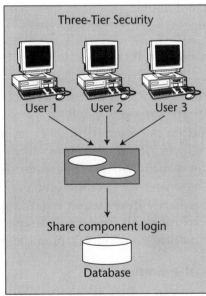

Figure 8.3   Two-tier client/server security requires each client to supply a valid login to gain access to the database, while three-tier architectures permit the middle-tier components to log in to the database on behalf of all clients.

Security in COM+

COM+ provides several security features that we can use to protect our COM+ applications. These services can be configured or implemented either declaratively at design time or programmatically at run time. Windows 2000 Component Services provide a rich, visual interface to implement security declaratively, while COM+ exposes a rich Application Programming Interface (API) for managing security programmatically.

The automatic security services that COM+ offers (role-based security and authentication) make it possible to implement all security functionality declaratively. When we turn on the services and configure them appropriately, COM+ handles the details of enforcing the security of our security policies. Additionally, if the automatic services are not sufficient for our applications requirements, we can extend them, building on the automatic security platform provided by COM+.

Which mechanisms you use to secure a given application depends on the particular requirements of that application. Some security choices affect how you write components, and some can significantly affect the application's design. Before you make any decisions about how to secure an application, you should consider its security requirements in the context of its overall design and choose the most suitable combination of security features. The following sections describe relevant COM+ security categories and features.

Role-Based Security

Role-based security is the central feature of COM+ application security. Using roles, we can administratively build an authorization policy for an application. Authorizing which users can access which resources can be performed at the component level, an interface level and, if necessary, at a method level. Roles also provide a framework for programmatically enforcing security when applications require more granular access control.

Role-based security is built on a general mechanism that enables you to retrieve security information regarding the original caller in the chain of calls to a component. This facilitates database auditing and logging when a COM+ application adopts its own security identity.

Client Authentication

Before you can authorize clients to access resources, you must be able to authenticate who they are. A COM+ application lets you turn on the authentication service administratively to enroll other more fundamental COM+ and Windows 2000 services. These services are transparent to the COM+ application.

Client Impersonation and Delegation

In some cases, an application needs to do work on behalf of a client using the client's identity, for example, when accessing a database that needs to authenticate the original client. This requires the application to impersonate the client. COM+ provides facilities for client impersonation, which can be configured administratively if proper support has been provided within the code of the application's components.

Multitier Application Security

In three-tier applications, determining where to enforce data access security can be an obstacle. In traditional client/server development, implementing security at the database is the easiest and most sure option. In fact, many database administrators are reluctant to trust any other security mechanism to secure data stores.

To implement security at the data tier, each user must have an individual database connection. If an application needs to scale, that is, accommodate an increasing number of users and transactions, the resource demands that are needed to support the increased database connections may be too burdensome. In fact they are often so significant that the advantages of multitier development are never realized. Consequently, when developing scalable, multitier applications, security should be implemented with COM+ applications in the middle tier. This enables the application to fully leverage the scalable services provided by COM+.

Enforcing Data Security at the Database

Since data is the most important thing to protect, the database is a natural place to implement security. As noted, however, the resources to support the required connections can be too expensive. Despite the preference of enforcing security at the middle tier, there may be a number of reasons to enforce security at the database. Consider the following:

- Your application is to be used by a limited number of users and is not expected to scale. Implementing security in the middle tier can actually diminish performance, because a price is being paid for features that are not required.

- More precise security access may be obtained with database authentication when the data is more intricately bound with specific users.

- Authenticating clients at the database enables more detailed auditing capabilities.

If you implement security at the database, the user identity needs to be passed through to the database. While it is possible to pass user security information to the database in parameters, COM+ applications can impersonate the original caller. In other words, component requests to the database are done on behalf of the original caller using its specific security information. Implementing security at the database can have consequences, which could be detrimental if the application needs to be scaled. Two of these consequences are that database connections from specific users cannot be pooled with other users and user impersonation is slower than when making a direct database request.

Enforcing Data Security in the Middle Tier

As a general rule, scalable multitier applications using COM+ should enforce security in the COM+ application at the middle tier. Doing so enables us to exploit the full capabilities provided by COM+. Ideally, we should secure our database objects in such a way the COM+ application is able to access them using its own security identity. The database simply authenticates the COM+ component entrusting it to properly authenticate and authorize clients requiring data access through its functionality. The benefits of this approach are as follows:

- Since one login is used for all clients, connections may be pooled.

- Overall security maintenance is reduced on both the database server and in the COM+ applications.

- When one COM+ application calls another COM+ application, we do not need additional logins or sessions. We can configure COM+ security to authenticate application-to-application calls.

Implementing Security in COM+ Applications

It is helpful to understand the resources that must be secured in the COM+ security model. Here are the primary goals of the COM+ security model:

- Activation control

- Access control

- Authentication control

- Identity control

Activation control specifies who is permitted to launch components. Once a component has been launched, *access control* determines who can touch the component's objects. In some cases, it might be acceptable for certain users to have access to certain areas of functionality, while other services of a component are restricted. For example, perhaps all users connecting over the Web are permitted to access certain areas of the component's functionality, but other services are reserved for authorized users only.

Authentication control ensures that a network transmission is authentic and protects the data from unauthorized viewers. Different authentication levels can be set so that all the data is encrypted before being transmitted.

Identity control specifies the security credentials under which a component executes. These credentials can be a specific user account configured for the COM+ application or the security credentials of the client activating it.

Security information for COM+ components is configured in two ways: declarative security and programmatic security. Declarative security settings are configured in the COM+ catalog external to the component. A system administrator typically configures declarative security. Programmatic security is incorporated into a component by the developer. Activation, access, authentication, and identity security settings for a component can be configured in the declarative manner via the COM+ catalog using the Component Services administrative tool. Access and authentication security can also be controlled programmatically by using several interfaces and methods provided by COM+. Activation and identity security cannot be controlled programmatically, because these settings must be specified before a component is launched.

Role-Based Security

If your COM+ application uses role-based security, several tasks need to be completed. When designing the components in your application, you define the roles that are necessary to protect access to the components. You also decide which roles to assign to the application's components, interfaces, and methods. During application integration, you use the Component Services administrative tool to add the defined roles to the application and assign each role to the appropriate components, interfaces, and methods.

The following list generally describes the tasks to be completed in configuring role-based security. The precise steps and options for accomplishing each task are described in the sections that follow.

- Turn on security for the application.

- Set security level for access checks.

- Turn on security for the component.

- Define roles for an application.

- Assign roles to the components.

Turn on Security for the Application

To turn on application authorization checking, you must enforce access checks for it. This will enable full role-based security. When designing your application, you may want to disable security so you can focus on the program's design and logic. Complete the following steps to enable access checks for an application:

1. In the console tree of the Component Services administrative tool, right-click the COM+ application for which you want to enable access checks and then click Properties.

2. In the application properties dialogue box, click the Security tab.

3. As shown in Figure 8.4, select the Enforce Access Checks for This Application checkbox.

4. Click OK.

After enabling access checks, you should select the appropriate security level.

Set Security Level for Access Checks

You have two choices for setting a COM+ application security level (see Figure 8.4):

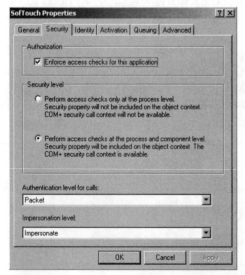

Figure 8.4   Under the Security tab of a COM+ applications property page, you can enable security authorization for the application and set its access security level.

Perform access checks only at the process level.   Security checks are performed only at the application level. Fine-grained role checking is turned off at the component, method, and interface levels. In addition, programmatic role-based security options are unavailable.

Perform access checks at the process and component level.   Security checks are performed at the object, interface, and method levels if so established. Programmatic role-based security also is enabled.

To select a security level:

1. In the console tree of the Component Services administrative tool, right-click the COM+ application for which you want to enable access checks and then click Properties.

2. In the application properties dialogue box, click the Security tab.

3. As shown in Figure 8.4, select either Perform Access Checks Only at the Process Level or Perform Access Checks at the Process and Component Level.

4. Click OK.

Any changes will be effective the next time the COM+ application is started.

Turn on Security for the Component

By default, component-level access checks are enabled when a component is installed. However, they are effective only when application-level access checks are enabled and the security level is set to perform access checks at the process and component level.

Disabling role checks for components that do not require security checks increases performance. Also, when debugging components, consider disabling security to better focus on the COM+ application's logic.

To enable or disable access checks at the component level:

1. In the console tree of the Component Services administrative tool, locate the COM+ application that contains the component for which you want to disable (or enable) role checks. Expand the view in the tree to view the components in the Components folder.

2. Right-click the component for which you want to enable role checks; then click Properties.

3. In the component properties dialogue box, click the Security tab.

4. Select the Enforce Component Level Access Checks checkbox to enforce component-level checks.

5. Click OK.

The new setting will take effect the next time the application is started.

Define Roles for an Application

COM+ roles represent the unit of privilege in a COM+ application. Once the security privileges have been defined for a COM+ application, roles are created that map to those levels of access privilege. This design is fulfilled when the application is deployed and system administrators populate the role with actual users and user groups.

To add a role to an application:

1. In the console tree of the Component Services administrative tool, locate the COM+ application to which you want to add the role. Expand the tree to view the folders for the application.

2. Right-click the Roles folder for the application; point to New, then click Role.

3. In the Role dialogue box, type the name of the new role in the box provided.

4. Click OK.

Once roles have been added to a COM+ application, they must be assigned to the appropriate components, interfaces, and methods. If role-based security has been chosen and enabled, and if roles have been added but not assigned, all calls to the application will fail.

Assign Roles to the Components

You can explicitly assign a role to any item within a COM+ application that is visible through the Component Services administrative tool. Doing so ensures that any users that are members of the role will be permitted access to that item and any other items that it contains. For instance, if you assign the role *DataEntry* to a component, then any member of *DataEntry* is allowed access to that component and any interfaces and methods it exposes. *DataEntry* will show up as an Inherited role for any of those interfaces and methods.

A method is accessible to callers only if you assign a role to the method's interface or the method's component, in which case the role will be inherited by the method. If no role is assigned, and access checks are enabled, all calls to the method will fail.

Before you can assign a role, you must define it for the application. All roles defined for the application will appear in the Roles Explicitly Set for Selected Item window on the Security tab for any components, methods, and interfaces within the application.

To assign roles to a component, method, or interface:

1. In the console tree of the Component Services administrative tool, locate the COM+ application for which the role has been defined. Expand the tree to view the application's components, interfaces, or methods, depending on what you are assigning the role to.

2. Right-click the item to which you want to assign the role; then click Properties.

3. In the Properties dialogue box, click the Security tab.

4. In the Roles Explicitly Set for Selected Item box, select the roles that you want to assign to the item.

5. Click OK.

Any roles that you have explicitly set for an item will be inherited by any lower-level items it contains and will show up in the Roles Inherited by Selected Item window for those items.

Declarative Security

The COM+ catalog is the underlying data store that holds all COM+ configuration data. Most COM+ administration involves reading and writing data stored in this catalog. The principal way we access the catalog is through the Administrative Tools—Component Services found on the Windows Start menu.

The COM+ catalog not only maintains COM+ security information, but also permits the control of many of the related settings. The ability to control these settings through the COM+ catalog is called *declarative security*. Security settings can also be configured programmatically; however, there is a considerable advantage to doing it declaratively.

By manipulating the catalog through component services, a knowledgeable administrator can flexibly configure and customize the COM+ security environment. COM+ then enforces all of these settings automatically. For example, you could specify that only users belonging to a specific group are permitted to launch or access a particular component. Once set, nothing more is required to prevent others from accessing the component. This significantly reduces the amount of security-related code you need to write.

Configuring Default COM+ Settings

Launching the Component Services administration tool and selecting the Default Properties tab from My Computer's Property page displays the options shown in Figure 8.5. These options enable the administrator to set

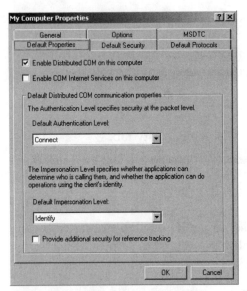

Figure 8.5 COM+ remote behavior configuration and default authentication and impersonation properties for COM+ applications can be defined on the Default Properties tab of the My Computer Properties page.

the default authentication and impersonation options on a machinewide basis for all COM+ applications.

The Enable Distributed COM on This Computer option enables DCOM and permits remote calls to and from this machine. When the system is first installed, this option is enabled. The Enable COM Internet Services on This Computer option determines whether COM+ Internet Services are available. (Doing so permits DCOM calls through TCP port 80.) By default, this option is disabled.

The Default Authentication Level setting specifies the base authentication level that will be used on this system, unless preempted programmatically or through other declarative settings. When the system is first installed, this setting is configured for connect-level authentication. The Default Impersonation Level setting specifies the base impersonation level that clients running on this system will grant to their servers, again assuming that a component does not modify its respective settings. From the client's point of view, anonymous-level impersonation is the most secure, because the component cannot obtain any information about the client. With each successive impersonation level, a component is granted further access to and use of the client's security credentials. When the system is first installed, this setting is configured for identity-level impersonation.

The Provide Additional Security for Reference Tracking option, when enabled, causes COM+ to perform additional callbacks to determine reference count calls. This helps assure that objects are not prematurely released. While this option can improve system security, it will slow execution speed.

The Component Services administration tools Default Security tab as shown in Figure 8.6 enables the administrator to configure default access and launch permissions on a machinewide basis. These settings are used for components that do not provide their own settings. Clicking the Edit Default button presents a list of users and user groups that can be explicitly allowed or denied permission. When the system is first installed, only administrators, the system account, and users granted launch permissions can launch an application. It is generally not recommended to change these values. Instead of changing the machinewide default settings that affect all components, it is preferable to adjust the security settings using the role-based mechanism described in the *Role-Based Security* section earlier in this chapter.

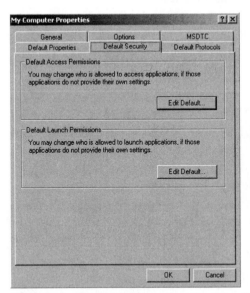

Figure 8.6   The Default Security tab of the COM+ My Computer Properties page permits setting default access and launch permissions on COM+ applications that do not supply their own.

Configuring Component Identity

Most declarative security settings at the COM+ application level were discussed in the *Role-Based Security* section earlier in this chapter. One setting, the Identity property, remains. This setting enables the administrator to determine in which user account the application will execute. You set this property on the Identity tab of the COM+ application's Property page as shown in Figure 8.7. There are two possible user accounts under which the application can execute: the interactive user, which is the currently logged-on user launching the application and a user account created specifically for the COM+ application (called This User).

When configured to run as an interactive user account, the COM+ application will be run under the identity of the user currently logged on. The application impersonates the user by taking on the user's security mantle. The following design problems must be addressed when configuring a component for execution as the interactive user:

- A user must be logged on for the component to execute.
- Users will log on with varying privileges, thus endowing the COM+ application with many rights if an administrator accesses the application, or very few rights if a guest seeks access.

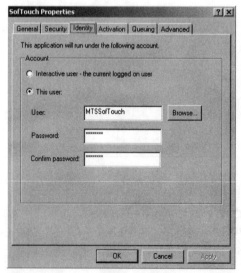

Figure 8.7 The Identity tab of the COM+ application Properties page permits the application to either impersonate the original caller or execute under its own user account.

- If the user logs off while the component is running, the component dies.

This user configuration setting may be useful in those situations where users directly interact with the COM+ application. It is not recommended for other types of data or middle-tier components.

The second identity setting is to configure the component for execution under a specific user account (This User). As shown in Figure 8.7, selecting This User enables you to specify a valid Windows user or group account under which the COM+ application executes. When an attempt is made to launch the component, COM+ automatically initiates a system logon using the specified user account. As part of the logon procedure, a new, noninteractive logon context is created for the component. This logon context, as with most logged-in users, may create objects and launch applications. However, being noninteractive, these objects and applications are not visible to other logged-in users and can't accept direct user input. This setting is often the best option for components serving many client programs simultaneously, since all instances of the component are loaded into this one logon context.

The permissions necessary to create this logon context when the COM+ application is launched are automatically assigned by the Component Services administration tool to any user account specified on the Identity tab shown in Figure 8.7. You can use the Browse button to select any current Windows user or group.

Programmatic Security

Configuring security declaratively gives the administrator a great deal of design flexibility and relieves the application developer from writing security-related code. However, declarative security may not always be the best answer. Certain features of the COM+ security model can be accessed only via a programming interface. In these cases taking programmatic control of security settings may be your only solution.

So when can you use programmatic security and what can you do with it? If role-based security has been enabled for the COM+ application containing your component, you have access to programmatic security in that component. You can check role membership to determine whether particular sections of code should execute, you can access security information using the security call context object, and you can determine whether security is enabled for the current call.

You can call the IsCallerInRole method to determine whether an object's direct caller is a member of a particular role. This functionality is useful when you want to ensure that a certain block of code is not executed unless the caller is a member of a particular role. For example, you could use this method to ensure that only users in a particular role perform transactions exceeding certain thresholds.

For example, if you are developing COM+ components for a Visual Basic application, you call the GetSecurityCallContext function and then use the security call context to call the IsCallerInRole, as shown in the following example:

```
If (GetSecurityCallContext.IsCallerInRole("Manager")) Then
    ' Go ahead and perform the transaction
Else
    ' Display an error message
End If
```

In cases in which role-based security is disabled, the IsCallerInRole method always returns true, which can lead the component to grant permissions to ineligible users. To overcome this problem, the IsSecurity-Enabled method can be called to determine whether role-based security is currently being enforced by COM+.

Finally, COM+ programmatic security comes to our aid in data access. Database auditing does not work as expected under the three-tier security model, because all users access the database through the same user ID (the COM+ application user account). To implement database auditing and logging in your COM+ application, use the GetOriginalCallerName method. This returns the Windows name of the original component caller, even if the COM+ component was called directly by another component. Calls to the database can pass the underlying user initiating the data modifications as a parameter. This in turn can be used in any manner the database administrator requires to facilitate required logging or auditing.

Best Practices

- Before deploying applications to production, stage them on a quality assurance server. This server should have the same security settings (NTFS permissions, MTS Roles, and SQL Server users) as the production server. Failure to properly test an application's security mechanisms invariably results in permission problems when put into production.

- COM+ provides a flexible and robust model for role-based application security, relieving the developer from coding the application's security plumbing. However, it is imperative for security that requirements be designed along with the application logic. The developer determines what roles are necessary in an application and allows operations on the data based on role membership. The only security consideration left to deployment is which Windows users or groups belong to which roles.

- If your application has any database auditing or logging requirements and the COM+ application does not impersonate the original caller, you must design for this in your business components and data services. Without user impersonation (recommended), the built-in database auditing features may not be useful, since all users access the database through the same user ID. To implement logging in your component, use the GetOriginalCallerName method. This returns the Windows username, even if the component was called directly by another component. This information can be passed as a parameter to the database to facilitate any required auditing or logging requirements.

- Every COM+ application should have at least one role. If there are differing levels of access, then there must be a role for each type of access.

- Create a Windows group called MTS Packages. Add each COM+ account that you create to this group. This is just for convenience when mapping a Windows user ID to a SQL Server login using the SQL Security Manager.

- Create a Windows user account for each COM+ application to run under. Consider starting the username with "MTS" followed by the name of the COM+ application.

- If the COM+ application uses programmatic security to check role membership, make the check fail-safe. For example, if the component is not in a COM+ context or if COM+ security is not enabled, the check should fail. The following Visual Basic code shows an example:

```
Private Function IsInRole(ByVal strRole As String) As Boolean
On Error GoTo HandleError
    Dim Ctxt As ObjectContext
    Set Ctxt = GetObjectContext()
    If Ctxt is Nothing Then ` Not running under MTS
        IsIinRole = False
        Exit Function
    End If
    If Not Ctxt.IsSecurityEnabled() Then ` Forgot to enable security
        IsInRole = False
         Exit Function
    End If
    IsInRole = Ctxt.IsCallerInRole(strRole)
    Exit Function

HandleError
    IsInRole = False
    Exit Function
End Function
```

REVIEW QUESTIONS

1. List the three logical services an application performs and briefly describe their roles in an application.

2. Briefly define tiers and services. Compare and contrast the roles of each in application development.

3. Define the client/server architecture and discuss the considerations in choosing a two-tier or three-tier application model.

4. Discuss the security issues inherent in multitier, distributed applications.

5. Describe how COM+ addresses these security issues.

6. Since connection pooling requires database logins to be identical, describe how you would implement a security model that would permit this feature.

Introducing the SQL Server Agent Service

SQL Server Agent runs on any server that is running instances of Microsoft SQL Server 2000 or earlier versions of SQL Server. SQL Server Agent is the service that allows you to automate administrative tasks. As such, you must start the SQL Server Agent service before your local or multiserver administrative tasks can run automatically. SQL Server Agent is also supported on the Microsoft Windows 98 operating system, but SQL Server Agent cannot be used with Windows Authentication when run on Windows 98. Windows Authentication can only be used after a login to the Windows 2000 domain. Existing Windows 2000 users and groups are granted access to SQL Server. SQL Server Authentication requires that logins be created in SQL Server, and you must supply the password with the account. More information on Windows and SQL Server Authentication can be found in Chapter 4, "Establishing Login Security."

SQL Server Agent is responsible for:

- Running SQL Server tasks scheduled to occur at specific times or intervals (*jobs*).

- Detecting specific conditions for which administrators have defined an action, such as alerting someone through pages or email, or a task that will address the conditions (*operators and alerts*).

- Running replication tasks defined by administrators (*replication*).

SQL Server Agent is similar to an auxiliary operator responsible for handling the repetitive tasks and exception-handling conditions defined through the other SQL Server automation components.

This chapter first provides a review of the configuration of the SQL Server Agent service account. Then it moves to an overview of jobs, operators, and alerts. This chapter also addresses specific security concerns related to jobs. The chapter then describes the email integration features of SQL Server. Finally, the chapter addresses replication and its security concerns.

SQL Server Agent Service Account

The SQL Server Agent is started in and runs as a Windows service. This service appears in the list of installed services in the Services dialogue box. The Services dialogue box is available from the Control Panel.

The two most important services to Microsoft SQL Server are the SQL Server service and the SQL Server Agent service. The *SQL Server service* handles all query processing and server configuration. The *SQL Server Agent service* manages all the automated processes, which can include jobs, operators, alerts, and replication.

For Microsoft SQL Server and SQL Server Agent to run as services in Windows, they must be assigned a Windows user account to use when they start up. This account is necessary for the service to log on to the system. Typically, both SQL Server and SQL Server Agent are assigned the same user account. However, it is possible to customize the settings for each service.

You have two choices for the configuration of the service account: the Local System Account and a Domain User Account. For email, replication, and multiserver jobs to function correctly, the SQL Server Agent service must be configured to start with a domain account. The account should be a local administrator on the SQL Server machine, and all instances of SQL Server should be configured to use the same account. More information about the configuration of the SQL Server Agent account is available in Chapter 3, "Exploring Initial Security Parameters."

You configure the properties of the SQL Server Agent service using SQL Server Enterprise Manager. To configure the general properties of the SQL Server Agent service, you should perform the following steps:

1. Open Enterprise Manager.

2. Click to expand your instance of SQL Server.

3. Click to expand the Management container.

4. Right-click the SQL Server Agent and select Properties, as shown in Figure 9.1.

5. Configure the General, Advanced, and Connection tabs as you deem necessary. The Job System tab is described in more detail later in the section *Job Security*. The options for configuration are detailed next.

In the General tab, you can configure the location of the error log file, enable the recording of execution trace messages (for troubleshooting), and enable the error file to be written as a non-Unicode file (resulting in a smaller log file size). Recording of execution trace messages can generate large files. You can also configure a recipient on the network to receive a Net Send pop-up message notification of errors recorded by the SQL Server Agent service. Configuring a mail session for the SQL Server Agent service is covered later in this chapter in the section *Setting Up SQLAgentMail*.

To configure advanced properties of the SQL Server Agent service, click the Advanced tab in the SQL Server Agent Properties dialogue box as shown in Figure 9.2.

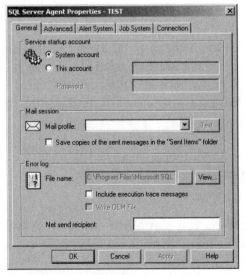

Figure 9.1   The SQL Server Agent Properties dialogue box allows for the customization of the SQL Server Agent service.

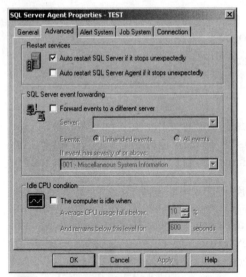

Figure 9.2 The Advanced tab of the SQL Server Agent Properties dialogue box provides additional control over the SQL Agent Service.

In the Advanced tab, you can configure the SQL Server Agent service to restart automatically if it stops unexpectedly by selecting the Auto Restart SQL Server Agent if It Stops Unexpectedly checkbox. This feature requires local administrator rights by the SQL Server Agent service account (either by granting them to the domain user account or using the local system account). By default, the SQL Server service is configured to restart automatically.

In the SQL Server Event Forwarding group box, you can configure the SQL Server Agent service to forward some or all SQL Server events to another server. You can use this feature to enable centralized alert management for a group of servers. Plan carefully, because this generates additional network traffic and load on the centralized server, and creates a single point of failure.

NOTE When configuring SQL Server Event Forwarding, the server you set for messages to be forwarded to must be a registered server in Enterprise Manager.

In the Idle CPU Condition group box, you can also define when the processor is considered idle. You define the idle condition by specifying a percentage below which the average processor usage must fall for a defined length of time. This feature requires local administrator rights granted to the SQL Server Agent service account (either by granting them

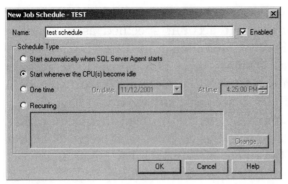

Figure 9.3   Jobs can be scheduled for a specific time or based on an event such as the SQL Server Agent service starting or the CPU becoming idle.

to the domain user account or using the local system account). Idle conditions are used to schedule jobs. One of the options for a job schedule is executing the job when the CPU becomes idle, as shown in Figure 9.3.

You configure the Connection properties of the SQL Server Agent service by clicking the Connection tab in the SQL Server Agent Properties dialogue box as shown in Figure 9.4.

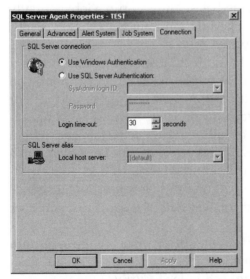

Figure 9.4   The Connection dialogue box is used to bypass the default connection options for the SQL Server Agent. By default the SQL Server Agent connects to another server using the SQL Server service account.

By default, the SQL Server Agent service connects to the local SQL Server 2000 instance using the domain user account specified as the service account. However, in the SQL Server Connection group box, you can specify that all connections to the local instance use a SQL Server login account that is a member of the sysadmin server role. You can also modify the login timeout value from the default of 30 seconds. Finally, if you have configured nondefault client Net-Libraries, you might need to specify a SQL Server alias that you previously created using the Client Network Utility. More details on aliasing and the Client Network Utility are addressed in Chapter 7, "Implementing Front-End Application Security."

Jobs, Operators, and Alerts

SQL Server Agent is a Windows service that executes jobs, notifies operators of actions on the server, and fires alerts. Jobs, alerts, and operators (which are discussed separately in the sections that follow) run in the security context of the SQL Server Agent service. Additionally, the full integration of these features depends on email integration with Exchange Server or another compatible email system.

Jobs

SQL Server Agent jobs automate administrative tasks (such as a backup statement) and run them on a recurring basis. You can run a job manually or schedule it to run in response to schedules and alerts. SQL Server jobs are configured as part of the SQL Server Agent.

A job can be created to run on the local machine or as a multiserver job, which can include steps that run on multiple machines. To run jobs on multiple servers, you must set up at least one master server and one or more target servers. The master server is responsible for the job configuration and the reporting of the success or failure status of the job. Each target server downloads its list of responsibilities from its master server. Each target server runs its own job steps and reports the status back to its master server. Multiserver jobs are dependent on the SQL Server Agent service on all SQL Servers being configured to start with the same domain user account.

Anyone can create a job, but only its owner or members of the sysadmin role can edit a job. More information about job security and configuration is described later in this chapter in the section *Job Security*.

Jobs can easily be created in Enterprise Manager. As you decide on the job you would like to configure, you should consider the following:

- Jobs are made up of steps. Each job can be configured to have one or more steps. Job steps can be Transact-SQL statements, ActiveX Script tasks, replication-related events, and operating system commands.

- Each job has an owner. The ownership of the job determines to some extent the security context the job steps will run in. Ownership of jobs is addressed in more detail later in this section.

- Jobs can be scheduled. After you create a job, it can be configured to run immediately or scheduled for a specific time or event.

- Jobs can notify operators of the resulting status of the action. The operator notification can be through email, pager notification, or Net Send.

To create a job for your instance of SQL Server you should perform the following steps:

1. Open Enterprise Manager.

2. Click to expand your instance of SQL Server.

3. Click to expand the Management container.

4. Click to expand SQL Server Agent.

5. Right-click Jobs and select New Job.

6. The New Job Properties dialogue box will appear as shown in Figure 9.5.

7. On the General tab you will need to give the job a name and select its owner.

8. Steps, Schedules, and Notifications can be configured from their appropriate tab.

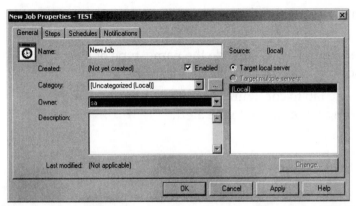

Figure 9.5   New jobs are created and managed from Enterprise Manager.

Defining Alerts

Alerts are useful in creating a proactive approach to database administration. In far too many cases administrators spend time running around putting out the fires that result as applications that rely on SQL Server fail. Alerts allow the administrator some control over these errors and allow for a configured action based on the error received. Alerts can either be based on errors that have already occurred or they can be created on a system-based performance condition (threshold). Errors and messages, or events, are generated by Microsoft SQL Server and entered into the Microsoft Windows application log. SQL Server Agent constantly reads the application log and compares events to alerts that you have defined. If no alert is defined, then no action is taken. The alert can be configured to notify an operator or execute a job. When an error occurs or a threshold is met, you can fire an alert, which in turn executes a job to take an action to respond to the event. For instance, you may want to define an alert that monitors the percentage of log space used on your production database. When a threshold is met, such as 75 percent full, the alert is fired. You could then have the alert execute a job that backs up the log. (The backup log statement truncates the inactive portion of the log.) This job immediately responds to the alert, thereby avoiding a bigger problem later on.

Alerts are also easily configured through Enterprise Manager. To create an alert you should perform the following series of steps:

1. Open Enterprise Manager.
2. Click to expand your instance of SQL Server.
3. Click to expand the Management container.
4. Click to expand SQL Server Agent.
5. Right-click Alerts and select New Alert.
6. The New Alert Properties dialogue box will appear as shown in Figure 9.6.
7. Configure the General tab to include the name, type of alert (event or performance condition), and historical information.
8. Use the Response tab to configure Operator notification and the execution of jobs as a response to the alert.

Operators

Operators are objects for notification of job status and alert firing. The operator is a representation or a user or group. An operator can be used for three types of notification:

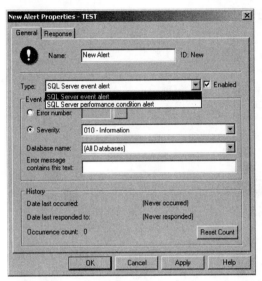

Figure 9.6   New alerts are created from this dialogue box page to act on SQL Server errors or performance conditions.

- *Email notification* depends on the integration of email services. SQL Agent Mail must be configured to use this option. The details of the email configuration are addressed later in this chapter in the section *Setting Up SQLAgentMail.*

- *Pager notification* depends on pager integration software. SQL Server and Microsoft Exchange Server do not include pager software. If your organization has a pager software solution, this option can be used.

- *Net Send notifications* are pop-up messages that are configured to pop up on the computer screen. They are beneficial because they interrupt whatever the user is doing. They cannot be relied on as the only notification, because if the machine isn't on or the user isn't logged on, the message cannot be received.

Operators should be configured using Enterprise Manager. To configure an operator, follow these steps:

1. Open Enterprise Manager.

2. Click to expand your instance of SQL Server.

3. Click to expand the Management container.

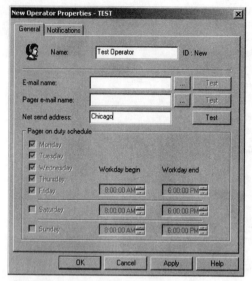

Figure 9.7 Use the New Operator Properties dialogue box to add a new operator to notify of specified alerts or job status.

4. Click to expand SQL Server Agent.

5. Right-click Operators and select New Operator.

6. The New Operator Properties dialogue box will appear as shown in Figure 9.7.

7. Operators must be given a name and email, pager, and Net Send information.

NOTE The primary attributes of an operator are name and contact information. It is recommended that you define operators before you define alerts. If operators are set up first, they are visually available in Enterprise Manager when you create the alerts, so notification configuration of alerts is easy.

Job Security

Using SQL Server Agent, you can create and schedule jobs that automate routine administrative tasks. In this section, you learn to create simple and complex jobs. You learn to configure permissions for jobs owned by users who are not members of the sysadmin server role. You learn to execute these jobs manually or according to a schedule. You also learn to use operators for notification of the success, failure, or completion of a job. Finally, you learn to review job properties and job execution history.

Implementing Jobs

Database administrators create jobs to perform predictable administrative functions (such as backing up databases or importing data) either according to a schedule or in response to events and conditions. Jobs can be simple operations containing only a single job step or they can be extremely complex operations containing many job steps with control of flow logic. SQL Server Agent is responsible for the management and execution of all jobs. SQL Server Agent must be running for jobs to execute. Jobs can be created on the local server or on one or more target servers in a multiserver administration configuration.

Types of Job Steps

SQL Server 2000 supports jobs containing operating system commands, CmdExec commands, Transact-SQL statements, Microsoft ActiveX scripts, and replication tasks. A single job can contain all of these types of commands, although each job step can contain only a single type of command. It is common for a single job to consist of multiple steps.

NOTE Have a design for the steps that need to be included with the job. *Evaluate* your needs before you add the job. The logic and troubleshooting will be easier if you are clear on what you need to accomplish.

- Operating system commands (such as .bat, .cmd, .com, or .exe) must contain the absolute path to the executables, the executable command (including switches and options), and a process exit code. All operating system commands issue an exit code upon completion of execution indicating the success or failure of the command. An exit code of 0 (zero) indicates that the command completed successfully. Any other exit code indicates a type of command failure. Responses to different types of failures can be programmed into the job logic. Chapter 11, "Managing Data Transformation Services," provides an example of using the DTSRUN command to execute a DTS package. DTSRUN is an example of an operating system command. More information on operating system commands and exit codes can be found in SQL Server Books Online.

■ Transact-SQL statements must identify the database in which the statement will execute and provide the statement, function, stored procedure, or extended stored procedure to be executed. A single job step can contain multiple batches of Transact-SQL statements with embedded GO commands. Members of the sysadmin role can write job steps to run on behalf of another database user.

■ ActiveX scripts must identify the scripting language used by the job step and provide the ActiveX script commands. An ActiveX script can also be compiled and run as a CmdExec executable. Common ActiveX Scripting languages include VBScript and Jscript.

Permissions and Ownership of Jobs

By default, jobs are owned by the creator of the job and operate in the security context of that login, regardless of who executes the job. A member of the sysadmin role can modify ownership when necessary. A system administrator can assign a job to any owner regardless of the owner's security context.

Ownership of a job, by itself, does not grant the right to execute any particular job step. Permission to execute each Transact-SQL job step is verified by the SQL Server service using permissions granted within SQL Server. By default, permission to execute CmdExec and ActiveX job steps is granted only to jobs owned by members of the sysadmin server role. If this is not changed, only members of the sysadmin role will be able to own jobs that include ActiveX or CmdExec job steps. When owned by a member of the sysadmin role, these job steps run in the security context of the SQL Server Agent service account.

Permission to run CmdExec and ActiveX scripting job steps can be granted to users who are not members of the sysadmin fixed server role. These job steps owned by a nonsysadmin role run in the security context of a specified Windows account called the *proxy account* and inherit the rights granted to that account.

Configuring the Proxy Account

If you plan to create jobs containing CmdExec and ActiveX job steps that will be owned by (or executed in the context of) users who are not members of the sysadmin server role, you must configure the proxy account.

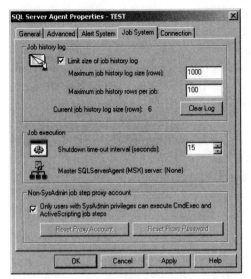

Figure 9.8 You can configure the proxy account to allow nonsysadmin job owners to configure operating system and ActiveX Script job steps.

1. Open Enterprise Manager.
2. Click to expand your instance of SQL Server.
3. Click to expand the Management container.
4. Right-click the SQL Server Agent and select Properties.
5. Select the Job System tab as shown in Figure 9.8.
6. Click the Only Users with SysAdmin Privileges Can Execute CmdExec and ActiveScripting Job Steps checkbox.

NOTE The account information provided for the proxy account must be an existing local or domain user account. You should then assign this account the permissions you want nonsysadmins to inherit when their jobs are run. If the service account used by the SQL Server service does not have administrator privileges, you will be prompted for the user credentials of an administrator.

Multiple Job Steps and Job Responses

Each job can have a workflow configured for the execution of job steps. A job step either succeeds or fails. You can determine the order in which your job steps run based on the status of another step. For instance, on the success of a job step, you can configure the job step to continue to the next step or a specific job step. You can also configure the job step to quit and report success or failure. For example, you could have a job step that was responsible for executing a DTS package that will transfer data from one server to another. If this process succeeds, you may want to execute another step that backs up the database. If the job step fails, you may want to dump the data to a text file so it is at least accounted for. You would define the backup step and the dump-to-text file as different steps. You would then need to configure the workflow so that if the DTS package executed successfully, the backup step runs. If the DTS package fails, then the workflow would execute the task to dump the data to a text file. In this case workflow is important because you don't want both the backup and the dump-to-text file steps to run.

You can configure operators to be notified of the success, failure, or completion of the job. Without operators who are designated to receive notification, the reports of success and failure of the job do not get transmitted to users. Operators are configured through Enterprise Manager, similar to jobs. Operators can be notified via an email, a pager notification, or a Net Send message. The email option depends on the SQLAgentMail configuration, which is addressed later in this chapter in the section *Setting Up SQLAgentMail*. Otherwise, by default, failure of a job is automatically logged to the Windows application log, which can be viewed in Event Viewer.

Reviewing Jobs and Job History

The Details pane of the Jobs container in SQL Server Enterprise Manager displays information regarding all jobs for the SQL Server 2000 instance. Information regarding each job is displayed in columns. Click a column heading to sort the jobs based on that column. Notice the Enabled column. If you are troubleshooting a job that does not run, verify that it is enabled. Information is displayed regarding the status of a job (such as executing or not running), the last time a job ran, and the next time it is scheduled. You can view the job history by right-clicking a job and selecting Job History as shown in Figure 9.9.

Job Properties

To view or modify the properties of a job, right-click the job and then click Properties (or double-click the job). Users who are not members of the sysadmin server role can only view or modify jobs they own.

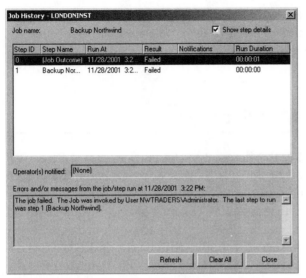

Figure 9.9   Job History is used to troubleshoot jobs that are not executing properly.

Job History Log

To review the execution history of a job, right-click the job and then click Job History as shown in Figure 9.10. Information is displayed regarding each time the job was run, its result, who invoked the job, and whether operators were notified.

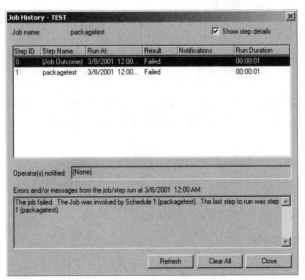

Figure 9.10   A job history helps to troubleshoot a failed job.

NOTE While viewing a job history, it is beneficial to show the job step details. This displays the details for each of the steps taken. In many cases, this is the only place an error message is displayed.

Setting SQL Server Mail Services

SQL Server 2000 can connect with Microsoft Exchange Server and other mail services to provide two email options: SQL Mail and SQLAgentMail. Both services require a MAPI client application (such as Microsoft Outlook) on the local SQL Server 2000 computer and a MAPI messaging profile. A MAPI messaging profile requires the use of a domain user account. The SQL Server service and SQL Server Agent services should both be configured to use the domain user account. In many cases, SQL Mail and SQLAgentMail use the same domain user account for administrative convenience.

SQL Mail is the mail service of the SQL Server service. This is useful in allowing the developer to programmatically use the email functions. The SQL Server service uses the xp_sendmail extended stored procedure to send email from Transact-SQL batches, scripts, stored procedures, and triggers. It establishes a mail session only as needed; therefore, the system overhead for SQL Mail configuration is minimal.

The following example uses the xp_sendmail extended stored procedure to send an email message to Andy regarding the current SQL Server 2000 performance. This query could be scheduled to run periodically to notify a DBA of the current performance information.

```
EXEC xp_sendmail 'Andy@Softouch.trn' ,
@subject = 'Performance Information' ,
@query = 'SELECT * FROM master.dbo.sysperfinfo'
```

The content of the email sent can include several types of information. The following is a list of contents that can be used for sending xp_sendmail messages.

- A result set from a query
- A message string
- A Transact-SQL statement or batch for execution
- A page for an electronic pager

SQLAgentMail is the mail service of the SQL Server Agent service. This is the more common of the mail services and is essential for many of the processes described in this chapter. Email notification to an Operator depends on this service. The SQL Server Agent service starts a mail session when the service starts. By default SQLAgentMail is not configured and will not start until you complete the configuration process. This service is then used as the basis for job and alert notification processes.

Configuring a Messaging (Mail) Profile

Both SQL Mail and SQLAgentMail require the installation of a MAPI client (such as Microsoft Outlook) on the local SQL Server 2000 computer. After initial testing and installation, this client should not be used because of possible conflict. The mail services of SQL Server use the mapi32.dll for email functions. This is the same .dll used by Outlook. Using them both on the same machine increases the chances of corrupting the mapi32.dll. This could result in either Outlook or your SQL Server services to stop working. Typically, on your production server this is not a problem because a user is not using the server as a workstation.

Next, you must create a messaging profile (also called a mail profile) for the domain user account used by the SQL Server services and SQL Server Agent services. First this requires an email account configured in Exchange Server or your messaging system. You can create the messaging profile by using Outlook or the Mail program located in the Control Panel. If the services use a different account during startup, then two profiles must be generated. In general, you must log on to Windows 2000 as the domain user to configure the messaging profile for that domain user. A messaging profile includes information about the email account such as email server, personal address books, and email storage information.

When you create a profile using either the MAPI client or the Mail program in Control Panel, the default messaging profile name in the Profile Name text box for a domain user is MS Exchange Settings. You can use the xp_get_mapi _default_profile extended stored procedure to determine the default profile name (if any) for the SQL Server service domain user account. The mail program can be used to edit any of the profile properties.

Setting up SQL Mail

After configuring and testing the messaging profile for the SQL Server service domain user account, you are ready to set up SQL Mail. You configure SQL Mail by following these steps:

1. Open Enterprise Manager.
2. Click to expand your instance of SQL Server.

3. Click to expand the Support Services container.

4. Right-click SQL Mail and select Properties. The SQL Mail Configuration dialogue box will appear.

5. Select the appropriate profile and click the OK button.

If the messaging profile does not appear in SQL Server Enterprise Manager, verify that the SQL Server service is using the domain user account for which the messaging profile was created. Also verify that the domain user account has full control permissions on the HKEY_LOCAL_MACHINE\SOFTWARE \Clients\Mail Registry key.

Setting Up SQLAgentMail

After configuring and testing the messaging profile for the SQL Server Agent service domain user account, you are ready to set up SQLAgentMail through the following procedure:

1. Open Enterprise Manager.

2. Click to expand your instance of SQL Server.

3. Click to expand the Management container.

4. Right-click SQL Server Agent and select Properties. The General tab of the SQL Server Agent Properties dialogue box will appear.

5. Click the drop-down box to select the appropriate mail profile as shown in Figure 9.11. After the profile has been selected, you can test the profile.

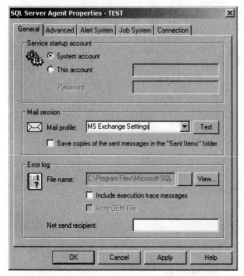

Figure 9.11 The SQLAgentMail requires a valid MAPI profile.

Replication

This section of the chapter introduces the security concerns related to replication. The first part of the section introduces replication to build a foundation that is necessary to explain the security references. First you will be introduced to the replication components; then the security considerations for replication will be addressed. More information about the steps necessary for configuring replication can be found in SQL Server Books Online.

Replication Components

The components discussed in the following sections are the core of SQL Server replication. Although the three components are separate logically, a single server can have multiple components configured. It is common for the machine that plays the role of the publisher to also be configured as the distributor. In a multimaster replication model (all machines can update and receive changes), it is common for a single server to be configured as a publisher, distributor, and subscriber.

Publisher

The *Publisher* is a server that makes data available for replication to other servers. In addition to being the server where you specify which data is to be replicated, the Publisher also detects which data has changed and maintains information about all publications at that site. Usually, any data element that is replicated has a single Publisher, even if it may be updated by several Subscribers or republished by a Subscriber. The data is made available to the Subscriber by configuring a Publication. The Publication is the table or subsets of a table that are available for replication.

Distributor

The *Distributor* is a server that contains the distribution database and stores metadata, history data, and transactions. The Distributor can be a separate server from the Publisher (remote Distributor), or it can be the same server as the Publisher (local Distributor). The role of the Distributor varies depending on which type of replication you implement, and in general its role is much greater for snapshot replication and transactional replication than it is for merge replication.

Subscribers

Subscribers are servers that receive replicated data. Subscribers subscribe to publications, not to individual articles within a publication, and they subscribe only to the publications that they need, not necessarily all of the publications available on a Publisher. Subscribers access data from the Publication by creating a Subscription. The Subscription can be either a push or pull subscription. The push subscription is configured from the Publisher machine and the overhead for the distribution of data is performed at the Publisher. It the Subscription is a pull subscription, the overhead and configuration are performed from the Subscriber machine.

Types of Replication

SQL Server supports three types of replication: snapshot, transactional, and merge. Each type of replication is explained below in more detail.

Snapshot Replication

Snapshot replication is a full replication and therefore is typically just used as a starting point for transactional and merge replication. Snapshot replication is implemented by the Snapshot Agent and the Distribution Agent. The Snapshot Agent prepares snapshot files containing schema and data of published tables and database objects, stores the files in the snapshot folder, and records synchronization jobs in the distribution database on the Distributor. By default, the snapshot folder is located on the Distributor, but you can specify an alternative location instead of or in addition to the default. (For more information, see the section later in this chapter labeled *Alternative Snapshot Locations.*)

The Distribution Agent moves the snapshot held in the distribution database tables to the destination tables at the Subscribers. The distribution database is used only by replication and does not contain any user tables.

Transactional Replication

Transactional replication is incremental in nature and has been around since the early versions of SQL Server. It is the most common form of replication.

Transactional replication is implemented by the Snapshot Agent, Log Reader Agent, and Distribution Agent. The Snapshot Agent prepares snapshot files containing schema and data of published tables and database objects, stores the files in the snapshot folder, and records synchronization jobs in the distribution database on the Distributor.

The Log Reader Agent monitors the transaction log of each database configured for transactional replication and copies the transactions marked for replication from the transaction log into the distribution database. The Distribution Agent moves the initial snapshot jobs and the transactions held in the distribution database tables to Subscribers.

Merge Replication

Merge replication is new to SQL Server 2000. Merge replication is implemented by the Snapshot Agent and Merge Agent. The Snapshot Agent prepares snapshot files containing schema and data of published tables, stores the files in the snapshot folder, and inserts synchronization jobs in the publication database. The Snapshot Agent also creates replication-specific stored procedures, triggers, and system tables.

The Merge Agent applies the initial snapshot jobs held in the publication database tables to the Subscriber. It also merges incremental data changes that occurred at the Publisher or Subscribers after the initial snapshot was created, and reconciles conflicts according to rules you configure or a custom resolver you create.

The role of the Distributor is limited in merge replication, so implementing the Distributor locally (on the same server as the Publisher) is common. The Distribution Agent is not used at all during merge replication, and the distribution database on the Distributor stores history and miscellaneous information about merge replication.

Security Considerations

When considering security in Microsoft SQL Server 2000, replication is similar to other applications in SQL Server 2000. Your determining factors will be a balance between how secure the data needs to be and how accessible the data needs to be for your environment. In many cases the needs for security have to be compared with the overhead of the additional configuration. Replication is a prime example of this.

Replication security is one of the biggest concerns with the replication process. In many cases, troubleshooting replication depends on your understanding of the replication security issues detailed in Table 9.1. Several of the security issues described in the table are more fully explained in the sections that follow.

Table 9.1 Replication Security Issues

SECURITY	DESCRIPTION
Role Requirements	By mapping user logins to specific SQL Server 2000 roles, SQL Server 2000 allows users to perform only those replication and database activities authorized for that role. Replication grants certain permission to the sysadmin fixed server role, the db_owner fixed database role, the current login, and the public role.
Connection to Distributor	SQL Server 2000 provides a secure administrative link between the Distributor and Publisher. Publishers can be treated as trusted or nontrusted clients.
Publication Access Lists	Publication access lists (PALs) allow you to determine which logins have access to publications. SQL Server 2000 creates the PAL with default logins, but you can add or delete logins from the lists.
Agent Login Security	SQL Server 2000 requires each user to supply a valid login account to connect to the server. Replication Agents are required to use valid logins when connecting to Publishers, Distributors, and Subscribers. However, agents can also use different logins and security modes when connecting to different servers simultaneously.
Password Encryption	Passwords used in SQL Server 2000 replication are encrypted automatically for greater security.
Security and Replication Options	Filtering replicated data can be used to increase data security, and there are additional security considerations when using dynamic snapshots, immediate updating, and queued updating.
Security and Replication over the Internet	Different types of replication over the Internet have different security levels. Additionally, when transferring replication files using FTP sites, precautions must be taken to secure the sites and still make them accessible to Replication Agents.

SQL Server Agent Service Configuration

The SQL Server Agent service (SQLServerAgent) at the client should not use the Local System account. It should be configured to use a standard domain account. The SQLAgent account is the security context under which the Snapshot Agent, Merge Agent, and Distribution Agent are running by default. Replication Agents use the SQL Server Agent service account for their security context. If the service account is configured as the Local System account, many of the agents and replication processes will not work.

NOTE The Replication Agents are processes that run on behalf of the user to perform the necessary functions for the replication process. Some of the agents, like the Snapshot Agent, need to be started before the replication process will function correctly.

Each SQL Server Agent service connects to one or more servers (Publisher, Distributor, or Subscribers, depending on the agent) and must have a valid login to that instance of SQL Server to complete the connection. The agent login will determine the success status of replication. If the SQL Server Agent service is started with an account that is a local administrator, the Replication Agents will default to that security context and there shouldn't be any problem. Replication is easiest to configure and manage when all servers involved in the process use the same domain account for the SQL Server Agent service.

Replication Agent Login Security

Replication implements login security by requiring a user to have a valid login account and password to connect to a Publisher, Distributor, or Subscriber. Replication Agents run under SQL Server Agent service and use the associated logins and passwords to connect to the various replication objects and to perform their roles in the synchronization process.

Snapshot Replication

The Snapshot Agent connects to the publication database on the Publisher and to the distribution database on the Distributor. The Snapshot Agent also writes to the snapshot folder when storing the snapshot files. The SQL Server agent service must have access to both of these locations.

Transactional Replication

The agents used in transactional replication must have the following functionality:

- The Log Reader Agent connects to the publication database at the Publisher and to the distribution database at the Distributor.
- With a push subscription, the Distribution Agent is, by default, located on the Distributor and connects first to the distribution database on the Distributor. While connected to the Distributor, the

Distribution Agent connects to the subscription database at the Subscriber. The Distribution Agent also reads from the snapshot folder when applying the snapshot files.

- With a pull subscription, the Distribution Agent is, by default, located on the Subscriber and connects first to the subscription database on the Subscriber. While connected to the Subscriber, the Distribution Agent connects to the distribution database at the Distributor. The Distribution Agent also reads from the snapshot folder when applying the snapshot files.

Merge Replication

The agents used in merge replication must have the following functionality:

- With a push subscription, the Merge Agent is located on the Distributor and connects first to the distribution database on the Distributor. While connected to the Distributor, the Merge Agent connects to the subscription database at the Subscriber and then to the publication database at the Publisher. The Merge Agent also reads from the snapshot folder when applying the snapshot files.

- With a pull subscription, the Merge Agent is located on the Subscriber and connects first to the subscription database on the Subscriber. While connected to the Subscriber, the Merge Agent connects to the distribution database at the Distributor and then to the publication database at the Publisher. The Merge Agent also reads from the snapshot folder when applying the snapshot files.

- Merge replication requires an entry for the Publisher in the sysservers table at the Subscriber. If the entry does not exist, either SQL Server will attempt to add the entry when you create a merge publication or the Merge Agent will attempt to add the entry. If the login used does not have sufficient access to add the entry in sysservers, an error will be returned.

NOTE For an agent that holds simultaneous connections, Microsoft SQL Server allows you to configure the login for each connection independently. For example, if the Snapshot Agent connects to the Publisher *and* to the Distributor, each connection can use a different login.

Agent Connectivity

When implementing replication, make sure that the Replication Agents can communicate with all servers involved in the replication topology. One way to test agent connectivity is to log in to the required server and database using SQL Query Analyzer with the same login that the Replication Agent will be using (or typically the login that SQL Server Agent is using).

You must be a SQL Server 2000 system administrator to enable the server for replication. After replication is enabled, you do not need to be a SQL Server 2000 system administrator to set up publications and subscriptions, or to invoke or schedule the Replication Agents. You must be in the db_owner role to create publications. Anyone who is added to the publication access list (PAL) can create pull subscriptions to that publication (but only to that publication). PALs are described more fully later in this chapter in the section *Publication Access Lists.*

Snapshot Folder Security

The snapshot folder is used to store the information (schema and data) that need to be replicated from the Publisher to the Subscriber. It is important to monitor the location of this folder to assist in managing security and drive space. If security for this folder is not set accurately, the snapshot will fail. Also, if there is not enough space on the hard drive for the files that need to be created by the snapshot, the process will fail.

Location of Snapshot Files

The folder in which the snapshots are stored must be available to all Subscribers on the network. To ensure secure access to the initial snapshot files of your replicated data, it is recommended you use an explicit share instead of an administration share (for example, C$) for which you cannot grant specific permissions. The administrative share is used as a default only because it will always exist on Windows 2000 (but it cannot be accessed except by an administrator account). When configuring distribution, you can define the default location for all snapshot files. After creating a publication, you can define the location of the snapshot files using the Publication Properties dialogue box (see Figure 9.12).

Alternative Snapshot Locations

Alternative snapshot locations enable you to store snapshot files in a location other than or in addition to the default location, which is often located on the Distributor. Alternative locations can be on another server, on a network share, or on removable media (such as CD-ROMs or removable hard disks). When specifying the snapshot location on a network share, it is recommended that you dedicate the share for snapshot storage and files that have the same security standards. Next, give the Replication Agents Write permission on the share in the snapshot location and in appropriate folders so the agents can write the snapshot files there.

Subscribers that need to access the snapshot files will need Read permission to the snapshot location and appropriate folders. If the appropriate Subscribers cannot share the snapshot folder, the Replication Agents cannot access the folder and replication fails.

If your application requires the ability to create pull subscriptions on a server running the Windows 98 operating system, you must change the snapshot folder to a network path accessible by Replication Agents running at the Publisher and Subscribers. You can change the local path to a network path by sharing the folder manually.

Security Mode of the Publisher

Connections to a server (Publisher, Distributor, or Subscribers) can use Windows Authentication or SQL Server security. Windows Authentication is generally preferred for greater security and ease of use; however, connections to Windows 98 servers must use SQL Server security because Windows Authentication is a feature only on Windows NT 4.0 and Windows 2000.

It is recommended that the Subscriber connection have DBO permissions in the subscription database to make sure the proper permissions are granted.

Publication Access Lists

When you create a publication, SQL Server creates a publication access list (PAL) for the publication. The PAL contains a list of logins that are granted access to the publication. The logins included in the PAL are members in the sysadmin fixed server role and the current login.

The PAL functions similarly to a Windows 2000 access control list. When a user or Replication Agent attempts to log in to a Publisher, SQL Server 2000 first checks to see if the login is in the PAL. If you must further expand or restrict access to a publication, you can add or delete logins in the PAL using SQL Server Enterprise Manager or the sp_grant_publication_access and sp_revoke_publication_access stored procedures.

A snapshot, transactional, or merge publication may be secured with a PAL programmatically or through SQL Server Enterprise Manager.

NOTE A replication agent login for the Publisher and Distributor must exist in the PAL before it can access the publication. The user login must also exist in the publication database or the database must allow guest users. If you are using a remote Distributor, the logins must exist at both the Publisher and the Distributor before they can be added to the PAL. Because the Replication Agents can run under SQL Server Agent, the account under which SQL Server Agent runs on a Windows platform must be in the PAL.

If you have a large number of user logins to add to the PAL, consider making them all members of a single Windows 2000 group and then adding the Windows 2000 group to the PAL. You can grant or revoke access to a publication by performing the following steps:

1. Expand a server group and then click the Publisher name.
2. On the Tools menu, point to Replication and then click Create and Manage Publications.
3. Expand the database and then click the publication.
4. Click Properties and Subscriptions.
5. Click the Publication Access List tab as shown in Figure 9.12.
6. Add or remove the login to access the publication.

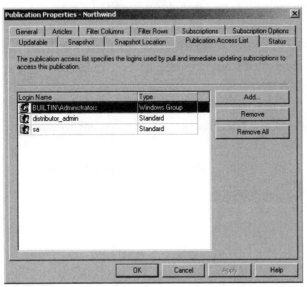

Figure 9.12   Publication Access List controls the users who can subscribe to a publication.

> **NOTE** If a remote Distributor is used, the new logins must exist in the
> publication access lists at the Publisher and the Distributor. If the pull
> subscription login is not in the publication access list, an error appears at the
> Subscriber.

Best Practices

- Use a domain account for the SQL Server Agent login account.
- Make sure all servers that are involved in replication or multiserver jobs are configured to use the same domain user account for the SQL Server Agent service.
- Use a proxy account to allow other than system administrators to run job steps that include operating system commands and ActiveX Script steps.
- Create performance condition alerts to notify you of system-related errors and security events.
- Configure a MAPI profile to enable SQLAgentMail.
- Use a system administrator account for job ownership whenever possible. There may be cases when a developer needs to support jobs on the production server and has to be the owner of the job to view the details of the job. Avoid this where politically possible.
- Verify security of the snapshot folder. The snapshot folder has to be available through a shared point for the replication process to succeed.
- Start the Replication Agents if the process doesn't appear to work initially.
- Use publication access lists to control the individuals who can subscribe to a publication.

REVIEW QUESTIONS

1. What is the purpose of the proxy account?
2. Why is job ownership important?
3. What is a multiserver job?
4. What is a MAPI profile and how is it created?
5. What is the difference between snapshot and transactional replication?
6. What are the purposes of the Replication Agents?
7. What is the snapshot folder used for?

CHAPTER

Managing Distributed
Data Security

Among the primary concerns for organizations over the last few years has been the ability to reuse data for multiple applications. Many applications need to access data in another database. The distributed data options available in SQL Server allow you to use the data across multiple servers for a single application.

Additionally, many applications have mission-critical status for an organization and you may not be able to afford downtime. Chapter 2, "Designing a Successful Security Model," addressed the Clustering service as an option for implementing a fault-tolerant solution. This chapter addresses the distributed data options for creating fault-tolerant solutions.

This chapter first introduces linked servers. Linked servers allow you to create a continuous connection to another server. You can reference objects on the other server in a manner similar to their being stored locally. You can also maintain transactional consistency across servers.

The chapter then describes the log shipping feature of SQL Server 2000. Log shipping is a feature that allows for the creation and maintenance of a read-only standby server.

Finally this chapter describes the Federated Database Servers feature of SQL Server. Federated Database Servers allows you to partition a database across multiple servers to give the appearance that multiple databases are actually one. This feature allows your Enterprise and Internet applications to scale with ease.

Linked Servers

Microsoft SQL Server allows you to create links to OLE DB data sources called *linked servers.* Configuring a linked server allows the connection information to be supplied once. The supplied connection information is used for the security context between the servers for the initial connection. When you run a query that executes against the server you are connected to and a linked server, your user information is used just for the authentication at the first server. The server you are connected to connects to the linked server on your behalf to execute the rest of the query. When this connection is made, the security context used to authenticate at the linked server is key. You can allow the server to pass your current user credentials or map you to another user's credentials on the linked server. This section first provides an overview to linked servers, then addresses accessing objects on other servers, and finally details the security concerns related to linked servers.

Linked Server Overview

Linked server configuration is easily accomplished from Enterprise Manager. You will need to have the connection information about the server you are trying to connect to. After linking to an OLE DB data source, you can perform any of the following actions:

- Reference rowsets from the OLE DB data sources as tables in Transact-SQL statements. You can include the tables and views from the linked server within your Transact-SQL statements.

- Pass commands to the OLE DB data sources and include the resulting rowsets as tables in Transact-SQL statements. You can use this to execute remote stored procedures.

- You can create distributed transactions. The consistency and autonomy of your transaction can be maintained across multiple servers.

Your distributed queries can access multiple linked servers. You can read from one server and update another. You have the flexibility to treat the data on the linked server as though it is local. Your ability to access data on the other server depends on your having permission to the objects you reference. In general, Microsoft SQL Server requires distributed transactions support from the corresponding OLE DB provider whenever data from more than one linked server is likely to be updated in a transaction. Hence, the types of queries that are supported against linked servers depend on the level of support for transactions present in the OLE DB providers. You can configure a linked server to any OLE DB data source, such as:

- Microsoft Access
- Oracle
- Microsoft Exchange
- Microsoft Directory Services
- Any ODBC data source

You can easily create and manage linked servers from Enterprise Manager. To set up a linked server, you should perform the following steps:

1. Open Enterprise Manager. Click to expand your server group.
2. Click to expand the server that you want to link to another server.
3. Click to expand the Security container.
4. Right-click Linked Servers and choose New Linked Server. The Linked Server Properties dialogue box will appear as shown in Figure 10.1.
5. If you choose SQL Server you do not need to supply any additional information other than the name of the server. If you select another data source, you will need to select the provider name from the drop-down box. Most data sources will also require additional connection information.
6. Click OK to create the linked server.

NOTE Alternatively, you could use the sp_addlinkedserver and sp_droplinkedserver system stored procedures to create and manage linked servers.

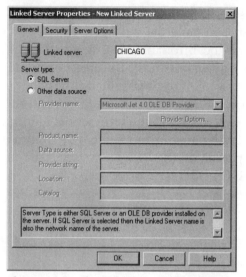

Figure 10.1 The Linked Server Properties dialogue box is used to create a linked server.

Reference Objects on Linked Servers

After a linked server is defined, a four-part name in the form *server.database. owner.object_name* can be used in Transact-SQL statements to reference data objects from the linked server. Table 10.1 identifies each of the pieces of the four-part name.

When working with local servers, it is not always necessary to fully qualify your object names. The server name defaults to local server, the database name defaults to the database you are connected to, the object

Table 10.1 Four-Part Object Names

PART NAME	DESCRIPTION
Server	Name of the linked server
Database	Name of the database
Owner	Owner of the object
Object_name	Name of the object being referenced

name defaults to your username, and if the object is owned by the database owner (DBO) it is automatically resolved. Because these defaults are assumed by SQL Server, when interacting with local data most individuals just reference the object name.

When using linked servers it is always best to fully qualify the object names. The default assumptions of SQL Server will not work, because you are not working with the local server. In addition to the local server default not working, the DBO is not automatically resolved across servers, so it also must be explicitly defined. If you fully qualify your object names, you will also eliminate confusion related to the location of your objects.

Linked Server Security Requirements

During a linked server connection (for example, when processing a distributed query), the sending server provides a login name and password to connect to the receiving server on the client's behalf. You will need to configure what information should be sent to the other server.

You have the ability to configure individual local logins and how they are mapped to the remote server. This is configured in the top half of the dialogue box as shown in Figure 10.2. For every client that is not configured in the top half of the dialogue box, you have four options for the security context used to connect to the other server, also shown in Figure 10.2. Those four options are as follows:

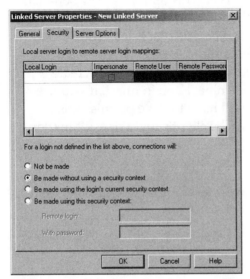

Figure 10.2 For a distributed query to be successful, the linked server security settings must be configured.

Not Be Made.   When this option is selected, if the user does not have an explicit mapping between the servers, the connection will not be allowed.

Be Made without Using a Security Context.   This option is commonly confused with the previous option. When it is selected, the connection to the other server is allowed but it is not limited by a specific user account. The user information is not passed to the other server. This is appropriate when you are using a data source that does not require authentication, such as Microsoft Access or Microsoft Excel.

Be Made Using the Login's Current Security Context.   This option uses the user's current login information and passes it to the other server. This will pass the user's Windows Authentication information to the other server. If the user is a known login on the other server, the connection will be successful. This option depends on security account delegation. More information on security account delegation can be found in Chapter 4, "Establishing Login Security." This option is only beneficial when you are using Windows Authentication and when the logins on both servers are very similar.

Be Made Using This Security Context.   With this option enabled you are also prompted for a username and password as shown in Figure 10.3. This option allows SQL Server to use the credentials you define here and pass them to the other server. This option is very beneficial if you are using SQL Server Authentication or if you do not have security control over the linked server. The other database administrator may be much more willing to provide you with a single account to access some of the data than to have to create every login that exists on your machine. Keep in mind, if you use this option the user you supply will have to have permissions to perform the action of your query. The client's login doesn't matter to the linked server.

NOTE You can also use the sp_addlinkedsrvlogin and sp_droplinkedsrvlogin to create and manage login mappings between servers.

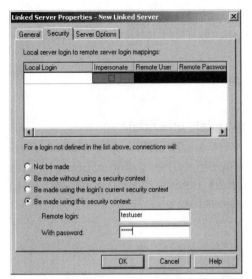

Figure 10.3   When you configure SQL Server to pass a specific security context, you must supply the username and password of the login on the other server.

Log Shipping

In SQL Server 2000 Enterprise Edition, you can use log shipping to feed transaction logs from one database to another on a constant basis. This sets up a destination server to be a read-only standby server. In this section the machine that is shipping the logs will be referred to as the primary and source server. The machine that is receiving the logs will be referred to as the secondary, destination, or standby server. The source server will back up its database and then ship it to the destination server. The source server continually backs up the transaction logs from a source database and then copies and restores the logs to a destination database. In addition to shipping the logs, the process should also keep the destination database synchronized with the source database. This new feature of SQL Server allows you to implement a backup server and also provides a way to offload query processing from the main computer. The destination servers can be used for read-only purposes. Some common uses for the destination server could include:

- High overhead reporting functions
- DBCC CHECKDB
- Long Running Queries used to populate other data sources

This section outlines the security concerns related to log shipping. Then it moves to the configuration of log shipping. The configuration includes the steps to set up the process and then details the steps necessary to change roles when the primary server goes down.

Security Suggestions

Log shipping is not difficult to configure. It is just precise, and you must follow the previously mentioned steps to get it to work correctly. The following list summarizes your key security concerns. If you follow these security suggestions, you can decrease the administrative overhead related to log shipping.

- Make sure the SQL Server and SQL Server Agent startup accounts are local administrators on both machines.
- Make sure the startup accounts have access to the transaction log share points.
- You must be a system administrator to change log shipping roles.
- Remember to run your Data Transformation Services (DTS) package to synchronize the logins of both servers before changing roles.

Log Shipping Configuration

Log shipping is easiest to configure through the Database Maintenance Plan Wizard. Before you begin the wizard, you should consider the following facts about log shipping:

- The user configuring log shipping must be a member of the sysadmin server role in order to have permission to configure the database for log shipping.
- Only one database at a time can be configured for log shipping. If you try to select more than one database, the option for log shipping is disabled in the wizard.

■ The startup account used for your SQL Server and SQL Server Agent services must have access to the database maintenance plan, the destination server, and the source server.

NOTE If both instances of SQL Server that are used for log shipping use the same service account for starting the SQL Server and SQL Server Agent service, log shipping will be easier to configure. It is also helpful to have the account be a local administrator on both physical machines.

■ You can only ship logs to a hard drive. You can't use the backup to tape options when configuring log shipping.

When you start the wizard you will be presented with a checkbox to configure log shipping as shown in Figure 10.4. The wizard can be used to configure the following items:

■ Synchronize the frequency of transfer and verification of the databases.

■ Specify which destination servers might assume the role of the source server.

■ Register new servers to be configured for log shipping.

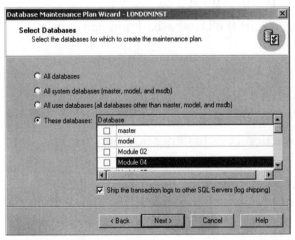

Figure 10.4   Log shipping is an option available from the Database Maintenance Plan Wizard.

- Create the source databases on all destination servers. When adding a destination database through the Database Maintenance Plan Wizard, you have the option of creating the databases on the destination server or using existing databases. Databases that already exist must be in standby mode.

- Set a restore delay. This delay defines how old a transaction log must be before it is restored. If something goes wrong on the source server, this delay provides extra time before the corrupted log is restored on the destination server.

- Set a backup schedule.

Log shipping is easily configured using Enterprise Manager. In fact, through Enterprise Manager you can configure log shipping from a SQL Server 2000 instance or a SQL Server 7.0 instance. If you are going to configure shipping from a 7.0 instance the server must have Service Pack 2 applied and the Pending Upgrade database option must be enabled. You can enable this option by typing the following code:

```
EXEC sp_dboption 'database name', 'pending upgrade', 'true'
```

NOTE Before you configure log shipping, you must create a share on the primary database to make the transaction logs available. This share should be created at the location where the log backups are configured for storage.

To configure log shipping you should walk through the Database Maintenance Plan Wizard and perform the following steps:

1. From Enterprise Manager, start the Database Maintenance Plan Wizard.

2. On the Welcome screen, click Next.

3. In the Select Databases screen, select the These Databases checkbox, and then select the Database to Log Ship.

4. Select the Ship the Transaction Logs to Other SQL Servers (Log Shipping) checkbox.

5. Continue through the wizard, specifying the rest of the database maintenance options until you get to the Specify the Transaction Log Share screen as shown in Figure 10.5. Click Next.

6. Enter the location of the share point you created for log shipping and click Next.

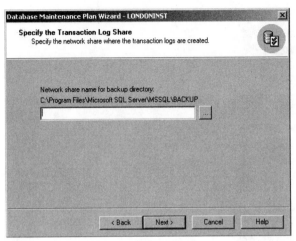

Figure 10.5 The Transaction Log Share is the network share you created for log backup storage.

7. From the Specifying the Log Shipping dialogue box, click Add to add a destination database.

8. In the Add Destination Database dialogue box, select the destination server name.

9. The server must be registered in Enterprise Manager and running Microsoft SQL Server 2000 Enterprise Edition to appear in the drop-down list. If you want this destination to become an available source destination, you must select the Allow Database to Assume Primary Role checkbox as shown in Figure 10.6. If this box is not selected, this destination database will not be able to assume the source desti-nation role in the future.

10. If the source database does not exist on the destination database, select the Create and Initialize New Database checkbox.

11. The Database Name box will default to the source database name. If you want a different database name on the destination server, spec-ify a new name. (If you have chosen to allow this destination data-base to assume the source role, you cannot change the database name from the default.)

12. If you have selected the Create and Initialize New Database check-box in step 10, you must specify the file directories for the data and log on to the destination database in the For Data and For Log boxes.

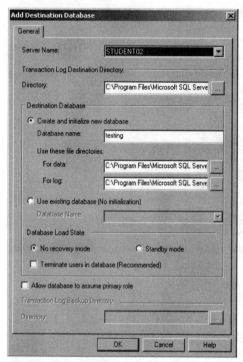

Figure 10.6 The Allow Database to Assume Primary Role checkbox enables the destination server to be promoted to the source server when problems arise.

13. If the source database already exists on the destination database, select the Use Existing Database checkbox. This completes the Add Destination Database dialogue box and you have successfully created a destination for the log shipping. Click OK to return to the Specify Log Shipping Destinations dialogue box.

14. Click Next.

15. The Initialize the Destination Databases dialogue box appears. You will either have to perform a full backup at this point or supply the location of a recent backup file.

16. Click Next.

17. The Log Shipping Schedules dialogue box appears as shown in Figure 10.7. View the default log shipping schedule. If you would like to alter the schedule, click Change to edit the schedule properties.

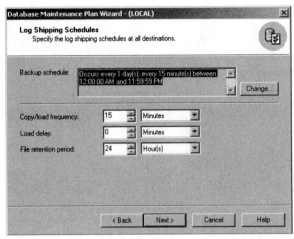

Figure 10.7   Use the Log Shipping Schedules dialogue box to configure the frequency of your log shipment.

18. From the Log Shipping Schedules dialogue box, you configure the Copy/Load Frequency option. This is configured in minutes and sets the frequency at which you want to back up data from the source server and load the data into the destination server.

19. The Load Delay option sets the delay, in minutes, that you want the destination database to wait before it restores the transaction log from the source server. (The default for this box is 0 minutes, which indicates that the destination database should immediately restore any transaction log backups.)

20. The File Retention Period option in the Log Shipping Schedules dialogue box is used to specify the length of time that must elapse before a transaction log can be deleted. After you have configured the time interval, click Next.

21. The Log Shipping Thresholds dialogue box is used to set the Backup Alert Threshold. This is the maximum elapsed time since the last transaction log backup was made on the source server. After the time exceeds this specified threshold, an alert will be generated by the monitor server.

22. The Out of Sync Alert option, also configured in the Log Shipping Thresholds dialogue box, is used to specify the amount of time

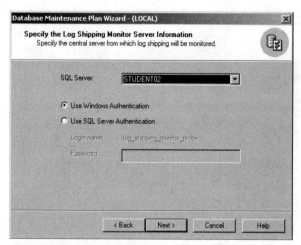

Figure 10.8   The Specify the Log Shipping Monitor Server Information dialogue box is used to configure the server that will monitor the log shipping process.

allowed to pass between the last transaction log backup on the source server and the last transaction log restore on the destination server. Click Next after you have configured the appropriate intervals.

23. In the Specify the Log Shipping Monitor Server Information screen, select the name of the server that will monitor log shipping as shown in Figure 10.8.

24. Click either Use Windows Authentication or Use SQL Server Authentication to connect to the monitor server. The log_shipping_monitor_probe login name is fixed and must be used to connect to the monitor server. If this is a new account, choose a new password. If the account already exists on the monitor server, you must specify the existing password. After you have chosen your method of Authentication, click Next.

25. The Reports to Generate dialogue box appears and is used to configure the location of all Database Maintenance Plan reports. You will need to finish the Database Maintenance Plan wizard by supplying information in the last couple of dialogue boxes. These options control the history storage and are not specific to log shipping.

26. When you come to the end of the wizard, click Finish to complete the process.

Figure 10.9   When you remove log shipping, the configuration is removed from all servers involved in the process.

It is much easier to remove log shipping than it is to configure it. After you no longer have the need to use log shipping, you can perform the following list of steps to remove it.

1. Open Enterprise Manager.
2. Click to expand your server group.
3. Click to expand the Management container.
4. Click Database Maintenance Plan.
5. In the details pane, right-click the database maintenance plans to delete and then click Properties.
6. Click the Log Shipping tab as shown in Figure 10.9 and then click Remove Log Shipping. This removes log shipping from all servers involved in the process.

Changing Log Shipping Roles

SQL Server 2000 allows the changing of log shipping roles through system-stored procedures. Hopefully, there will never be a problem that requires the change of roles from one server to another, but if a problem with the source server does occur, you should be prepared. Log shipping supports the changing of roles, which requires the following three steps. Although the steps are basic by themselves, the process is very procedural and needs to be configured properly as detailed over the next few pages.

1. Ensure that the secondary server has the database maintenance plan. If the secondary or destination server does not know about the process, it will not ship logs to anyone else.

2. Create a DTS package that transfers the logins from the current primary server to the secondary server.

3. Perform the role change to set the current secondary server as the current primary server.

Secondary Server Maintenance Plan

Before performing a log shipping role change, a maintenance plan for this log shipping pair must exist on the secondary server. A maintenance plan can be created using the Database Maintenance Plan Wizard or by adding a server as a secondary server using the Add Secondary dialogue box found in the user interface of the primary database maintenance plan.

Transfer Logins Package

The logins from the primary (source) server need to transfer to the secondary (destination) server to ensure that both machines are in sync from a security standpoint. The following steps should be taken to perform this login transfer:

1. Create a DTS package on the current primary server using DTS Designer.

2. Add a Transfer Logins task to your package, as shown in Figure 10.10.

3. In the Transfer Logins dialogue box on the Source tab, in the Source Server list, enter the source server (the current primary server).

4. Click either Use Windows Authentication or Use SQL Server Authentication, as applicable.

5. On the Destination tab, in the Destination Server list, enter the destination server (the current secondary server).

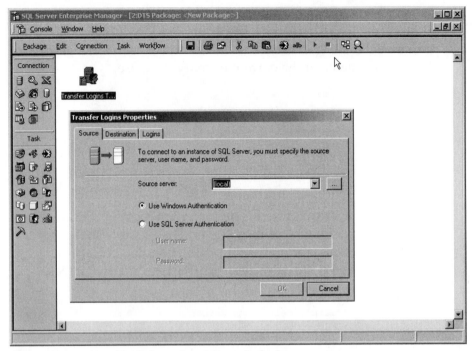

Figure 10.10   Use this dialogue box to transfer logins.

6. Click either Use Windows Authentication or Use SQL Server Authentication, as applicable.

7. On the Logins tab, click either All Server Logins Detected at Package Runtime or Logins for Selected Databases.

8. Save the package.

Changing Roles

After you have configured the logins at the destination server, you will now execute the stored procedures necessary to change the server roles. After this change the destination server will be the "primary server" and the source server will be the "secondary server." You must be a SQL Server administrator on both machines to perform a server role change. You will need to execute the following stored procedures:

1. Run sp_change_primary_role on the instance of SQL Server marked as the current primary server. The example shows how to make the primary database stop being the primary database. *current_primary_dbname* is the name of the current primary database.

```
EXEC sp_change_primary_role
    @db_name = 'current_primary_dbname',
    @backup_log = 1,
    @terminate = 0,
    @final_state = 2,
    @access_level = 1
GO
```

2. Run sp_change_secondary_role on the instance of SQL Server marked as the current secondary server. The example shows how to make the secondary database the primary database. *current_secondary_dbname* is the name of the current secondary database.

```
EXEC sp_change_secondary_role
    @db_name = 'current_secondary_dbname',
    @do_load = 1,
    @force_load = 1,
    @final_state = 1,
    @access_level = 1,
    @terminate = 1,
    @stopat = NULL
GO
```

3. Run sp_change_monitor_role on the instance of SQL Server marked as the monitor. The example shows how to change the monitor to reflect the new primary database. *new_source_directory* is the path to the location where the primary server dumps the transaction logs.

```
EXEC sp_change_monitor_role
    @primary_server = 'current_primary_server_name',
    @secondary_server = 'current_secondary_server_name',
    @database = 'current_secondary_dbname',
    @new_source = 'new_source_directory'
GO
```

The former secondary server is now the current primary server and is ready to assume the function of a primary server. The former primary is now not a member of the log shipping pair. You will need to configure the original primary as a secondary server to the new primary if you want it to participate in the log shipping process.

Federated SQL Server 2000 Servers

Microsoft SQL Server 2000 databases can be spread across a group of database servers capable of supporting the processing growth requirements of the largest Web sites and enterprise data processing systems built with Microsoft Windows. SQL Server 2000 supports updateable distributed partitioned views used to transparently partition data horizontally across a group of servers. Although these servers cooperate in managing the partitioned data, they operate and are managed separately from each other.

A group of servers that cooperate to process a workload is known as a *federation*. Although SQL Server 2000 delivers impressive performance when scaled up on servers with eight or more processors, it can support huge processing loads when partitioned across a federation. The federation depends on all machines involved in order to make them work together to act as a single database. They need very similar security settings to make sure that users can interact with all machines involved in the federation. Although the user sees one view of the data, security is configured separately for each server. This process will be easy to configure if the user setting up the federation is a system administrator.

A federated database tier can achieve extremely high levels of performance only if the application sends each SQL statement to the member server that has most of the data required by the statement. This is called *collocating* the SQL statement with the data required by the statement. Collocating SQL statements with the required data is not a requirement unique to federated servers. It is also required in clustered systems.

Although a federation of servers presents the same image to the applications as a single database server, there are internal differences in how the database services tier is implemented. Table 10.2 identifies the differences between a single server application and a federated server-tiered application.

Table 10.2   Single Server Applications versus Federated Database Servers

SINGLE SERVER	FEDERATED SERVERS
Only one instance of SQL Server needed.	One instance required for each member of the federation.
Production data is physically stored in a single database.	Each member has a database and the data is spread across the servers.

(continues)

Table 10.2 Single Server Applications versus Federated Database Servers *(Continued)*

SINGLE SERVER	FEDERATED SERVERS
Each table is singular.	The table from the original database is horizontally partitioned into tables on each of the member servers. Distributed partitioned views are used to make it appear as though the data is in a single location.
Connection is made to a single server.	The application layer must be able to collocate SQL statements to ensure that the server that has most of the data receives the request.

While the goal is to design a federation of database servers to handle a complete workload, you do this by designing a set of distributed partitioned views that spread the data across the different servers. If the design is not solid in the beginning, the performance of your queries will suffer as the servers try to build the result sets required by the queries.

This section discusses the details of configuring the distributed partitioned view. Thereafter, the considerations for updating, inserting, and deleting data are introduced. Finally, this section addresses the security concerns related to Federated Database Servers.

Creating a Partitioned View

A partitioned view joins horizontally partitioned data from a set of member tables across one or more servers, making the data appear as if from one table. SQL Server knows the difference between local views and distributed partitioned views. In a local partitioned view, all participating tables and the view reside on the same instance of SQL Server. In a distributed partitioned view, at least one of the participating tables resides on a different server. In addition, SQL Server differentiates between partitioned views that are updateable and views that are read-only copies of the underlying tables. Although the view that is created may be updateable, the user that interacts with the view must still be given permission to update the distributed view. The permissions for these partitioned views are similar to regular views; you just have to configure the permission on each server referenced in the partitioned view. More information on setting permission for views is found in Chapter 5, "Managing Object Security."

Before implementing a partitioned view, you must first partition a table horizontally. The original table is replaced with several smaller member tables. Each member table has the same number of columns and the same configuration as the original table. If you are creating a distributed partitioned view, each member table is stored on a separate member server. The name of the member databases should be the same on each member server. This is not a requirement, but will help eliminate confusion.

You design the member tables so that each table stores a horizontal slice of the original table based on a range of key values. The ranges are based on the data values in a partitioning column. The range of values in each member table is enforced by a CHECK constraint on the partitioning column, and ranges cannot overlap. For example, you cannot have one table with a range from 1 through 200000, and another with a range from 150000 through 300000, because it would not be clear which table contains the values from 150000 through 200000. For example, if you are partitioning a Customer table into three tables, the CHECK constraint for these tables could appear as follows:

```
-- On Server1:
CREATE TABLE Customer_33
  (CustomerID   INTEGER PRIMARY KEY
              CHECK (CustomerID BETWEEN 1 AND 32999),
  ... -- Additional column definitions)


-- On Server2:
CREATE TABLE Customer_66
  (CustomerID   INTEGER PRIMARY KEY
              CHECK (CustomerID BETWEEN 33000 AND 65999),
  ... -- Additional column definitions)


-- On Server3:
CREATE TABLE Customer_99
  (CustomerID   INTEGER PRIMARY KEY
              CHECK (CustomerID BETWEEN 66000 AND 99999),
  ... -- Additional column definitions)
```

NOTE You need to have the permission to create tables on all servers involved in the federation.

After creating the member tables, you define a distributed partitioned view on each member server. The view name should also be the same on each server. This allows queries referencing the distributed partitioned view name to run on any of the member servers. The system operates as if a copy of the original table is on each member server, but each server has only a member table and a distributed partitioned view. The location of the data is transparent to the application.

Creating distributed partitioned views requires several steps, which must be configured. To perform the necessary configuration options, you should perform the following three steps:

1. Each member server has to be configured as a linked server on every other member server. This is necessary to allow every server to run a query and access the other servers when necessary. The security settings of the linked servers must be configured to allow all users to authenticate against all servers.

2. Set the lazy schema validation option, using sp_serveroption, for each linked server definition used in distributed partitioned views. This tells the query optimizer not to request meta data from the remote table until it actually needs data from the remote table. This optimizes the execution of the query and may prevent unnecessary retrieval of meta data. You need to be a member of the system administrators (sysadmin) role to set this value.

3. Create a distributed partitioned view on each member server. The views use distributed SELECT statements to access data from the linked member servers and merge the distributed rows with rows from the local member table. To complete this step, you must have the permission to create views on all servers. The following example demonstrates a distributed partitioned view. The SELECT statement must be performed against all servers involved in the federation.

```
CREATE VIEW Customers AS
    SELECT * FROM CompanyDatabase.TableOwner.Customers_33
UNION ALL
    SELECT * FROM Server2.CompanyDatabase.TableOwner.Customers_66
UNION ALL
    SELECT * FROM Server3.CompanyDatabase.TableOwner.Customers_99
```

Updateable Partitioned Views

If a local or distributed partitioned view is not updateable, it can serve only as a read-only copy of the original table. An updateable partitioned view can exhibit all the capabilities of the original table. This can be an excellent option for security. If you want the users to be able to view the data but not update it, this option should be used. This is beneficial if your data is being loaded from a source other than the user who is analyzing the data.

A view is considered an updateable partitioned view if the view is a set of SELECT statements whose individual result sets are combined into one using the UNION ALL statement. Each individual SELECT statement references one SQL Server base table. For the view to be updateable, the additional rules discussed in the following sections must be met.

Table Rules

Member tables are defined in the FROM clause in each SELECT statement in the view definition. Each member table must adhere to the following standards:

- Member tables cannot be referenced more than once in the view.
- Member tables cannot have indexes created on any computed columns.
- Member tables must have all PRIMARY KEY constraints on an identical number of columns.
- Member tables must have the same ANSI padding setting.

Column Rules

Columns are defined in the select list of each SELECT statement in the view definition. The columns must follow these rules:

- All columns in each member table must be included in the select list.
- Columns cannot be referenced more than once in the select list.
- The columns from all servers involved in the federation must be in the same ordinal position in the select list.
- The columns in the select list of each SELECT statement must be of the same type (including data type, precision, scale, and collation).

Partitioning Column Rules

A partitioning column exists on each member table and, through CHECK constraints, identifies the data available in that specific table. Partitioning columns must adhere to these rules:

- Each base table has a partitioning column whose key values are enforced by CHECK constraints.
- The key ranges of the CHECK constraints in each table do not overlap with the ranges of any other table.
- Any given value of the partitioning column must map to only one table.

- The CHECK constraints can only use these operators: BETWEEN, AND, OR, <, <=, >, >=, =.

- The partitioning column must be in the same ordinal location in the select list of each SELECT statement in the view. For example, the partitioning column is always the same column (such as first column) in each select list.

- Partitioning columns cannot allow nulls.

- Partitioning columns must be a part of the primary key of the table.

- Partitioning columns cannot be computed columns.

- There must be only one constraint on the partitioning column. If there is more than one constraint, SQL Server ignores all the constraints and will not consider them when determining whether or not the view is a partitioned view.

Distributed Partition View Rules

In addition to the rules defined for partitioned views, distributed partition views have these additional conditions:

- A distributed transaction will be started to ensure atomicity across all nodes affected by the update.

- The XACT_ABORT SET option must be set to ON.

- The smallmoney and smalldatetime columns in remote tables are mapped as money and datetime, respectively. Consequently, the corresponding columns in the local tables should also be money and datetime.

- Any linked server cannot be a loopback linked server, that is, a linked server that points to the same instance of SQL Server.

- A view that references partitioned tables without following all these rules may still be updateable if there is an INSTEAD OF trigger on the view. The query optimizer, however, may not always be able to build execution plans for a view with an INSTEAD OF trigger that are as efficient as the plans for a partitioned view that follows all of the rules.

Data Modification

In addition to the rules defined for updateable partitioned views, data modification statements referencing the view must adhere to the rules defined for INSERT, UPDATE, and DELETE statements, as described in the sections that follow. The permission to perform these statements is handled at each server. To aid in troubleshooting, all of the servers should have an identical security configuration for the database used in the federation. For instance, if a user needs permission to perform the INSERT statement, it must be given at all servers.

INSERT Statements

INSERT statements add data to the member tables through the partitioned view. The INSERT statements must adhere to the following standards:

- All columns must be included in the INSERT statement even if the column can be NULL in the base table or has a DEFAULT constraint defined in the base table.

- The DEFAULT keyword cannot be specified in the VALUES clause of the INSERT statement.

- INSERT statements must supply a value that satisfies the logic of the CHECK constraint defined on the partitioning column for one of the member tables.

- INSERT statements are not allowed if a member table contains a column with an identity property.

- INSERT statements are not allowed if a member table contains a timestamp column.

- INSERT statements are not allowed if there is a self-join with the same view or any of the member tables.

UPDATE Statements

UPDATE statements modify data in one or more of the member tables through the partitioned view. The UPDATE statements must adhere to the following guidelines:

- UPDATE statements cannot specify the DEFAULT keyword as a value in the SET clause even if the column has a DEFAULT value defined in the corresponding member table.

- The value of a column with an identity property cannot be changed; however, the other columns can be updated.

- The value of a PRIMARY KEY cannot be changed if the column contains text, image, or ntext data.

- Updates are not allowed if a base table contains a timestamp column.

- Updates are not allowed if there is a self-join with the same view or any of the member tables.

- The DEFAULT keyword cannot be specified in the SET clause of the UPDATE statement.

DELETE Statements

DELETE statements remove data in one or more of the member tables through the partitioned view. DELETE statements are not allowed if there is a self-join with the same view or any of the member tables.

Security Considerations for Federated Servers

The following security suggestions can make the management of Federated Database Servers lighter. The configuration of Federated Database Servers is very procedural and if security is not configured correctly, you will not get the intended results.

- The individual configuring the federation should be a system administrator on all servers. This is technically not required for each step, but it will make all configurations possible from a single login.

- The Distributed Partitioned Views do not have to be updateable. If it is inappropriate for users to make modifications to the data, don't allow the view to be modified.

- The databases at each server are configured separately, although they appear to the user as a single entity. You should remember this as you troubleshoot failed statements. If the security across the servers is not similar, you will need to check security settings at each server individually.

- The startup account for the SQL Server and SQL Server Agent service should be the same across all servers and should be a local administrator on all machines.

- All logins that need to execute queries against the federation should be created on all servers.

- The database users and roles on all servers should be identical for the distributed database.

- All users who need to perform queries against the federation will need permission to the view. The permission must be equivalent to the action the users need to perform. For instance, if you need a user to insert into the view, that user must have INSERT permission to the view definition at each server.

- Configure security account delegation to allow the servers to pass Windows Authentication information to each other. If you want to use the Windows account information, you need to allow the servers to pass the user information on behalf of the users.

Best Practices

- Set up linked servers to allow for distributed transactions. Without linked servers, transactional consistency cannot be maintained across servers.

- Configure security account delegation to integrate Windows Authentication with linked servers.

- Use the same startup account for the SQL Server service and the SQL Server Agent service for all services that need distributed data support.

- Verify that the service account is a local administrator on all servers that participate in the distributed data options.

- Use the Database Maintenance Plan Wizard to configure log shipping. The process is very procedural in nature, and the wizard will make sure you complete all the necessary steps.

- Use Federated Database Servers for large enterprise applications and Web farms. It is only beneficial for very large database solutions.

REVIEW QUESTIONS

1. What is a linked server?

2. Why should I consider the log shipping feature?

3. What are the necessary steps for promoting a secondary server to a primary server when using log shipping?

4. Which of the distributed database features depend on the Enterprise Edition of Microsoft's SQL Server 2000?

5. What is horizontal partitioning?

6. What is the purpose of a distributed partitioned view?

7. How can Federated Database Servers slow down performance?

8. How could Federated Database Servers be used to speed up query and application performance?

Managing Data Transformation Services

Many organizations need to centralize data to improve corporate decision-making. However, their current data may be stored in a variety of formats and in different locations. Data Transformation Services (DTS) addresses this vital business need by providing a set of tools that lets you extract, transform, and consolidate data from disparate sources into single or multiple destinations supported by DTS connectivity. By using DTS tools to graphically build DTS packages or by programming a package with the DTS object model, you can create custom data movement solutions tailored to the specific business needs of your organization.

DTS is used to manage your data and with the management of data comes security concerns. You need to make sure that your data is protected appropriately in all circumstances and across all data sources. You want to make sure that you take the appropriate security precautions to access the data across multiple systems. Additionally, if you have created a complex DTS package, you want to secure the package to restrict those who can modify or execute it.

This chapter first describes the DTS feature of SQL Server 2000. This section includes a description of DTS packages and their core components (connections, tasks, and workflow).

This chapter also describes and demonstrates the tools that can be used with DTS. The first part of this chapter describes the tools used to create and manage packages. The chapter then describes the execution tools available with DTS. Finally, this chapter moves to the security concerns related to creating, executing, scheduling, and modifying DTS packages.

DTS Packages

A DTS package is an organized collection of connections, DTS tasks, transformations, and workflow constraints assembled with a DTS tool and saved to be executed at a later time. Each package contains one or more steps that are executed sequentially or in parallel when the package is run. When executed, the package connects to the configured data sources, copies data and database objects, transforms data, and notifies other users or processes of events. Packages can be edited, password-protected, scheduled for execution, and retrieved by saved version. Because DTS packages perform such a wide range of options, securing the data and the connections to the data is a prime concern. Some of the security options available in DTS depend on your choice of storage locations for your DTS packages. DTS allows you to store your packages in one of these four places:

Microsoft SQL Server.   Packages stored in this location are most often referred to as local packages, and they are actually stored as part of the MSDB database. This location allows you to use passwords (user password for execution of the package and owner password for modification of the package) as security options, but you have no ability to store the package lineage. This is the most common storage method.

SQL Server 2000 Meta Data Services.   This location involves packages stored in the repository. By default the repository is also part of the MSDB database. When you store your package in the Meta Data Services, you have the ability to track the lineage of the package data. This allows you to see a history of the data that was manipulated by the package. Although tracking the lineage of the package provides the most information about the package, it also slows down the package's execution performance. When you store your package in Meta Data Services, you also lose the ability to assign user and owner passwords. This storage option is the weakest from a security standpoint.

Structured storage file.   This location option stores the package as a COM structured storage file in the operating system. When you use this option for storage, you can't find the package using Enterprise Manager. You will have to know the location of the file. This storage option limits your security constraints to permissions at the operating system level. If the user trying to execute or modify the package does not have permission to the file from the operating system perspective, that user cannot interact with the package.

Microsoft Visual Basic file.   This storage location option is new to SQL Server 2000. With this option you can open the file from Visual Basic and manipulate the package and program against the package. From a security standpoint, you have the same restrictions as a structured storage file.

DTS Connections

To successfully execute DTS tasks that copy and transform data, a DTS package must establish valid connections to its source and destination data and to any additional data sources (for example, lookup tables). You need to configure a connection object for each of the source and destination locations. Each of these connections has its own connection properties, which provide the security credentials to be used when the package connects to the data source.

Because of its OLE DB architecture, DTS allows connections to data stored in a wide variety of OLE DB-compliant formats. In addition, DTS packages usually can connect to data in custom or nonstandard formats if OLE DB providers are available for those data sources and if you use Microsoft Data Link files to configure those connections. DTS allows the following types of connections:

A data source connection.   These are connections to: standard databases such as Microsoft SQL Server 2000, Microsoft Access 2000, Oracle, dBase, Paradox; OLE DB connections to ODBC data sources; Microsoft Excel 2000 spreadsheet data; HTML sources; and other OLE DB providers. You should keep in mind that each of these data sources has a different security model. You need to supply security credentials that are sufficient for access to the data source from which you are requesting a connection. In some cases, such as Microsoft Access and Excel, the security credentials may be optional. In others, such as SQL Server and Oracle, the user credentials are required for connectivity to the data source.

A file connection. DTS provides additional support for text files. The security available at the file level is typically limited to the file system in which the file is stored. You will need to have permissions to open the file if you are extracting data from the file. You will need to have permission to modify the file if you are writing data to the file.

A data link connection. These are connections in which an intermediate file outside of SQL Server stores the connection string. The connection string is similar to that of the data source connection in that it includes the user information that will be required to connect to the database.

When creating a package by using the DTS Import/Export Wizard, in DTS Designer, or programmatically, you configure connections by selecting a connection type from a list of available OLE DB providers. The properties you configure for each connection vary depending on the individual provider for the data source. The security information you supply is the security context in which the connection is made.

You need to supply an account with enough permission to perform the tasks you are requesting from the connection. When you use Windows Authentication as your security credentials for the connection, you need to recognize that the security context changes depending on the user who is executing the package. If the package is being executed manually by a user, the user's current Windows login is used for the connection credentials.

If you have scheduled the package to be executed as part of a job, the security context depends on the owner of the job. More information on the security context of the job owner is found later in this chapter in the section *DTS Tools.* You should perform the following steps to create a connection to a SQL Server database from the DTS Designer:

1. Open Enterprise Manager.
2. Click to expand your server group.
3. Click to expand the server where you want to create the package.
4. Click to expand Data Transformation Services.
5. Right-click Local Packages and select New Package. The DTS Designer should appear as shown in Figure 11.1.
6. Click to expand the Connection menu item.
7. Select Microsoft OLE DB Provider for SQL Server.

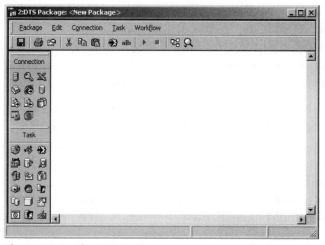

Figure 11.1 The DTS Designer can create complex DTS packages that can execute multiple tasks against multiple data sources.

8. From the Connection Properties dialogue box, you need to name the connection, choose the server you are connecting to, supply the database you are connecting to, and your security credentials for connecting to the database, as shown in Figure 11.2.

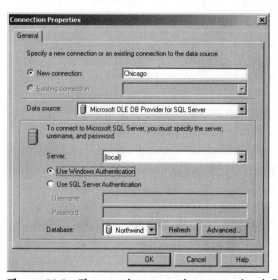

Figure 11.2 The security connection properties define the user credentials used when the connection is made to the data source.

You can configure a new connection within the DTS Designer or use an existing one. You can also use the same connection many times in a single package. This can be useful in organizing the package. You can minimize the number of icons on your DTS Designer screen by reusing connections. Before configuring a connection, you should consider the following items:

Each connection can be used by only one DTS task at a time, because the connections are single-threaded.   When you are designing a complex package, you may want to create multiple connections to the same data source. This allows each of the tasks within the package to use a separate connection object. This results in faster-running packages and easier troubleshooting when a package task is failing. In general, each task should have its own connection object to each data source it needs to access.

If you have configured two tasks to use the same connection, they must execute serially rather than in parallel.   If two tasks use different connection objects, they may execute in parallel. Additionally, if two tasks that you have configured use separate connections that refer to the same instance of SQL Server, they will, by default, execute in parallel. A package transaction requires all of the steps of the transaction to run in serial. You will need to manage the workflow properties to ensure that the tasks you add to the package transaction execute in the order that you want. More information about managing the package workflow is supplied later in this chapter in the section *DTS Package Workflow.*

If you plan to run a package on different servers, you may need to edit the direct connections made in a package.   (For example, if the original data sources will be unavailable or you will be connecting to different data sources.) A direct connection is a connection to the server where the package is being created. If the package is ported to another machine, the direct connections may need to be edited to point to the correct server. To simplify editing, consider using a data link file, where the connection string is saved in a separate text file. You could then update the text file to update all of the direct connections. Alternatively, consider using the Dynamic Properties task to change the connection information at run time. You can use the Dynamic Properties task to supply the server and security credentials that should be used when connecting. This information, supplied at run time, can be altered based on the variables at the time of execution.

When scheduling a package, consider the security information you have provided.   If you used Windows Authentication when configuring a connection, the SQL Server Agent authorization information is used to make the connection rather than the account information you used when designing the package. If the security settings for these accounts are different, you may get an authentication failure when the package executes.

DTS Tasks

A DTS task is a set of functionality executed as a single step in a package. Each task defines a work item to be performed as part of the data movement and data transformation process, or as a job to be executed. DTS supplies a number of tasks that are part of the DTS object model and can be accessed graphically, through DTS Designer, or programmatically. These tasks, which can be configured individually, cover a wide variety of data copying, data transformation, and notification situations. The supplied tasks allow you to perform the following:

Importing and exporting data.   DTS can import data from a text file or an OLE DB data source (for example, a Microsoft Access 2000 database) into SQL Server. Alternatively, data can be exported from SQL Server to an OLE DB data destination (for example, a Microsoft Excel 2000 spreadsheet). DTS also allows high-speed data loading from text files into SQL Server tables. When importing and exporting data, you are limited to the security of the data sources and data destinations. For example, if the source of your data is an Access database that doesn't have security set on it, you will not have any restrictions in your access to the data. You should be familiar with the security models of all the sources and destinations involved in the import or export process.

Transforming data.   DTS Designer includes a Transform Data task that allows you to select data from a data source connection, map the columns of data to a set of transformations, and send the transformed data to a destination connection. DTS Designer also includes a Data Driven Query task that allows you to map data to parameterized queries. Both of these options allow you to make changes to the data as it is being moved. Data transformations are addressed in the *DTS Transformations* section that follows.

Copying database objects.   With DTS, you can transfer indexes, views, logins, stored procedures, triggers, rules, defaults, constraints, and user-defined data types in addition to the data. You can also generate the scripts to copy the database objects. You need to have administrative permissions to both databases involved in the transfer process. You also need to transfer the objects between SQL Server databases. When you use this option, you should be careful of object ownership issues. If the user running the DTS package is not a system administrator on both SQL Server systems, the destination objects will be owned by the user account that executed the package instead of the DBO. For more information on object ownership, you should refer to Chapter 2, "Designing a Successful Security Model."

Sending and receiving messages to and from other users and packages. DTS includes a Send Mail task that allows you to send email notification if a package step succeeds or fails. The Send Mail task depends on an email profile created on your server for the SQL Server Agent service account. To make this work correctly, your SQL Server Agent service account should be a member of the Windows 2000 local administrators group. DTS also includes an Execute Package task that allows one package to run another as a package step and a Message Queue task that allows you to use Message Queuing to send and receive messages between packages. One package can supply information to another package as a global variable.

Executing a set of Transact-SQL statements or Microsoft ActiveX scripts against a data source.   The Execute SQL and ActiveX Script tasks allow you to write your own SQL statements and scripting code and execute them as a step in a package workflow. This is helpful if you want to perform some action before or after you transfer the data, such as dropping your indexes or backing up the database. Keep in mind that the credentials defined by your connection properties determine your security context on the other server. For example, if the user's account information you provide does not have the permission to drop indexes, you will not be able to execute the package step that drops the indexes. DTS cannot be used as a method of bypassing normal SQL Server security.

Extending the existing COM model.   Because DTS is based on an extensible COM model, you can create your own custom tasks. You can integrate custom tasks into the user interface of DTS Designer and save them as part of the DTS object model.

DTS Transformations

A DTS transformation is one or more functions or operations applied against a piece of data before the data arrives at the destination. The source data is not changed. Because you are not changing the source data, you only need select permission on the data you are accessing to perform the transform. For example, you can extract a substring from a column of source data and copy it to a destination table. The particular substring function is the transformation mapped onto the source column. You also can search for rows with certain characteristics (for example, specific data values in columns) and apply functions only against the data in those rows.

Transformations make it easy to implement complex data validation, data scrubbing, and conversions during the import and export process. The permissions required against the source data are generally minimal. To move the new transformed data to the data destination, you will need to have the ability to insert and update against the destination table. You can use transforms against column data to perform any of the following:

Manipulate column data.   For example, you can change the type, size, scale, precision, or nullability of a column.

Apply functions written as ActiveX scripts.   These functions can apply specialized transformations or include conditional logic. For example, you can write a function in a scripting language that examines the data in a column for values over 1000. Whenever such a value is found, a value of -1 is substituted in the destination table. For rows with column values under 1000, the value is copied to the destination table.

Choose from among a number of transformations supplied with DTS.   An example would be a function that reformats input data using string and date formatting, various string conversion functions, and a function that copies the contents of a file specified by a source column to a destination column.

Write your own transformations as COM objects and apply those transformations against column data.   Through COM objects you can perform more advanced logical language evaluations that are not fully supported by VBScript. This can then be executed from your DTS package.

DTS Package Workflow

You have control over the order in which your package tasks execute. The DTS package workflow defines the order in which the tasks of your package execute. The default is for up to four task to execute in parallel. Tasks that use different data sources will try to run in parallel and tasks that use the same data source will run in serial.

Precedence constraints allow you to link two tasks together based on whether the first task executes successfully or unsuccessfully. You can use precedence constraints to build conditional branches in a workflow. You should have a solid design of the steps that are required for your DTS package. If you design the required steps before you begin using the DTS Designer, you will have a clearer picture of what needs to be configured from the DTS Designer.

DTS Tools

DTS includes several tools that simplify package creation, execution, and management. The DTS tools can be broken into two categories: management and execution tools. They are discussed separately in the sections that follow.

Management Tools

DTS provides two primary tools for the management of DTS packages. Your selection criteria for the appropriate tool are completely dependent on your package requirements. The Import/Export Wizard is easy to use but lacks the functionality required for many packages. The DTS Designer is much more complex, but can be used to provide the full functionality of DTS. More details about each of these tools can be found in SQL Server Books Online or the help files within the DTS tool. Two management tools can enhance your ability to interact with DTS packages: The *DTS Import/Export Wizard*, which is used to build packages, can be used to import, export, and transform data, and to copy database objects. The Wizard is limited to one source and one destination connection. It is limited to some basic transfer and transformation tasks. The Wizard does allow you to define the connection security settings for the source and destination. The Wizard also allows you to determine the storage location of the package. Based on this option, if you choose SQL Server or structured file, you can also configure package passwords to secure the package. Package passwords are discussed in more depth in the section later in this chapter named *DTS Security Concerns*.

The *DTS Designer*, a graphical application, lets you construct packages containing complex workflows, multiple connections to heterogeneous data sources, and event-driven logic. The Data Transformation Services node in the SQL Server Enterprise Manager Console tree is used to view, create, load, and execute DTS packages. This is also where you launch the

DTS Designer and configure some of the DTS Designer settings. From the DTS Designer you can configure the package passwords as well as error log files. Many of the security settings related to error checking can only be configured through the DTS Designer.

Execution Tools

In addition to the management tools discussed in the preceding sections, the following execution utilities can also run DTS packages. These utilities are especially beneficial when you are trying to schedule a package for later execution. The dtsrun utility is used to execute a package as an operating system command. The dtsrunui tool is a graphical interface used to run and schedule DTS packages.

dtsrun

The dtsrun command is useful in scheduling your DTS packages to be run as a step in a SQL Server job. You need to recognize that the dtsrun command is executed as an operating system command. This is not a Transact-SQL statement. The fact that dtsrun is an operating system command affects both the syntax that you use to execute the package and the security context in which the package runs.

The syntax you use for your dtsrun commands is case-sensitive and the switches supplied need to be separated with the proper characters. You can either use the / (forward slash) or the - (hyphen) to separate the switches used for your dtsrun command. The switches available with the dtsrun command allow you to set the following options:

Configure connection settings.   You can specify the server name or filename, identify how the package was saved, and provide security credentials.

Pass the user password.   The user password must be supplied for the package to be executed. By default, packages do not have a user password configured. Therefore the user password need only be supplied when a user password is set at the time the package is saved.

Set scheduling options.   You can specify regular package execution through the SQL Server Agent.

Configure log settings.   You can identify and enable an event log file.

Apply global variable settings.   You can add new global variables and change the properties of existing global variables. Modifications to package global variables are in effect only for the duration of a dtsrun utility session. When the session is closed, changes to package global variables are not saved.

Define encryption options.   You can encrypt the command prompt options to be executed by the dtsrun command, allowing you to create an encrypted dtsrun command for later use.

The dtsrun command is typically run as a scheduled command that is part of a SQL Server job. When this is the case, the security context becomes a little confusing. The security context of the owner of the job defines the credentials that will be used to execute the package. The security information of the job owner is also used to determine the security context of the connections and tasks within the DTS package. If a member of the system administrator's role owns the job, the package will be executed in the security context of the SQL Server Agent service account. The service account should be a member of the local administrator's group. If this is the case, the package execution will most likely succeed during the connection phase of the package. If the owner of the job is not a member of the system administrator's role, the job step that executes the package will fail by default. As detailed in Chapter 9, "Introducing the SQL Server Agent Service," operating system steps that are not owned by the system administrator will fail. Information about overcoming this obstacle can be found in Chapter 9.

dtsrunui

The DTS Run utility (dtsrunui) allows you to execute a package using the graphical user interface. The parameters available can be used to execute the package at a later time. The dtsrunui has the same runtime options as the dtsrun command. Dtsrunui is a graphical interface version of the dtsrun command. For more information on the types of parameters you can supply with this utility, refer to the previous section, "dtsrun." The dtsrunui utility simplifies the process of executing and scheduling package execution. To execute a package using the dtsrunui utility, you should perform the following steps:

1. Click the Start button and select the Run command.

2. In the Run dialogue box, type dtsrunui. The DTS Run utility should appear as shown in Figure 11.3.

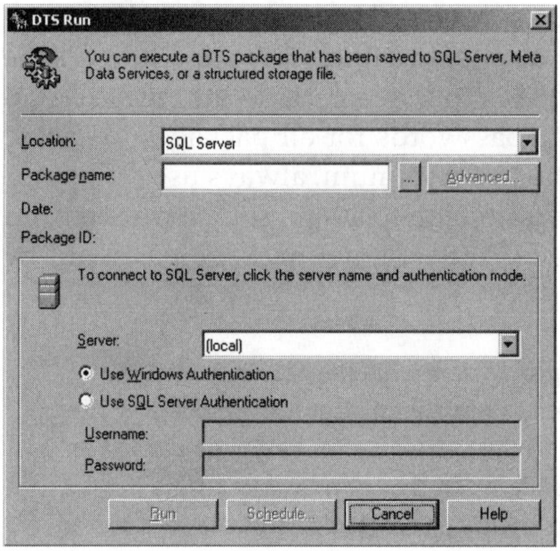

Figure 11.3   The DTS Run dialogue box can execute DTS packages.

DTS Security Concerns

This section consolidates and expands on the security concerns introduced earlier in this chapter. This section first addresses passwords that can be assigned to the DTS packages. It then moves to issues related to scheduling and ownership of DTS packages. Next, this section moves to the security issues related to data link files. Finally, it addresses connection security in a little more detail.

DTS Package Passwords

When you save a package to Microsoft SQL Server or as a structured storage file, you can assign the package passwords. You use DTS passwords in addition to the Windows Authentication or SQL Server Authentication passwords you use to connect to an instance of SQL Server. Two types of DTS package passwords are available for your packages. The *owner password* is required if a user wants to execute or modify the package. When you supply the owner password, you must also supply a user password. The *user password* can be assigned by itself or in conjunction with the owner password. Package users with access to only the user password can execute the package. However, they can neither open nor edit the package unless they have access to the owner password. It is strongly recommended that you use DTS package passwords for all packages to ensure both package and database security. At a minimum, always use DTS package passwords when connection information to a data source is saved and Windows Authentication is not used. You assign a package password by performing the following steps:

NOTE Although passwords are helpful in controlling access to your DTS package, they do not prevent another system administrator from deleting the package. You should make a backup of the package after you have altered its structure. If the DTS package was stored in SQL Server or in Meta Data Services, backing up the MSDB database backs up the package. If the package is stored in a structured file or Visual Basic file, you should back the package up by making a copy of the file.

1. Open an existing package.
2. On the Package menu, click Save or Save As.
3. In the Location list, click either SQL Server or Structured Storage File, as shown in Figure 11.4.
4. Enter an Owner password.
5. Enter a User password.

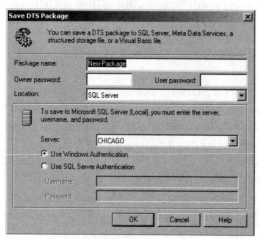

Figure 11.4 Package passwords control the users who can modify and execute your package.

Package Execution Scheduling

Usually a package run from DTS Designer, the DTS Import/Export Wizard, the dtsrunui utility, or a dtsrun command executes under the security context of the user who is currently logged in. However, a package that is scheduled for execution runs under the security context of the SQL Server Agent job that runs the package. The owner of that job may or may not be the same as the user currently logged in. Consider the following situations for job ownership.

For packages created under a Windows NT 4.0 or Windows 2000 account, the job runs under the security context of the account that started SQL Server Agent. This should be your SQL Server service account that was created on the domain.

If the job is owned by a login belonging to the sysadmin fixed server role, the security context of the package defaults to the account used to start the local SQL Server Agent. If the server is registered using Windows Authentication, the owner of the job is the account of the SQL Server Agent. If the server is registered using SQL Server Authentication, the owner of the job is the SQL Server login.

If the job is owned by a login that is not a member of the sysadmin fixed server role, by default the package that is scheduled as a job step will not run. If the proxy account is enabled, the package runs under the context of the proxy account with the rights and permissions of that account. More information on the proxy account can be found in Chapter 9, "Introducing the SQL Server Agent Service."

Ownership conflicts can occur when the security context used for the package execution is not the same context as for the user who created the package. This can also be a problem if the user is the same but the permissions assigned to the user are different from the development to the production server. For instance, a developer may be responsible for creating the packages. When the developer creates the packages on the development server, the developer is a member of the system administrator role and the job is executed in the context of the SQL Server agent service account. When the package is moved to production, the user is no longer a system administrator. So the package now executes in the context of the proxy account. If the permissions assigned to the proxy account are not the same as those that are assigned to the SQL Server Agent service, a problem may arise. The following types of problems are possible with ownership conflicts:

- File paths specified in the package may not be visible in a different security context. That is, a different user executing the package may not have access to the same share points as the package creator. For example, the user who executes a query may not have the same mapped network drives as the creator. This would result in the user executing the package not having the same drive letters that the package is referencing. To guard against this problem, use Universal Naming Convention (UNC) names rather than file paths when specifying external files.

- The owner of the SQL Server Agent job who runs the package does not have permission to access the paths pointed to or connections made in the package. For example, the owner of the job may only have local server access. If this problem arises, view the security context of the job in SQL Server Enterprise Manager and log out of that instance of SQL Server. Then log back in to that same instance of SQL Server using the security context of the job and attempt to run the package.

- For packages that call COM components in Microsoft ActiveX scripts, the called components must exist on the same workstation on which the package is running. Also, the SQL Server Agent job account must have permission to run the job.

For all of these scenarios, copying external files used by the package onto the same server as the executing package may preempt package failures caused by ownership problems. In cases where COM components are used by a scheduled package, the called components must be loaded onto the same computer on which the instance of SQL Server is installed and SQL Server Agent must have permission to use the objects. Otherwise, the package will not execute successfully.

NOTE If you schedule a DTS package with a user password instead of an owner password, the scheduled job will not report a failure unless the package is set to fail on the first failed step. This is because the user does not have permission to read the package status after the package is run. This behavior will not occur if the package is scheduled using the owner password. It is always important to test your packages thoroughly before putting them into production.

Data Link Files

Microsoft Data Link (.udl) files are unencrypted text files you can use to encapsulate a connection string in a package. It is strongly recommended, from a security perspective, that you not include password information in a data link file, because the information would be visible to anyone viewing the text file. If you intend to use data link files to store a connection string, you should consider using Windows Authentication for the connection. Windows Authentication does not require login information to be placed in the data link file. It requires only a flag indicating that a trusted connection will be used. This connection method is secure for data link files. Do *not* use SQL Server Authentication for the connection. SQL Server Authentication requires you to place login and password information in the data link file. Therefore, this information would not be secure.

Connection Security

By default, the Windows Authentication or SQL Server Authentication information used to connect to a data source is saved along with the package. To control the persistence of the authentication information, use the Persist Security Info option in the Advanced Connection Properties dialogue box in DTS Designer. This option only exists for SQL Server connections. By default the value is set to 1 for all SQL Server connections. This sets the property on, which causes the authentication information to be persistent. There may be reasons for disabling the persistence of the Windows Authentication or SQL Server Authentication information in a package. For example, suppose you want to create a package that will be tested in a different environment from the one in which the package was created. In that case, you may not want the security information from the connections saved along with the package, because that information cannot be used to reconnect in the new environment. Make package connections with data links that resolve their settings from a data link file and use Windows Authentication for the connections. This increases package portability and maintains package security. To disable the persistence of authentication information, you should perform the following steps:

1. Open an existing package in the DTS Designer.
2. On the DTS Designer design sheet, double-click a connection.
3. In the Connection Properties dialogue box, click Advanced, which leads to the dialogue box shown in Figure 11.5.
4. When the value is set to 1, the connection security credentials are saved with the package. When the value is set to 0, the security information is not saved when the package is saved. Under the Value column, click the value for the Persist Security Info property.
5. Change the value to 0.

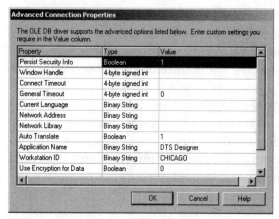

Figure 11.5   The Persist Security Info property controls the package connection security.

Best Practices

- Test your package execution multiple times on the test server before moving the package to production. Your test server and production server should be configured with the identical security context. This will help to ensure that you have worked out the bugs in the package execution.

- Know the job owner of your scheduled packages. The job owner determines the security context in which the package will execute. You will specifically need to know if the job owner is a member of the sysadmin server role.

- When using Windows Authentication for the connection security credentials, remember the security context of the package could change based on the user who is executing the package. If the package is scheduled, the security context depends on the owner of the scheduled job.

- Assign user and owner passwords to your packages to help prevent unwanted modification and execution of your package. If you assign an owner password, you are also required to supply a user password.

- Make sure your SQL Server Agent service account is a member of the local administrator's group. The security of context of this account is used in the execution of many scheduled jobs and could affect your DTS packages.

- If you are storing your packages in SQL Server, back up your MSDB database after you perform modifications to your package. Passwords do not prevent the deletion of your package.

- Use Windows Authentication for data link files. Data link files store the connection properties in a plain-text format. If the user credentials are stored in the file, anyone who has access to the text file could also have access to the security credentials used for connection to a database server. When you use Windows Authentication, the user information is not stored with the file.

REVIEW QUESTIONS

1. What are the core components of a DTS package?

2. What are the management tools available to create and modify packages?

3. What are the security concerns related to scheduling packages as SQL Server jobs?

4. Where can packages be stored?

5. What is the advantage to storing packages as a Visual Basic file?

CHAPTER

12

Exploring Analysis
Services Security

Analysis Server is used in conjunction with SQL Server 2000. Technically, it is not part of SQL Server; it is a separate product. Analysis Server extends the normal relational functionality of SQL Server to help optimize the analytical nature of a data warehouse. The purpose of the product is to give the end user a fast, easy to use, and intuitive look at the data needed for analysis.

It is common for normal transactional databases to suffer in either input or analytical performance. If you are running all analysis and all transaction processing against the same database, some of the decisions that you need to make will cause one of the two to suffer in performance. For example, indexes are created to speed up the retrieval of data. To achieve the performance increase for data retrieval, indexes also take up additional hard drive space. Indexes also slow down the inserts and updates that are sent to the database, because the database has to update or insert the data in the index as well as in the data in the table. When a user inputs data into the database, the database and the index both have to be updated. Analysis Server allows you to separate the two processes. Your transactional system can be optimized for modifications, while your reports and analysis work are performed against the data stored in Analysis Server databases.

Analysis Server has its own security model, which is separate from that of SQL Server. Analysis Server depends on Windows Authentication, and the security configuration for the online analytical processing (OLAP) databases and cubes depends on the Windows user and group account information. Because the data warehousing architecture is built on top of SQL Server, you have to first account for the security infrastructure of the data that you are transferring to Analysis Server. Then you have to account for the data as it is stored in the OLAP databases.

The focus of this book is on security. If you are just starting out with SQL Server Analysis Services, you should refer to *Microsoft SQL Server 2000 Analysis Services Step by Step* by Microsoft Press, 2001.

This chapter first introduces Analysis Server. This portion of the chapter defines the components that make up Analysis Server and defines some key terms, because the terminology is very different from a normal relational database environment. The chapter then moves to a comparison of data warehousing and OLAP. The terms *data warehousing* and *OLAP* are often used interchangeably, but are actually two separate layers in Analysis Server architecture.

The chapter then introduces an overview to the components of an OLAP cube, which are the multidimensional objects used to store OLAP data. The chapter next describes the storage options for OLAP cubes and then addresses processing of OLAP cubes. Finally, this chapter tackles the security concerns of Analysis Server. This product has its own security model, which is different from the model we have introduced for SQL Server so far. The security model of Analysis Server is not complicated, but because it is different from the rest of SQL Server security, it often adds some complication.

Analysis Server

Analysis Server is the service component of SQL Server 2000 Analysis Services. It is specifically designed to create and maintain multidimensional data structures and provide multidimensional data in response to client queries. This allows for the analysis of data on multiple axes. As an example you could easily view the total invoices for a customer by the date of the invoice, the location of the invoice, and the products on the invoice. The data is summarized into levels, so when viewing the invoices by time you could also view the total amount of invoices for a year, quarter, month, or day. In multidimensional data structures you also can define the dimensions that you want to analyze and the level at which you want to view the data (such as year, quarter, month, and day.) The calculations are run at a scheduled interval so users are not waiting for the totals to calculate each time they change levels or dimensions. In contrast, a database table stores data in a two-dimensional format. The table allows for the retrieval and storage of data based on columns and rows. A cube can store and retrieve data in more dimensions. Multidimensional structures allow for flexible, fast, and summarized retrieval of data.

Analysis Server is a means of separating your transactional data from your analytical data to decrease the contention for data access. This can also be used as a security strategy. If you have users that just need access to the data for analytical purposes, they no longer need access to the transactional processing system. Similarly, if you have users that don't need access to the analysis data, you don't have to give them access to the OLAP databases.

Analysis services are made up of two main components: Microsoft online analytical processing (OLAP) databases and the data mining tool. The following sections describe the role of each of these components. Then key terms Analysis Server are defined to provide an introduction to the terminology of the product and lay a foundation for the security concerns addressed later in the chapter.

OLAP Databases

OLAP databases provide an analytical alternative to the standard relational database architecture. The purposes when designing an OLAP database are to provide fast query response time, flexible viewing options, and multidimensional analysis. The following are the characteristics of an OLAP database:

- They are denormalized to facilitate fast user queries.
- They have a robust engine to provide fast numeric analysis.
- They are intuitive to users.
- They are separate from the transactional processing system, which can provide an additional layer of security.

OLAP databases are multidimensional. They use cubes to allow for the viewing of numeric data summarized by varying characteristics. Cubes are described in greater detail later in this chapter in the section *Introduction to Cubes.*

OLAP databases are excellent for applications that revolve around an analytical process. The following applications are good candidates for OLAP databases:

- Financial reporting applications
- Sales/Marketing analysis applications
- Executive Information Systems
- Statistical analysis packages
- Any application that requires heavy calculations for analytical purposes

Data Mining

Data mining is the process of finding meaningful patterns from large amounts of data. You configure data mining models to search for the patterns within your data. This information could be used for historical analysis and for predicting future outcomes. You start with data mining by creating a model.

A *data mining model* is a virtual structure that represents the grouping and predictive analysis of relational or multidimensional data. In many aspects, the structure of a data mining model resembles the structure of a database table. However, while a database table represents a collection of records, or a record set, a data mining model represents an interpretation of records as rules and patterns composed of statistical information, referred to as cases. The structure of the data mining model represents the case set that defines the data mining model, while the data stored represents the rules and patterns learned from processing case data.

The data mining model of SQL Server is also easy to use. The data mining discovery process analyzes the data, and users don't have to perform all of the analysis. This allows users to see more meaningful angles of their data without having full access to all of the data that the data mining model is analyzing. Users can see the results of the data analysis without requiring permission to all of the data that is used to build the final analysis. This can be used to allow users to perform the data analysis necessary without decreasing the security of the data used for the analysis.

Microsoft supports two different techniques (algorithms) for data mining: Microsoft Clustering and Microsoft Decision Trees. The following sections describe these options.

Microsoft Clustering

The Microsoft Clustering algorithm is an expectation method that uses iterative refinement techniques to group records into clusters that exhibit similar, predictable characteristics. Often these characteristics may be hidden or nonintuitive. This information can be used to determine the likelihood of a future action based on the clustering criteria.

Microsoft Decision Trees

The Microsoft Decision Trees algorithm is based on the notion of classification. The decision tree is used to display a predictable model. You can use some of the columns to determine the statistical probability of a known result. For instance, if you had a customer table and the ability to track outstanding debt, you could use the decision tree to supply columns of the customer table to the decision tree. The Decision Tree would analyze each of the columns to determine which one is the largest factor in the outstanding debt. With this you could determine whether information such as income, location, or gender has the largest effect on outstanding debt. This provides a statistical analysis that is unavailable anywhere else in SQL Server.

The Decision Tree algorithm builds a tree that predicts the value of a column based on the remaining columns in the set of data. Therefore, each node in the tree represents a particular case for a column. The decision on where to place this node is made by the algorithm, and a node at a different depth than its siblings may represent different cases of each column. The Microsoft Decision Tree builds a hierarchical structure that you can navigate through to see the predicted results The tree is displayed in a user-friendly interface that allows for navigation up and down the tree as shown in Figure 12.1.

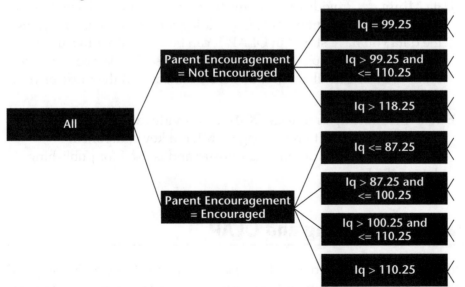

Figure 12.1 The Microsoft Decision Tree creates a hierarchy of predicted results that can be used to determine most likely causes of your database actions.

Key Terms

Analysis Server has a very different design from SQL Server. With the new options there is also a new set of terms that have to be defined to help explain the role of this product and its features. The following list of terms provides a background of Analysis Server and its components:

Analysis Manager.   Provides a graphical user interface for accessing the analysis services, such as building cubes, managing security, and browsing data sources. This is the main utility for configuration and management of Analysis Server.

Data Warehousing Framework.   Consists of a set of components and APIs that implement SQL Server's data warehousing features.

Data Transformation Services (DTS).   Assists in loading and transforming data into a data mart or data warehouse. DTS consists of an Import Wizard and an Export Wizard that allow for movement of data as well as data transformation. DTS also provides the DTS Designer to customize existing packages and create new complex DTS packages. DTS is covered in more depth in Chapter 11, "Managing Data Transformation Services."

Repository.   Contains a number of interfaces, database schema models, and predefined data transformations to fit into the Data Warehousing Framework. Because data transformations occur on a regular basis, their definitions can be stored for reuse.

Data Mining.   Provides algorithms for defining and implementing multidimensional cubes. The data mining tool is useful in analyzing the data you have stored in OLAP. It can be used either to cluster your data into groups that are similar or to use the Decision Tree to build a hierarchichal analysis structure to help find the cause of your predicted model.

Extensible Markup Language (XML).   Provides a standard formatting and data representation language. XML is a key component of application-to-application data transfer and is used for publishing data to the Internet.

Data Warehousing and OLAP

Although sometimes used interchangeably, the terms data warehousing and online analytical processing (OLAP) apply to different components of systems often referred to as decision support systems or business intelligence systems. Components of these types of systems include databases and applications that provide the tools that analysts need to support organizational decision-making.

A *data warehouse* is a database containing data that usually represents the business history of an organization. This historical data is used for analysis that supports business decisions at many levels, from strategic planning to performance evaluation of a discrete organizational unit. Data in a data warehouse is organized to support analysis rather than to process real-time transactions as in online transaction processing systems (OLTP).

Data Warehouse Design

Before you can create an OLAP database and define cubes to navigate through your data, you must first supply the source for the OLAP database. The source is generally a data warehouse. The key to making your OLAP database efficient is the design of your data warehouse. Although a data warehouse is referred to as a single entity, it is common to have multiple fact tables for a single data warehouse and multiple data warehouses for your entire organization. Although these data warehouses are managed separately, they are commonly referred to as a single entity.

If is not configured correctly, the Analysis Services will never work correctly or efficiently for you. This book focuses on security and therefore the design topics presented here are for introductory purposes only. For more information on designing your data warehouse, you should read The *Data Warehouse Lifecycle Toolkit: Expert Methods for Designing, Developing, and Deploying Data Warehouses* (John Wiley & Sons, 1998).

Your data warehouse should have the following characteristics:

- The data should be organized around subject areas. These areas should match the needs or structure of your organization. For example, you may have a sales data warehouse and a legal analysis data warehouse that use different data. Often, these smaller subsets of data that are organized by subject areas are referred to as *data marts.* The data from the data marts can then be rolled up (summarized) into a single data warehouse.

- The data should be nonvolatile and mass loaded. It is normal for a data warehouse to be truncated and reloaded every evening or every week. The analysis expectations should match the requirements of the database load.

- The data should be in a format that is easily understood. Many data warehouse client applications provide direct access to the data, as it is formatted, in a data warehouse. You should avoid meaningless codes for descriptive fields. For example, a region may be better displayed to a user as North instead of as a meaningless code such as RN. A meaningless code is a representation of data that has no meaning to the end user. Codes are appropriate in a data warehouse when they are the common term used by the end user.

■ The data should provide the means for analysis at multiple levels of granularity. For instance, if you are tracking the sales of your organization, you may want to track the date and time of the transaction. Your data warehouse should provide means for users to analyze data at the year, quarter, month, and day levels.

Now that we have addressed some of the characteristics of the data in your data warehouse, let's move to the details of the design process. This section will first introduce the star schema, describe the fact table and its components, and finally describe the dimension table characteristics.

Star Schema

The data warehouse is typically structured into what is referred to as a *star schema*. A star schema includes the fact table and multiple dimension tables. OLAP cubes use the star schema as its data source. The following characteristics help define the star schema structure:

■ The center of the star is the *fact table*. The fact table keeps the instances of the action you are tracking. For instance, if you were tracking sales entries to the invoice level, the fact table would have one record for each invoice.

■ The points of the star are the *dimension tables*. These tables are used to describe the information that is stored in the fact table. Each of the dimension tables stores information that describes a fact. If the fact is a sales action, the dimension tables could be customers, inventory, time, and location. Each of the dimension tables has a primary key. That column is also in the fact table as a foreign key. The dimension tables are directly related to the fact table. The dimension tables are not related to each other. Each of them describes a portion of the fact.

■ When you create a dimension table that has another table joined to it that is not the fact table, you have created a *snowflake schema*. It is called a snowflake because the tables no longer represent the star schema and the points extend out to include more tables. The details about the action you are monitoring may now be two or more tables away from the fact table. This increases the amount of joins necessary to retrieve data and will most likely slow performance.

Fact Table

Each data warehouse or data mart includes one or more fact tables. Central to a star or snowflake schema, a fact table captures the data that measures the organization's business operations. A fact table might contain business sales events such as cash register transactions or the contributions and expenditures of a nonprofit organization. Fact tables usually contain large numbers of rows, sometimes in the hundreds of millions of records when they contain one or more years of history for a large organization.

A key characteristic of a fact table is that it contains numerical data that can be summarized to provide information about the history of the organization. Each row of the fact table has columns that are foreign keys to each of the dimension table's primary keys. The fact table also includes a multipart index that contains as foreign keys the primary keys of related dimension tables, which contain the attributes of the fact records. Fact tables should not contain descriptive information or any data other than the numerical measurement fields and the index fields that relate the facts to corresponding entries in the dimension tables.

The most useful measures to include in a fact table are numbers that are additive. Additive measures allow obtaining summary information by adding various quantities of the measure, such as the sales of a specific item at a group of stores for a particular time period. Nonadditive measures, such as inventory quantity-on-hand values, can also be used in fact tables.

When designing a fact table, the most important step is to identify the granularity of the table. Microsoft most commonly refers to the granularity as *fact table grain*. The grain is not a configuration option. It is a statement of the level of detail that you want to track. You must be familiar with the user analysis needs to choose an appropriate grain. For instance, if you owned a retail store you could have the option of storing data by an invoice or a line item within the invoice. You should have many more line items than invoices. If you choose to define your grain at the line item level, you should be prepared to take the additional storage. You should only store data at the level that is appropriate for user analysis. If there is no analysis at the line item level, then don't store data to that level of detail. When you are choosing the grain for your fact table, you should consider these items:

- You will not be able to analyze data at any detail greater than your grain. If you choose the grain at the invoice level, you will not have access to the line item information.

- Your grain should match the level of detail required by the users analysis specifications. Don't store data at a more detailed level than needed by the users.

- The measures should be consistent with the grain. Your comparative values should identify your grain (fact) of the fact table. For instance, you should not store an invoice total price in a fact table that is tracking information at the line item level. It would be more appropriate to define measures specific to the line item. This could include quantity or unit price.

- The fact table grain is the most important decision you will make pertaining to the amount of hard drive space the data warehouse absorbs. Take care in choosing the level of data you need to track. The last level of detail is generally the level that adds the most data. For example, if you choose to store data at the day-by-day level instead of at the monthly level, you will increase your number of members of the bottom level from 12 (months) to 365 (days) per year.

Dimension Tables

Dimension tables surround the fact table. They are the points of the star schema created with your data warehouse design. In a star schema, each of the dimension tables is directly related to the fact table. Dimension tables are descriptive in nature and provide the details of each of the facts described by the fact table.

For example, if you create a data warehouse to track the sales of your products, the fact table would keep a row to represent each of the sales. The fact table would have columns that are foreign keys to the primary keys in the dimension tables. The dimension tables provide the descriptions and details for each of the sales.

Some common dimension tables you may want to consider to track a sale would include the customer who purchased the product, the time of the sale, the location of the sale, the salesperson who sold the product, and the product that was sold. Each of these details would be stored in its own dimension table. The primary key of each of these dimension tables would also be a column in the fact table as the primary key. The fact table simply combines the details for a specific sale. The characteristics of dimension tables are as follows:

- They are used as the source for cube dimensions.

- They provide the context or description of the information stored in the fact table.

- They typically have far fewer records than the fact table.
- They create hierarchies. For instance, a time dimension table could have separate columns to represent yearly, quarterly, monthly, and daily data.

Introduction to Cubes

The cube is the very core of OLAP technology. A *cube* is a set of data that is a subset or summarization of the data source. In most cases this data source is from the data warehouse that you have created. The data source for a single cube is generally a single fact table from the source data warehouse. Cubes are made up of dimensions and measures. Although dimensions and measures are different objects from the dimension tables and measures that were defined in the data warehouse section, they generally correlate to each other. Dimensions and measures will be further defined in the next section. This section of the chapter defines an overview to the cube structure. Next, the section introduces the storage options for cubes. Finally, this section introduces the processing options for cubes.

A cube is a data structure that is interfaced from a client application. The cube structure is multidimensional in nature. It is often compared to a spreadsheet pivot table. Client applications interface with the cube to view the data they need to analyze. The client applications use the pivot table service to interact with the OLAP databases. The pivot table service can be used with Microsoft Office 2000 or later. The pivot table service can also be implemented from the pivot table control, which is an ActiveX control. This control allows for Web access to OLAP databases.

Excel and the Web Pivot control are examples of the Microsoft clients that are available to interface with cubes. These front-end applications spare the user from having to write language-based queries. Additionally, users who have Analysis Manager installed on their machines can use the Cube Browser of Analysis Manager to view the data. The cubes store summary information and precalculated data. The data can be easily navigated, similar to a pivot table, as shown in Figure 12.2.

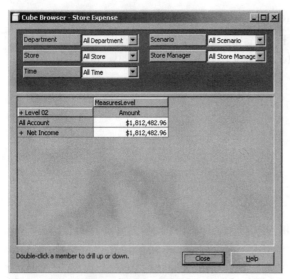

Figure 12.2 The Cube Browser is an easy tool for browsing through cube data. You can use the drop-down boxes to drill up and down through the dimensions of your cube.

The precalculated data is referred to as an *aggregation*. The aggregations are saved and can easily be retrieved by the users. This creates a quick response time for the end user. The aggregations are created for a cube before end users access it. An Analysis Server can support many different cubes, such as a cube for sales, a cube for inventory, and a cube for customers.

Every cube has a schema, which is the set of joined tables in the data warehouse from which the cube draws its source data. The central table in the schema is the fact table, which is the source from which the cube draws its measures. The other tables are dimension tables—the sources of the cube's dimensions.

A cube is defined by the measures and dimensions that it contains. Measures are comparative additive values that will be used for the detailed analysis. The dimensions are the descriptive information about the measures. For example, a cube for sales analysis may include the measures Item_Sale_Price and Item_Cost and the dimensions Store_Location, Product_Line, and Fiscal_Year. This cube enables users to separate Item_Sale_Price and Item_Cost into various categories by Store_Location, Product_Line, and Fiscal_Year.

Each cube dimension can contain a hierarchy of levels to specify the categorical breakdown available to users. For example, a Store_Location dimension may include the level hierarchy: Continent, Country, Region, State_Province, City, Store_Number. Each level in a dimension is of finer granularity than its parent. For example, continents contain countries, and states or provinces contain cities. Similarly, the hierarchy of the Fiscal_Year dimension includes the levels Year, Quarter, Month, and Day. When a user is moving to a more detailed level, the process is referred to as *drilling down*. When the user accesses a level that is less detailed or up in the hierarchy, the process is referred to as *drilling up*.

Dimension levels are a powerful data modeling tool, because they allow users to ask questions at a high level and then expand a dimension hierarchy to reveal more detail. For example, a user starts by asking to see Item_Cost values of products for the past three fiscal years. The end user may notice that 1998 Item_Cost values are higher than those in other years. Expanding the Fiscal_Year dimension to the Month level, the user sees that Item_Cost values were especially high in the months January and August. The user may then explore levels of the Store_Location dimension to see if a particular region contributed significantly to the high Item_Cost values or may expand into the Product_Line dimension to see if Item_Cost values were high for a particular product group or product. For more information about defining different types of dimensions and measures, refer to SQL Server Books Online

Cube Storage

Analysis Services offers three storage modes of cubes. Your data retrieval performance depends on the method in which you choose to store the data. All security access to the cubes is configured through Analysis Services. The storage option you choose does not change your options for security configuration. The following items describe your three options and the advantages and disadvantages of each. After the storage options are defined, this section introduces cube partitions and virtual cubes.

Multidimensional OLAP (MOLAP).   This option stores the underlying data for a cube along with aggregation data in a multidimensional structure. MOLAP storage provides the best query response time. Because all of the data used to create the cube is duplicated from the data source, MOLAP is generally the most expensive relative to hard drive space.

Relational OLAP (ROLAP).   This option stores underlying data for a cube along with the aggregation data in a relational database. ROLAP storage enables you to take advantage of your investment in relational technology and enterprise data management tools. ROLAP also optimizes the use of data storage by decreasing the amount of data that has to be duplicated.

Hybrid OLAP (HOLAP).   This option stores the underlying data for a cube in a relational database, and the aggregation data is stored in a high-performance multidimensional structure. HOLAP storage offers the benefits of MOLAP for aggregations without necessitating duplication of the underlying detail data. This is a mix between MOLAP and ROLAP.

NOTE **MOLAP is noticeably faster than the other storage options. You should consider investing in the drive space necessary to store your frequently accessed data in MOLAP. You can partition a cube into separate physical sections. Each partition can be stored in a different mode, in a different physical location, and with a level of aggregations appropriate to the data in the partition. The result is that you can fine-tune the performance and data management characteristics of your system. For example, in many analysis environments the current year is queried more often than previous years. You could use partitions to store the current year's data in MOLAP in one partition and another partition to store all other years in HOLAP. Partitioning allows you to take advantage of the speed of MOLAP without investing drive space for duplication of all of your data.**

NOTE **Cube partitioning is only available in the Enterprise Edition of Analysis Server.**

A virtual cube is a combination of multiple cubes in one logical cube, somewhat like a relational database view that combines other views and tables. When you create a virtual cube, you select measures and dimensions from the consolidated set of dimensions and measures in the underlying component cubes. Users see the virtual cube as a single cube. A virtual cube can also be based on a single cube to expose only selected subsets of its measures and dimensions. Because virtual cubes store only their definitions and not the data of their component cubes, they require virtually no physical storage space. You can use virtual cubes to create combinations and variants of existing cubes without using significant additional storage.

A virtual cube can provide a valuable security function by limiting the access of some users when viewing the underlying cubes. If some of a cube's information is sensitive and not suitable for all users, you can create a virtual cube from the existing cube and omit the sensitive information.

Cube Processing

When you process a cube, the aggregations designed for the cube are calculated and the cube is loaded with the calculated aggregations and data. Processing a cube involves reading the dimension tables to populate the levels with members from the actual data, reading the fact table, calculating specified aggregations, and storing the results in the cube. After a cube has been processed, users can query it.

After one of the following actions occurs, the cube will be unavailable until you process it:

- Building the cube and designing its storage options and aggregations
- Changing the cube's structure (measures, dimensions, and so on) and saving the changes to the cube
- Changing the structure of a shared dimension used in the cube
- Changing the data in the underlying source table

When you process the cube, you have the option of performing a Full Process, an Incremental Update, or a Refresh Data. Each of these options is appropriate for different situations. You should look at the modification that has occurred to the structure or data of the cube to determine which level of processing is most appropriate. The following sections introduce each option.

A *Full Process* performs a complete load of the cube. All dimension and fact table data is read and all specified aggregations are calculated. You must process a cube with the Full Process option when its structure is new or when the cube, its dimensions, or its measures have undergone structural changes.

An *Incremental Update* is appropriate when new data is to be added to a cube, but existing data has not changed and the cube structure remains the same. The Incremental Update option adds new data and updates aggregations. An Incremental Update does not affect the existing data that has already been processed. It usually requires significantly less time than the Full Process option. An Incremental Update can be performed while users continue to query the cube; after the update is complete, users have access to the additional data without having to disconnect and reconnect.

The *Refresh Data* option causes a cube's data to be cleared and reloaded and its aggregations recalculated. This option is appropriate when the underlying data has changed but the cube's structure remains the same. The Refresh Data option can be performed while users query the cube; after the refresh has completed, users have access to the updated data without having to disconnect and reconnect.

OLAP Security

After you have designed your data warehouse and OLAP solution, you need to account for the security structure of Analysis Server. The security model used by Analysis Server is quite different from the options you have in SQL Server 2000. In this section of the chapter, administrator security is introduced first; then you are introduced to securing user authentication with Analysis Server.

Next, the section addresses roles. Two types of roles exist in Analysis Server: cube and database roles. After this section, you will know the differences between the two and when to use one rather than the other. Finally, this chapter defines dimension and cell security options.

Administrator Security

Your administrator security defines who can configure and administer your Analysis Server. You should know how to add administrators and the details of managing your administrators group.

Administration security is integrated with Windows Authentication. You do not have the option of using SQL Server Authentication. All administrative access to Analysis Server is configured through Active Directory. The Analysis Manager tool does not have an administrative configuration option. When you install Analysis Server services, an OLAP Administrators group is added to your machine. OLAP Administrators is a local group. Any member of this group has full access to configure and administer your Analysis Server. You should perform the following steps to add an administrator to the OLAP Administrators group:

1. Open Active Directory Users and Computers.
2. Click to expand your domain.
3. Click to expand the Users container.
4. Right-click OLAP Administrators and select Properties.
5. Click the Members tab and select a user, as shown in Figure 12.3.
6. Click Add to add the new administrator.
7. When you have added all administrators, click the OK button to close the OLAP Administrators Properties dialogue box.

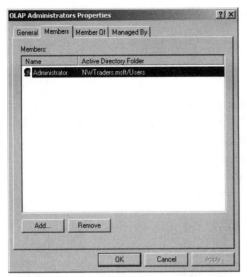

Figure 12.3   Members of the OLAP Administrators group can fully administer your Analysis Server.

The administrative security model of Analysis Server is not very detailed, but you should keep the following considerations in mind:

- The user account that was used to install Analysis Server is automatically part of the OLAP Administrators group.
- All administrators are given the same privileges.
- Analysis Server security depends on Windows Authentication.
- Administrators have full access when connecting through Analysis Manager or any other client.

User Authentication Security

Users can connect to Analysis Server through two different means. The client can either directly connect to Analysis Server or the client can use Internet Information Server (IIS) to connect to the server. A *direct connection* is made when the user attempts to connect to an Analysis Server by interfacing without using a middle tier. The client access completely depends on Windows Authentication. You don't have a choice to supply anything else. If your connection string offers a username and password that is not the current Windows login information, the connection string is ignored. If the user has not logged on to the Windows domain, the user will not have access to Analysis Server.

A *connection is made through IIS* when the user request is first made to the IIS server using an HTTP request. When the user connects through IIS, Analysis Server relies on the authentication of the Web server. If the user connection to IIS is unsuccessful, then binding to Analysis Server fails. IIS has several different authentication modes, which are addressed in more detail in Chapter 15, "Managing Internet Security."

Roles

Database roles in Analysis Server are not the same objects as database roles in SQL Server. Both types of roles are similar in that they group users. However, Analysis Server database roles can only have Windows 2000 users and groups as members. For the remainder of this section, the context of roles is the Analysis Server. Roles in Analysis Server have the following characteristics:

- Roles can be created at the database and cube levels.

- Roles are used to grant Windows users and groups access to a database or cube. The following section details the differences between the two types of roles.

- Roles must be manually created. There are no default database or cube roles.

- Roles that are created at the cube level are automatically added at the database level. All roles that are configured for a cube can also be used with other cubes in the same OLAP database.

- Roles are database specific. You cannot use the same role for multiple databases. The role is created as an object within the database, making it inaccessible to other OLAP databases.

Database Roles

Database roles give Windows users and groups access to an OLAP database. Within the Database Role Manager utility, you can specify the following properties.

- The Role name is the identifier for the role. It can be up to 50 characters in length. This name can't be changed after the role is created. The only option for changing names is removing the role and recreating it.

- The Enforce On property determines where the roles should be enforced. You can set a role to be enforced at the server or client level. The default is to enforce the role at the client. Client enforcement increases the performance by decreasing the number of round trips to the server. Server enforcement, while slower, is more secure because it guarantees that the client checks the current server settings.

- The Membership adds the Windows users and groups that will be part of the role.

- The Cubes option tab identifies the cubes at which this role is assigned.

- The Mining Models tab identifies the data mining models at which this role is defined.

- The Dimensions tab restricts access to specific dimensions and their members. This section only displays shared dimensions. Although this setting allows you to set security at a very granular level, it also increases the complexity to your security configuration. Whenever possible, it is best to limit your security to the cube level.

NOTE If you need to limit access to specific dimensions, consider creating virtual cubes to assist with security. When you create the virtual cube, don't include the dimensions that you need to restrict access to. Assign the role to the virtual cube and not the regular cube. By using this strategy, virtual cubes can assist you in decreasing the administrative overhead of security management. Virtual cubes are discussed in the *Introduction to Cubes* section earlier in this chapter.

Database roles are created and managed through Analysis Manager. You should perform the following steps to create a new database role:

1. Open Analysis Manager.

2. Expand your server.

3. Expand the database for which you want to create the role.

4. Right-click Database Roles and choose Manage Roles. The Database Role Manager dialogue box should appear as shown in Figure 12.4.

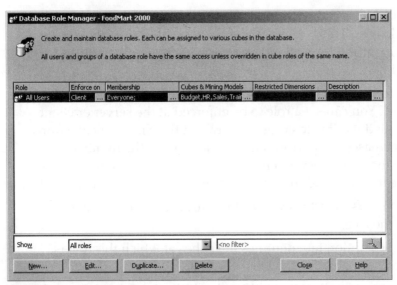

Figure 12.4 The Database Role Manager dialogue box creates and manages OLAP database roles.

5. Click New to create a new role, and then supply the name and other properties of the role.

6. Click the OK button to create the new role.

Cube Roles

The purpose of the cube role is to define user and group access to a cube. Cube roles can be created for normal or virtual cubes. The process of creating cube roles is similar to that of creating database roles. You need to start the role creation configuration process from the cube instead of the database. The dialogue box is similar, and most of the properties are the same. The following additional properties define a cube role:

- Cell security can be defined from a cube role. More information on cell security is found in the next section *Dimension and Cell Security.*

- Cube roles allow you to define drillthrough, cube linking, and SQL query permissions. Drillthrough allows users of this role to drill through the cube. Drillthrough is the process of requesting data at a more detailed level of the cube and the request being processed by the source data warehouse database. Cube linking allows role members to link to this cube from a remote machine. Linking provides a mechanism to store and access cubes across multiple servers. SQL query permissions allow the cube to be queried via Transact-SQL statements.

- The Cube Role Manager can be used to define security for both private and shared dimensions. Private dimensions can only be used in the cube in which they are created. All cubes in an OLAP database can access shared dimensions. Shared dimensions are then managed once for all cubes that use them. Roles created and modified at the database level only allow for security control over shared dimensions.

Dimension and Cell Security

After you have defined the security model for your OLAP databases and cubes, you have the choice of implementing dimension and cell security options. Dimensions and cells are more granular than databases and cubes, and therefore setting security at this granular level adds complexity to your system. You should document all cases in which you define additional security options (dimension or cell.) The following sections detail the options you have available through dimension and cell security.

Dimension Security

Dimension security can be implemented as a property of either a database role or a cube role. Therefore the property is viewed through the role editor for either a database or cube. The dimension options are more detailed than that of cube security and are modified through the Custom Dimension Security dialogue box as shown in Figure 12.5. The following options are available from the Custom Dimension Security dialogue box:

- Select Visible Levels determines the top and bottom levels that will appear for the members of the role. When a dimension is defined, you configure the levels at which the dimension can be analyzed. For instance, a time dimension may include year, quarter, month, and day as levels. The visible levels security option allows you to determine what appears as the top and bottom levels to the members of this role. To extend the example, you could configure this role to see quarter as the top level and month as the bottom level.

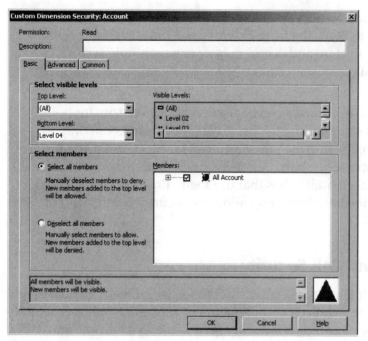

Figure 12.5 The Custom Dimension Security dialogue box controls the levels and members that a role can access.

- Select Members limits the members that can be viewed from the dimension of the cube. A member is the value of a level. For our time example, the members of year may be 1997, 1998, 1999, 2000, and 2001. In this case you could further restrict this role to only see the member 2001. Although this option is beneficial in some cases, member-level security can be time-consuming because of the number of members you may have to account for.

- The MDX builder is available from the advanced tab. You will notice that as you add dimension and member-level security options the multidimensional expressions (MDX) statements are being built for you.

NOTE MDX is the statement language used to query data from your cubes. It is multidimensional in nature, which provides additional flexibility over Transact-SQL. More information about MDX can be found in SQL Server Books Online.

- Visual Totals is available from the Common tab and affects the way that the data is calculated. By default, all member values are calculated regardless of whether the role can view the member information. When you enable this setting the members that are not visible are not included in your aggregation.

- Default Member is also available from the Common tab. This setting configures the default member for this role. If the user doesn't specify a member, the default member will be displayed automatically.

Cell Security

Cell-level security is the most granular level available for security configuration. The cell security is configured through the Cells tab in the Edit a Cube Role dialogue box as shown in Figure 12.6. There are three types of cell security: Read permission, Read Contingent permission, and Read/Write permission. The following items define these permission options:

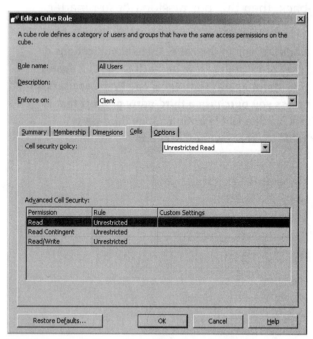

Figure 12.6 Cell security is the most detailed level of security available in Analysis Server. If you change the default values, document the changes you implement to assist in troubleshooting later.

- *Read permission* is used to determine the cells that are viewable by this role. The valid settings are Unrestricted, Fully Restricted, and Custom. Unrestricted leaves the cells with no security restrictions. All data can be viewed by the users. Fully Restricted denies access to all cells. Custom allows you to write an MDX statement to determine the cells that are viewable.

- *Read Contingent permission* has the same options for configuration as the Read permission. Read Contingent tells Analysis Server to check the access to the source cells of the cell you are trying to view. If you have access to the source cells you will be able to view the cell. If you don't have access to the source cells you are restricted from access to the target cell. A *source cell* is a piece of data that is stored directly from a fact or dimension table. A *target cell* is a calculated cell based on one or more source cells, and possibly other mathematical equations.

- *Read/Write permission* is used to determine whether the role can read and write to the cube. This depends on whether the cube was first enabled for write-back. If the cube that the cell resides in is not configured for write-back, then this permission doesn't matter.

NOTE *Write-back* allows modifications to the cube. These modifications do not update the data source; they are stored in a write-back table. This feature must also be supported by your client application. Excel and Web browsers do not support write-back; so unless you purchase a third-party product that is write-back enabled, write-back is not a viable option. Many third-party vendors use the write-back table to create what-if scenarios.

Best Practices

- Spend an appropriate amount of time designing your data warehouse. Your design is the key to an efficient OLAP database.

- Define an appropriate level of grain for your fact table. An overly detailed grain results in an overload of data, which results in the use of more hard drive space and slower response times. However, if you don't choose the grain at a level that is detailed enough, the users won't have access to the data they need to analyze. Your grain should match user analysis requirements.

- Strive to design a star schema. All of the dimension tables should be one step away from the fact table. This is not possible in all cases, but you should strive to make it happen where possible.

- Use MOLAP for your cube storage. MOLAP is fast and efficient for user queries. MOLAP requires more drive space, so plan your hardware accordingly. The other storage options should be used when lack of drive space is an issue.

- Create partitions to separate your data that is most often queried. Partitions allow you to physically separate your data so that queries only have to traverse the data that is meant for them.

- Try to set security options at the database and cube level. Dimension and cell-level security increase the complexity and are not appropriate for most cases. Keep in mind that the more complex your security design is, the tougher it will be to troubleshoot when you have problems.

- Use virtual cubes to limit user access to dimensions. Virtual cubes can be a subset of a cube. If you don't want a role to see certain dimensions, create a virtual cube that does not include the dimension you want to hide. You should then give the role access to the virtual cube instead of the regular cube.

- Limit access to the OLAP Administrators group. All members of this group have full access to everything within Analysis Server. There are no multiple levels of administration.

REVIEW QUESTIONS

1. What are the core components of Analysis Server?

2. What is the purpose of data mining?

3. What is the difference between a data warehouse and OLAP?

4. Why should you use a star schema instead of a snowflake schema when designing your data warehouse?

5. Why is the grain of the fact table so important?

6. What is a cube?

7. What are the differences between ROLAP and MOLAP?

8. Why should you consider partitions when designing a cube?

9. At what levels can roles be defined in Analysis Server?

10. What are the advantages and disadvantages of dimension-level and cell-level security?

Managing Current Connections

The current connections to your SQL Server affect the stability and performance of your server. Every connection is given its own execution context, which is a section of memory dedicated for the connection to exercise its statements. SQL Server manages these connections for you automatically. Each transaction performed by a connection is also managed by the transaction log-writing architecture of SQL Server. Within Enterprise Manager you can use the Current Activity window to view and manage the current connections to your server. You can also use Enterprise Manager to view the locks that have been set by SQL Server to avoid concurrency problems. In most cases the default methods of managing transactions are appropriate. This chapter focuses on the architecture that SQL Server uses to manage current user connections.

This chapter first tackles security concerns related to current activity. This topic has to be discussed first because, when addressing current activity, it is more important to know what is not available to you than to understand the features that are available. The chapter next provides a transaction log overview. The transaction log is used to write transactions before they are written to the data files. Within this section the checkpoint process and the Recovery models of SQL Server are introduced, among other architecture issues. The chapter then moves to a description of SQL Server's concurrency architecture, specifically the locking methods that are used to protect data from being modified by multiple users at the same time. The integrity of your data depends on the concurrency architecture of SQL Server. Locking is SQL Server's method of protecting the data that a user is modifying.

The chapter then addresses the options for monitoring the current activity of your SQL Server. This section includes the options that are available in Enterprise Manager as well as the system-stored procedures that can be used for monitoring. Throughout this chapter, the architecture is described to help explain the current activity options in SQL Server. Additionally, the chapter identifies the items that are not available in SQL Server 2000. Knowing what is not available is beneficial in planning and setting expectations for the system. Effective security management depends on knowing what is not available as well as the features that are available. After you read this chapter you will have a clear understanding of the transaction log architecture of SQL Server as well as the options you have for controlling the current connections on your SQL Server.

Security Concerns

When addressing the current activity of your SQL Server, it is important to note that most of your security considerations are set up for in the design and planning phase. You don't have as much control as you may like. You should know the architecture and what the system can do as you set your expectations. The following security considerations should be evaluated with regard to the current activity of SQL Server:

- Without a third-party utility you can't view the logical structure of the transaction log. Although you can see the files that are in use, you can't view the user transactions in the order in which they are logically written in the log. But several third-party products enable you to analyze the log. More information on some of these products can be found in Appendix B, "Third-Party SQL Server Security Management Tools." The fact that you can't directly view the transaction log is a security concern more from the standpoint of what you can't do than what you can do. For example, if a user performs a transaction that updates records to values that are incorrect, you have no recourse for rolling back that transaction if the transaction has already been committed to the log. Instead you have to manually change the data back or restore your database to the time just before the faulty transaction occurred.

- The locking architecture of SQL Server enforces security by preventing users from updating data that is currently in use by another user. The default locking mechanisms of SQL Server are appropriate for most cases. You should consider manually overriding the locking options only when you are not getting the results you want. To avoid deadlocks you should access the tables of your database in the same order for all transactions. For example, if you have customers, sales, and inventory tables on your system, you should determine the order in which all transactions should interact with the tables. If all transactions interact with tables in the same order, you will minimize locking problems with your data. Deadlocks are described in more depth later in this chapter in the *Locking Architecture* section.

- You can use the Current Activity window of Enterprise Manager to view current processes and connections. Doing so can be valuable in verifying user connections that are not wanted on the system. You can also send a message to a user or kill a user process to disconnect a user from a resource. The process of killing a user process is described later in this chapter in the *Current Activity* section.

- When the user connected to SQL Server is part of a group that has been granted access to SQL Server, the name that appears in Enterprise Manager is the group name. If you want to track information back to the Windows account, you will need to use the SQL Profiler utility. More information on SQL Profiler can be found in Chapter 14, "Creating an Audit Policy."

- Sp_who, sp_lock and KILL Transact-SQL statements can be used to view and manage current activity on SQL Server. More information on the implementation of these statements is found in the *Current Activity* section.

Transaction Log Overview

Each SQL Server database has a transaction log that records the transactions that take place and the modifications performed in each transaction. As a user performs work against the database, the record of the work is first recorded into the transaction log. Once the user has successfully written the data to the transaction log, the user is allowed to perform additional actions. The record of the modifications within the transaction log has three purposes:

Recovery of single transactions.   If an application issues a ROLL-BACK statement or if SQL Server detects an error in the processing of a transaction, the log is used to roll back the modifications that were started by the transaction. The developer can maintain consistency throughout the entire transaction regardless of the number of SQL statements that are included in the transaction.

Recovery of all uncommited transactions when the SQL Server service is started.   When SQL Server is stopped in a friendly manner, a checkpoint is performed on every database to ensure that all commited transactions are written to the database. More information on the checkpoint process is addressed later in this chapter in the section titled *Checkpoint Process*. If SQL Server is not stopped in a friendly manner and fails immediately (power failure, hardware failure, and so forth), the checkpoint doesn't have time to run. As a result the system can be left with transactions in the transaction log that are completed by the user but have not been written to the data file. When SQL Server is started, it runs a recovery of each database. Every modification recorded in the log that was not written to the data files is rolled forward (written to the database). A transaction that was not completed by the user but is found in the transaction log is then rolled back to ensure the integrity of the database.

Rolling a restored database forward to the point of failure.   After the loss of a database owing to a hardware failure or corrupted data files, you can restore your backups. After you have restored the appropriate full, differential, and transaction log backups, you can recover your database. When the last log backup is restored, SQL Server then uses the transaction log information to roll back all transactions that were not complete at the point of failure.

The transaction log is implemented on the hard drive. These files can be stored separately from the other database files. The log cache is managed separately from the buffer cache for data pages. This separation facilitates a speedy response time for the user. You can implement the transaction log on a single file or across several files. You can also define the files to autogrow when they fill up. The *autogrow* feature avoids the potential of running out of space in the transaction log.

This section first introduces the architecture of the log file, detailing both the logical and physical architecture of the transaction log. The section then introduces the write-ahead log features and the checkpoint process. Next the section identifies the Recovery models of SQL Server. Finally, this section addresses the maintenance of the transaction log file.

Transaction Log Architecture

Each database in SQL Server has its own transaction log. Each log needs to be monitored and maintained to ensure optimal stability and performance from your SQL Server databases. The transaction log is responsible for the integrity of each transaction that is performed against your server. Additionally, the transaction log provides a backup copy of the transactions that are made to your database. With the transaction log and the database files, you have two copies of each modification that is made to your database. The transaction log helps to provide fault-tolerant protection against system failure.

The transaction log architecture is made up of two separate views, or architectures: logical and physical. The *logical architecture* of the log presents the individual transactions that are performed against the data. Regardless of where the transaction is physically stored, the logical view presents all transactions serially. The *physical architecture* of the log consists of the files that reside in the operating system. These files are used to write the data and assist in presenting the data to the logical view. The following sections introduce the characteristics of the logical and physical views.

NOTE At the current time Microsoft does not ship a utility that enables you to view the contents of the transaction log. You can view the size of the log and the number of transactions currently in the transaction log, but the actual statements that have been performed against the log are not available. You can purchase third-party utilities that allow you to open and view the transaction log. You can use these log analyzer utilities to roll back individual user transactions that have already been committed to the database. The log analyzer utilities provide you with a level of security management that is unavailable with the tools included with SQL Server. More information about these utilities can be found in Appendix B, "Third-Party SQL Server Security Management Tools."

Logical Archictecture

The transaction log records in serial fashion modifications that are made to the data. Logically the first record is recorded as being at the beginning of the log, and the most recent modification would be stored at the end of the log. A log sequence number (LSN) identifies each log record. Each new log record is written to the logical end of the log with an LSN higher than the LSN of the record before it.

A log record may not be just a single statement. Log records for data modifications record either the logical operation performed or the before-and-after images of the modified data. Before-and-after images are used in instances where the data has been updated. A "before" image is a copy of the data before the update is applied, and an "after" image is a copy of the data after the operation is applied.

Every transaction that is sent to the SQL Server can result in many items being written to the log. The types of events that are stored in the log include:

- The start and end of each transaction
- Every INSERT, UPDATE, and DELETE statement
- All OBJECT creation statements

Transactions are written to the log in sequential order. Along with the transaction, the ID of the transaction and the date and time the transaction was performed are stored in the transaction log. These data allow the transaction log to maintain a chain of all the events that are associated with a single transaction. If necessary, the system can use the chain of events for a transaction to roll back the transaction. If a single step within the transaction fails, the system can use the transactional information from the log to roll back the transaction. A transaction rollback erases the events of the transaction as though it never existed. The transaction log secures your system by guaranteeing the consistency of your transactions. For example, if you have a transaction that transfers data from your checking account to your savings account, the transaction would have to include two update statements. One of the update statements has to subtract money from the checking account record. The other update statement has to add money to the savings account record. The integrity of your entire system depends on this process happening completely. If one of the updates fails, you want both of them to be erased. The transaction log is used to help guarantee this transactional consistency and protect your system from partially committed (incomplete) actions.

As a transaction is written to the log, it must also reserve space within the transaction log to store the information needed to roll back the transaction. All events involved in a rollback are also written to the transaction log. In general, the amount of space needed to roll back a transaction is equivalent to the amount of space taken for the transaction.

Physical Architecture

The transaction log is a physical file or a set of files. The files that are used for a database are defined when the database is created or altered. The information that is written to the log has to be physically stored in the log files. SQL Server 2000 segments each physical log file internally into a number of virtual log files. As an administrator or developer you typically do not see the virtual log files. Virtual log files are not a fixed size. SQL Server dynamically allocates the space for each virtual log file based on the size of the log and the intended rate of usage. SQL Server attempts to maintain a small number of virtual log files.

Transaction log files can be configured to autogrow when the transaction log fills up. The amount of growth can be set in kilobytes (KB), megabytes (MB), gigabytes (GB), terabytes (TB), or a specified percentage. The autogrow properties can be set when a database is created or altered. You can set the parameters by either using the ALTER DATABASE command in Transact-SQL or entering the values in Enterprise Manager. The following steps can be taken to modify the autogrow parameters of a database from Enterprise Manager:

1. Open Enterprise Manager.

2. Click to expand your server group.

3. Click to expand the server where your database resides.

4. Click to expand the Databases container.

5. Right-click on the database you want to alter and select Properties.

6. Click the Transaction Log tab. This should appear as shown in Figure 13.1.

7. In the bottom left-hand corner you can alter the Automatically Grow File parameters.

8. Click OK to set the new parameters.

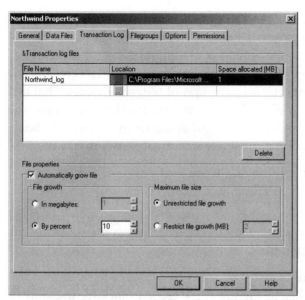

Figure 13.1 Enterprise Manager can alter the properties of a database's transaction log.

Write-Ahead Transaction Log

SQL Server uses a write-ahead transaction log. This means that all modifications are written to the log before they are written to the database.

All modifications have to perform their action against a piece of data that is stored in the buffer cache. The *buffer cache* is an area of memory that stores the data pages that users have retrieved to modify or analyze. The modification of a record is performed first on a copy of the data that is stored in the buffer cache. The modifications are stored in cache and are not written to the data files until either a checkpoint occurs or the modifications have to be written to disk because the area of memory that is caching the modifications is being requested for a new data page to be loaded. Writing a modified data page from the buffer cache to disk is called *flushing the page*. A page modified in the cache but not yet written to disk is called a *dirty page*.

At the time a modification is made to a page in the buffer, a log record is built into the log cache and records the modification. The log record must be written from the log cache to the transaction log before the data page is flushed. If the dirty page were flushed before the log record, the transaction log would not have a complete record of the transaction and the transaction could not be rolled back. The SQL Server service prevents a dirty page from being flushed before the associated log record is written from cache to the log file. Because log records are always written ahead of the associated data pages, the log is referred to as a *write-ahead log*.

Checkpoints

Checkpoints are used to verify that the transactions that have been completed in the log are written to the database. A checkpoint keeps track of all the transactions that have been written to the database and all the transactions that were not completed at the time of the checkpoint. The checkpoint process is used to help maintain a reference point to track the data that has been written to the database file. Checkpoints are used to minimize the portion of the log that must be processed during the recovery of a database. When a database is in recovery, it must perform the following actions:

- The log might contain records that were written to the log but not written to the data file yet. These modifications are rolled forward (applied to the data file).

- All transactions that were partially completed when the service stopped are rolled back (erased as though they never existed).

Checkpoints flush dirty data and log pages from the buffer cache to the data files. A checkpoint writes to the log file a record marking the start of the checkpoint and stores information recorded for the checkpoint in a chain of checkpoint log records. Checkpoints occur automatically in most cases, including under the following scenarios:

- A CHECKPOINT statement is executed by a user or application.
- An ALTER DATABASE statement is performed.
- The services of a SQL Server instance are shut down appropriately by shutting down the machine or performing the SHUTDOWN statement against the server.
- Checkpoints occur as transactions are performed. By default, checkpoints are carried out every minute or so based on the resources and transactions that are currently in use.

NOTE SQL Server 2000 generates automatic checkpoints. The interval between automatic checkpoints is based on the number of records in the log, not on an amount of time. The time interval between automatic checkpoints can vary greatly. The time interval can be long if few modifications are made in the database. Automatic checkpoints occur frequently if a considerable amount of data is modified.

SQL Server Recovery Models

SQL Server provides three Recovery models (Full, Bulk-Logged, and Simple) to simplify backup and recovery procedures, simplify recovery planning, and define trade-offs between operational requirements. Each of these models addresses different needs for performance, disk and tape space, and protection against data loss. For example, when you choose a Recovery model, you must consider the trade-offs between the following business requirements:

- Performance of a large-scale operation (for example, index creation or bulk loads)
- Data loss exposure (for example, the loss of committed transactions)
- Transaction log space consumption
- The simplicity of backup and recovery procedures

Depending on what operations you are performing, more than one Recovery model may be appropriate. After you have chosen a Recovery model or models, you can plan the required backup and recovery procedures. The following sections discuss the three Recovery models separately.

Full Recovery

The Full Recovery model uses database backups and transaction log backups to provide complete protection against media failure. If one or more data files are damaged, media recovery can restore all committed transactions. In-process transactions are rolled back.

Full Recovery provides the ability to recover the database to the point of failure or to a specific point in time. To guarantee this degree of recoverability, all operations, including bulk operations such as SELECT INTO, CREATE INDEX, and bulk loading data, are fully logged.

Full Recovery provides the maximum amount of recovery available. It is also the slowest of the models, because all transactions are fully written and stored in the transaction log.

Bulk-Logged Recovery

The Bulk-Logged Recovery model provides protection against media failure combined with the best performance and minimal log space usage for certain large-scale or bulk copy operations. The following operations are minimally logged; that is, the fact that they occurred is stored in the log file, but the details of the work performed are not stored in the log:

SELECT INTO. The SELECT INTO is used to create a temporary or permanent table from the results of a SELECT statement.

Bulk load operations (bcp and BULK INSERT). BULK INSERT and bcp are used to mass-load data into a table.

CREATE INDEX (including indexed views). CREATE INDEX is used to create indexes for the columns you want to search frequently.

Text and image operations (WRITETEXT and UPDATETEXT). These operations are used to write text and image data directly to the data file and bypass the log.

In the Bulk-Logged Recovery model, the data loss exposure for these bulk copy operations is greater than in the Full Recovery model. Whereas the bulk copy operations are fully logged under the Full Recovery model, they are minimally logged and cannot be controlled on an operation-by-operation basis under the Bulk-Logged Recovery model. Under the Bulk-Logged Recovery model, a damaged data file can result in having to redo work manually.

In addition, the Bulk-Logged Recovery model allows the database to be recovered only to the end of a transaction log backup when the log backup contains bulk changes. Point-in-time recovery is not supported.

In SQL Server you can switch between Full and Bulk-Logged Recovery models easily. It is not necessary to perform a full database backup after bulk copy operations are completed under the Bulk-Logged Recovery model. Transaction log backups under this model capture both the log and the results of any bulk operations performed since the last backup. To change the current Recovery model you should perform the following steps:

1. Open Enterprise Manager.

2. Click to expand your server group.

3. Click to expand the server that maintains the database you want to alter.

4. Click to expand the Databases container.

5. Right-click on your database and select Properties.

6. Select the Options tab to review your Recovery model as shown in Figure 13.2.

7. Click the drop-down list to choose the appropriate Recovery model.

8. Click OK.

Figure 13.2 You can change the Recovery model to control the amount of data that is stored in the transaction log.

Simple Recovery

In the Simple Recovery model, data is recoverable only to the most recent full database or differential backup. Transaction log backups are not used, and minimal transaction log space is used. After a checkpoint occurs, all transactions that have been successfully written from the log to the data file are truncated, and the space is reused. The Simple Recovery model is easier to manage than are the Full and Bulk-Logged models, but there is a higher risk of data loss exposure if a data file is damaged.

Log Maintenance

The transaction log is critical to the database. Maintenance and monitoring of the log are required to ensure that the transaction log is kept at an optimal size. The key issues for log maintenance are truncating the log to prevent it from growing uncontrollably and shrinking the log if it has grown to an unacceptable level. The following sections will more fully describe each of these options.

Truncating the Transaction Log

If log records were never deleted from the transaction log, the logical log would grow until it filled all of the available space on the disks that hold the physical log files. So at some point you need to truncate the log to help manage your disk space. The transaction log is truncated when you back up the log. Therefore it is a good idea to have regularly scheduled transaction log backups.

The active portion of the transaction log can never be truncated. The active portion is needed to recover the database at any time, so you must have the log images needed to roll back all incomplete transactions. The log images must always be present in the database in case the server fails, because the images are required to recover the database when the server is restarted.

Shrinking the Transaction Log

You can shrink the size of a transaction log file to free up hard drive space to the operating system. There are three different methods for physically shrinking the transaction log file:

- The DBCC SHRINKDATABASE statement is executed against the database.

- The DBCC SHRINKFILE statement is executed against the transaction log file.

■ An autoshrink operation occurs. Autoshrink is a database option that is not configured by default.

NOTE You must be a member of the system administrators server role or the db_owner database role to shrink the transaction log file.

Shrinking a log depends first on truncating the log. Log truncation does not reduce the size of a physical log file; instead it reduces the size of the logical log and marks as inactive the virtual logs that do not hold any part of the logical log. A log shrink operation removes enough inactive virtual logs to reduce the log file to the requested size. To truncate the log, you must be at least a member of the db_owner database role. System administrators can also truncate transaction log files.

The unit of size reduction is a virtual log. For example, if you have a 600 MB log file that has been divided into six 100 MB virtual logs, the size of the log file can only be reduced in 100 MB increments. The file size can be reduced to sizes such as 500 MB or 400 MB, but it cannot be reduced to sizes such as 433 MB or 525 MB.

Virtual logs that hold part of the logical log cannot be freed. If all the virtual logs in a log file hold parts of the logical log, the file cannot be shrunk until a truncation marks one or more of the virtual logs at the end of the physical log as inactive.

When any file is shrunk, the space freed up must come from the end of the file. When a transaction log file is shrunk, enough virtual logs from the end of the file are freed to reduce the log to the size that the user requested. The target_size specified by the user is rounded to the next higher virtual log boundary. For example, if a user specifies a target_size of 325 MB for our sample 600 MB file with 100 MB virtual log files, the last two virtual log files are removed. The new file size is 400 MB.

In SQL Server, a DBCC SHRINKDATABASE or DBCC SHRINKFILE operation attempts to shrink the physical log file to the requested size immediately (subject to rounding) if the following conditions are met:

■ If no part of the logical log is in the virtual logs beyond the target_size mark, the virtual logs after the target_size mark are freed and the successful DBCC statement is completed with no messages.

■ If part of the logical log is in the virtual logs beyond the target_size mark, SQL Server 2000 frees as much space as possible and issues an informational message. The message tells you what actions you need to perform to get the logical log out of the virtual logs at the end of the file. After you perform this action, you can then reissue the DBCC statement to free the remaining space.

In the following statement, DBCC SHRINKFILE is used to reduce the TestDB_Log file in the TestDB database to 1 MB:

```
USE TestDB
GO
DBCC SHRINKFILE (TestDB_Log, 1)
GO
```

Concurrency Architecture

When many people attempt to modify data in a database at the same time, a system of controls must be implemented so that modifications made by one person do not adversely affect those of another person. This process is referred to as *concurrency control*.

Two classifications exist for instituting concurrency control:

Pessimistic concurrency control.   A system of locks prevents users from modifying data in a way that affects other users. After a user performs an action that causes a lock, other users cannot perform actions that would conflict with the lock until the owner releases it. This process is called *pessimistic control* because it is mainly used in environments where there is high contention for data.

Optimistic concurrency control.   In optimistic concurrency control, users do not lock data when they read it. When an update is performed, the system checks to see whether another user changed the data after it was read. If another user updated the data, an error occurs. Typically, the user who receives the error rolls back the transaction and starts again. This situation is called *optimistic* because it is mainly used in environments where there is low contention for data.

SQL Server 2000 supports a wide range of optimistic and pessimistic concurrency control mechanisms. By default, SQL Server implements optimistic concurrency. Users can override the default by choosing an alternative type of concurrency, specifying a transaction isolation level for a connection and concurrency options on cursors. Altering the transaction isolation level is generally not necessary and may result in SQL Server locking your data for much longer than is necessary. For more information about the various isolation levels that can be implemented, refer to SQL Server Books Online. Alternatively, concurrency attributes can be defined in the properties of the database application programming interfaces

(APIs), such as ADO, OLE DB, and ODBC. For more information about the locking options that are available to you from the database APIs, refer to the syntax documentation of your programming tool.

Locking Architecture

A lock is an object that software uses to indicate that a user has some dependency on a resource. The software does not allow other users to perform operations on the resource that would adversely affect the dependencies of the user who owns the lock. Locks are managed internally by system software and are acquired and released based on actions that the user takes.

SQL Server 2000 uses locks to implement pessimistic concurrency control among multiple users who are performing modifications in a database at the same time. By default, SQL Server manages both transactions and locks on a per connection basis. For example, if an application opens two SQL Server connections, locks acquired by one connection cannot be shared with the other connection. Neither connection can acquire locks that would conflict with locks held by the other connection. Only bound connections are not affected by this rule.

SQL Server locks are applied at various levels of granularity in the database. Locks can be acquired on rows, pages, keys, ranges of keys, indexes, tables, or databases. SQL Server dynamically determines the appropriate level at which to place locks for each Transact-SQL statement. The level at which locks are acquired can vary for different objects referenced by the same query. For example, one table might be very small and have a table lock applied, while another larger table might have row locks applied. The level at which locks are applied does not have to be specified by users and needs no configuration by administrators. Each instance of SQL Server ensures that locks granted at one level of granularity respect locks granted at another level.

Five lock modes exist: shared, update, exclusive, intent, and schema. The lock mode indicates the level of dependency that the connection has on the locked object. SQL Server controls how the lock modes interact. The locks are a key in securing the data that is currently being read or modified. Ultimately, the lock is the object that prevents a user from modifying data that is currently being modified by another user, thus preventing update anomalies. For example, an exclusive lock cannot be obtained if other connections hold shared locks on the resource. Locks are held for the length of time needed to protect the resource at the level requested. The types of locks in SQL Server are shared locks, exclusive locks, update locks, intent locks, and schema locks.

- *Shared locks* are applied when the user is reading data. Shared locks can coexist with other shared locks, meaning that another user may read the data that you are currently reading. Shared locks are not compatible with exclusive locks.

- *Exclusive locks* are applied to records that are being modified. Exclusive locks are not compatible with shared locks.

- *Update locks* are used for large update operations. The update lock is a combination of a shared lock and an exclusive lock. The entire set of records that will be affected by the update are locked with a shared lock. The record that is currently being updated is then locked using an exclusive lock. Update locks prevent large update operations from having to apply exclusive locks to large amounts of data.

- *Intent locks* are used to prevent locks from layers that would affect a currently locked record. For instance, if a user was locking an individual record, an intent lock is placed on the data page that stores the record. The intent lock prevents a different user from locking the data page that the record is stored on.

- *Schema locks* are used to lock a table or database when the design of the table is being modified. Schema locks prevent users from adding data while the design of the table is under modification.

If a connection attempts to acquire a lock that conflicts with a lock held by another connection, the connection attempting to acquire the lock is blocked until one of the following events occurs:

- The conflicting lock is freed, and the connection acquires the lock that it requested.

- The time-out interval for the connection expires. By default, there is no time-out interval, but some applications set a time-out interval to prevent an indefinite wait.

- If several connections become blocked while waiting for conflicting locks on a single resource, the locks are granted on a first-come, first-served basis as the preceding connections free their locks.

- SQL Server has an algorithm to detect deadlocks, a condition in which two connections have blocked each other. If an instance of SQL Server detects a deadlock, it will terminate one transaction, allowing the other to continue.

NOTE When you write transactions you should plan around deadlocks. The tables that are referenced in your INSERT, UPDATE, and DELETE statements should be referenced in the same order for all transactions. You should standardize on the order in which statements are referenced to decrease the likelihood that two transactions will deadlock in the middle of execution.

SQL Server might dynamically escalate or de-escalate the granularity or type of locks. For example, if an update acquires a large number of row locks and has locked a significant percentage of a table, the row locks are escalated to a table lock. If a table lock is acquired, the row locks are released. SQL Server 2000 rarely needs to escalate locks; Query Optimizer usually chooses the correct lock granularity at the time the execution plan is compiled.

Current Activity

Enterprise Manager includes a Current Activity window. The Current Activity window can be used to view current use connections and locks, view the status of the current SQL statements, view objects that are currently locked, send messages to the user of a transaction, and kill current user transactions. Additionally, you can use the sp_who and sp_lock system stored procedures to view the current activity on SQL Server. This section first details the Current Activity windows from Enterprise Manager and then discusses the stored procedures from Transact-SQL.

Enterprise Manager

You should consider using the Current Activity window for troubleshooting problems that arise. The following information can be critical in assisting with the troubleshooting of current user activity:

- Current blocked and blocking transactions
- Currently connected users on an instance of SQL Server and the last statement executed
- Locks that are in effect

To view the details of the Current Activity window, perform the following steps:

1. Open Enterprise Manager.
2. Click to expand your server group.

Process ID ▲	Cont...	User	Database	Status	Open Trans...	Command
1	0	system	no database context	backgrou... 0		LAZY WRITER
10	0	sa	master	backgrou... 0		TASK MANAGER
11	0	sa	master	backgrou... 0		TASK MANAGER
12	0	sa	master	backgrou... 0		TASK MANAGER
2	0	system	no database context	sleeping ... 0		LOG WRITER
3	0	system	master	backgrou... 0		SIGNAL HANDLER
4	0	system	no database context	backgrou... 0		LOCK MONITOR
5	0	system	master	backgrou... 0		TASK MANAGER
51	0	NWTRADERS\Administrator	msdb	sleeping ... 0		AWAITING COMMAND
52	0	NWTRADERS\Administrator	distribution	sleeping ... 0		AWAITING COMMAND
53	0	NWTRADERS\Administrator	Northwind	sleeping ... 0		AWAITING COMMAND
54	0	NWTRADERS\Administrator	distribution	sleeping ... 1		AWAITING COMMAND
55	0	NWTRADERS\Administrator	msdb	sleeping ... 0		AWAITING COMMAND
56	0	NWTRADERS\Administrator	master	runnable ... 2		SELECT INTO
57	0	NWTRADERS\Administrator	master	sleeping ... 0		AWAITING COMMAND
58	0	NWTRADERS\Administrator	master	sleeping ... 0		AWAITING COMMAND
59	0	NWTRADERS\Administrator	master	sleeping ... 0		AWAITING COMMAND
6	0	system	master	backgrou... 0		TASK MANAGER
7	0	sa	no database context	sleeping ... 0		CHECKPOINT SLEEP
8	0	sa	master	backgrou... 0		TASK MANAGER
9	0	sa	master	backgrou... 0		TASK MANAGER

Figure 13.3   Current process information can be used to determine the number of users connected to SQL Server and the status of their connection and SQL statements.

3. Click to expand your server.

4. Click to expand the Management container.

5. Click to expand the Current Activity window.

6. Click the Process Info container. The Details pane should appear as shown in Figure 13.3.

In the Current Activity window that appears after you have followed this procedure, 21 columns provide information for a given SQL Server user. Table 13.1 identifies the columns used by the Current Activity window and the information they provide.

Table 13.1   Current Activity Window5 Information

COLUMN	DESCRIPTION
Process ID	SQL Server Process ID.
Context ID	The execution context ID that uniquely identifies the subthreads operating on behalf of a single process.
User	The ID of the user who executed the command.

Table 13.1   *(Continued)*

COLUMN	DESCRIPTION
Database	The database currently being used by the process.
Status	The status of the process (for example, running, sleeping, runnable, and background).
Open Transactions	The number of open transactions for the process.
Command	The command currently being executed.
Application	The name of the application program being used by the process.
Wait Time	The current wait time in milliseconds. When the process is not waiting, the wait time is zero.
Wait Type	The name of the last or current wait type.
Wait Resources	The textual representation of a lock resource.
CPU	Cumulative CPU time for the process. The entry is updated only for processes performed on behalf of Transact-SQL statements executed when SET STATISTICS TIME ON has been activated in the same session. The CPU column is updated when a query has been executed with SET STATISTICS TIME ON. When zero is returned, SET STATISTICS TIME is OFF.
Physical IO	Cumulative disk reads and writes for the process.
Memory Usage	The number of pages in the procedure cache that are currently allocated to this process. A negative number indicates that the process is freeing memory allocated by another process.
Login Time	The time at which a client process logged in to the server. For system processes, the time at which SQL Server startup occurred is displayed.
Last Batch	Last time a client process executed a remote stored procedure call or an EXECUTE statement. For system processes, the time at which SQL Server startup occurred is displayed.
Host	The name of the workstation.
Network Library	The column in which the client's network library is stored. Every client process arrives on a network connection. Network connections have a network library associated with them that allows them to make the connection.
Network Address	The assigned unique identifier for the network interface card on each user's workstation. When the user logs in, this identifier is inserted in the Network Address column.
Blocked By	Process ID (SPID) of a blocking process.
Blocking	The process ID (SPID) of a process that is blocked.

From Enterprise Manager you can also send the current user a message or kill the current statement the user is performing. This capability is beneficial in preventing unwanted access to resources and troubleshooting transactions that have been running for a long period of time.

NOTE You can use the DBCC OPENTRAN Transact-SQL statement to show the longest running transaction. This statement is useful for determining transactions that are causing other transactions to wait for locks.

To kill an existing connection from Enterprise Manager, perform the following steps:

1. Open Enterprise Manager.
2. Click to expand your server group.
3. Click to expand your server.
4. Click to expand the Management container.
5. Click to expand the Current Activity window.
6. Click Process to display the list of current users in the Details pane.
7. Right-click on and select Kill Process. A message appears asking if you are sure this is what you want to do.
8. Click Yes to confirm the kill.

You can send a message to the user who is connected to SQL Server by performing the following procedure:

1. Open Enterprise Manager.
2. Click to expand your server group.
3. Click to expand your server.
4. Click to expand the Management container.
5. Click to expand the Current Activity window.
6. Click Process to display a list of current users in the Details pane.
7. Right-click and select Send Message.
8. Type the message you want to send to the user and click OK.

Stored Procedures

The sp_who and sp_lock system stored procedures are available from Transact-SQL to provide similar information to Enterprise Manager, as described here:

- *sp_who* provides information about current Microsoft SQL Server users and processes. The information returned can be filtered to return only those processes that are not idle.

- *sp_lock* returns information about the current locks applied by SQL Server.

More information about the syntax required to execute these stored procedures can be found in SQL Server Books Online. You can also use the KILL statement to kill a current process or lock that you have viewed from one of these stored procedures.

Best Practices

- Back up the transaction log on a regular basis to help maintain the size of the log file. The backup transaction log option truncates the portions of the log that have been succesfully written to the data files.

- Use the Full Recovery model when you need to fully log every event. Although this is the slowest Recovery model option, it is also the option that allows for maximum recovery.

- Use the Bulk-Logged Recovery option when you need to import a large amount of data using a bulk import or bcp process. Bulk-Logged recovery minimally logs the transfer process, thus helping to keep the log size down and speed up the transfer process.

- After you have transferred a large amount of data into the database, perform a full backup of the database. Because the transfer was only minimally logged, the transaction log will not have a complete record of the data that was transferred. Full backup provides a good copy of the database for recovery purposes.

- Use a third-party tool to view the contents of the transaction log. Many tools are available to allow you to see the activity of the transaction log. You can also roll back transactions that have already been committed to the data files, thus helping to prevent unnecessary restores that back the system out of several changes. These third-party utilities provide security control that is not natively available in SQL Server 2000.

- Use the Current Activity window in Enterprise Manager to view the current connections. You should generally send users a warning message before you kill their connection.

REVIEW QUESTIONS

1. What is the difference between the logical view and the physical view of the transaction log?

2. What is the purpose of the checkpoint process?

3. When does a checkpoint occur?

4. When is it appropriate to use the Bulk-Logged Recovery model?

5. Why should you avoid the Simple Recovery model on a production server?

6. What are deadlocks? How can you help avoid them?

7. Give some examples of the information that can be viewed in the Current Activity window of Enterprise Manager.

Creating an Audit Policy

Auditing is the process of storing information about and reviewing actions that have occurred on your system. Generally, auditing is not used to prevent an activity from happening. It is the art of finding out the actions that have occurred and who carried out those actions.

Auditing, as with most additional features, requires overhead. The system has to keep some log of the activities that you want to be able to audit. To prevent excessive overhead, you should audit only the events that are necessary for your system requirements. Auditing can be an invaluable tool when you are trying to track the mission-critical events on your server. It should only be used, though, as a solution to a business requirement.

SQL Server 2000 provides auditing to trace and record activity that has happened on each instance of SQL Server (for example, successful and failed login attempts). SQL Server 2000 also provides an interface, SQL Profiler, for managing audit records. Auditing can be enabled or modified only by members of the system administrator's role, and every modification of an audit is an auditable event. The level of auditing that is available in SQL Server may not meet the requirements of the application you are creating. Auditing can also be written into the application and stored in the SQL Server database with the other data elements of your application. This process may require the altering of your table schema to keep track of the users who are modifying the data.

This chapter first identifies the built-in options for auditing, providing a detailed description of server auditing and C2-Mode auditing, which can be enabled from the sp_configure stored procedure. The chapter then moves to a description of the SQL Profiler utility and a definition of how the utility can be used to audit activity on your SQL Server. Finally, this chapter addresses auditing within an application. This process requires the intervention of the application developer to ensure that the application and database used for the application have the appropriate code included to allow for auditing of the required events. This section includes some suggested schema changes so that your application database can support the level of auditing you desire from your system.

Built-in Auditing Options

Microsoft has given SQL Server administrators some options for tracking system and user events. The auditing options allow for the tracking of these events based on the user identity of the individual performing the audited event. SQL Server provides two built-in options for auditing:

- *Server auditing*, which provides some level of auditing (including login access to the system) but does not require the same number amount of overhead and configuration as C2-Mode auditing.

- *C2-Mode auditing*, which requires that you follow very specific security policies. The setting is enabled from the Registry and is beneficial if you need detailed login information.

These two options are discussed in more detail in the separate sections that follow.

Server Auditing

Server auditing is configured through Enterprise Manager. When you configure server auditing, four levels of auditing are available:

None.   This option disables auditing and is the default setting for a newly installed instance of SQL Server.

Success.   This option makes possible auditing of successful login attempts. When this option is selected you get information recorded on both the SQL Server Authentication and Windows Authentication modes. The detailed information appears in both the Windows application log of the Event Viewer utility and the SQL Server error log. When the server is changed to this level of auditing, you must stop and start the SQL Server service in order for the modification to take effect.

Failure. This option enables auditing of failed login attempts. Similar in scope to the success audits, in this option the system is tracking failed login attempts and storing the information in the same log files that the success audit uses. Figure 14.1 is an example of a failed login attempt entry from the Windows 2000 application log. If you select the failure option, you have to restart the SQL Server service in order for the modification to take effect.

All. This option enables you to audit both successful and failed login attempts. When you change your configuration to this setting, you will also need to restart your SQL Server service. The details of the audit capture are stored in the same log files that the other auditing options use. This setting is the accumulation of the success and failure audits.

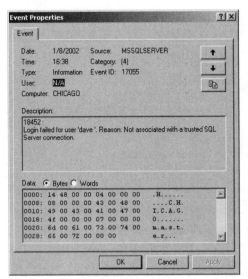

Figure 14.1 The application log of the Windows 2000 Event Viewer stores entries related to failed login attempts to SQL Server.

You can use Enterprise Manager to configure the appropriate level of server auditing for your environment. To configure server auditing, perform the following steps:

1. Open Enterprise Manager.

2. Click to expand your server group.

3. Right-click on your server and select Properties.

4. Select the Security tab as shown in Figure 14.2.

5. Under Audit Level click the bullet to select your chosen level of auditing and select OK.

6. From Enterprise Manager, right-click on your server and choose Stop.

7. Right-click on your server and choose Start. After the server is restarted, your changes will take effect.

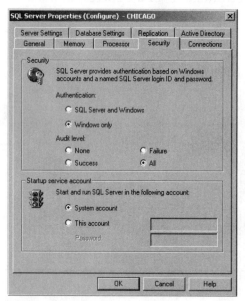

Figure 14.2 The SQL Server Properties dialogue box enables you to alter your configured level of auditing.

C2-Mode Auditing

The U.S. National Security Agency (NSA) created the C2 security rating. It was developed as a standard to rate the security of a server. This standard evaluates all levels of software from an application to an operating system. SQL Server 2000 has been certified as C2 compliant. For your server to meet the C2-compliant security level, you must have C2-Mode auditing enabled. Most of the settings for C2-Mode auditing are fixed settings, which are not controlled by you. The default auditing configuration is for the C2-Mode auditing to enable auditing of all objects in SQL Server. More information about the individual settings for each object can be found in the *SQL Server 2000 C2 Admin and User Guide*, which is located at www.microsoft.com/ downloads.

In Microsoft SQL Server 2000, you can use the C2-Mode auditing option to review both successful and unsuccessful attempts to access the objects at your server level or the objects within each database. With this information, you can document system activity and look for security policy violations. You should consider using the SQL Profiler tool in conjunction with C2-Mode auditing. SQL Profiler allows you to view the new events that are being audited after you have enabled C2-Mode auditing. With SQL Profiler, you can audit the users who access your mission-critical tables.

C2-Mode auditing tracks C2 audit events and records them to a file in the \mssql\data directory for default instances of SQL Server 2000, or the \mssql$instancename\data directory for named instances of SQL Server 2000. If the file reaches a size limit of 200 MB, C2 auditing will start a new file, close the old file, and write all new audit records to the new file. This process continues until SQL Server is shut down or auditing is turned off. If the log file causes the drive to fill up, all SQL Server services stop.

Before enabling and disabling C2-Mode auditing, consider the following:

- You must be a member of the sysadmin role to enable or disable C2-Mode auditing.
- C2-Mode auditing is an advanced option. If you are using the sp_configure system stored procedure to change the setting, you can change C2-Mode auditing only when Show Advanced Options is set to 1. You set this option by typing the following command:

```
Sp_configure 'show advanced options', '1'
```

- If the audit directory fills up, the instance of SQL Server stops. You can restart the instance of SQL Server if auditing is not set to start automatically. But if auditing is set to start automatically, you must free up disk space for the audit log before you can restart the instance of SQL Server.

NOTE You can restart the instance with the -f flag, which bypasses all auditing. This procedure is useful if you want to disable auditing until you can free up additional disk space or in an emergency situation where you do not have enough disk space to allocate to the 200 MB audit file. See the *Audit Log Files* section later in this chapter for further discussion of this procedure.

To enable C2-Mode auditing, set the C2-Mode auditing option to 1. This setting establishes the C2 audit trace and turns on the option to disconnect from the server if the server is unable to write to the audit file for any reason. After setting the option to 1, restart the server to begin C2 audit tracing. To stop C2-Mode audit tracing, set C2-Mode auditing to 0. You set the C2-Mode auditing option to 1 by typing the following command:

```
Sp_configure 'c2 audit mode', '1'
```

NOTE The default for C2-Mode auditing is to audit all counters. If all audit counters are turned on for all objects, there could be a significant performance impact on the server. Monitoring all audit counters is beneficial for troubleshooting a problem or tracking an individual event when there are signs of a problem, but this is not typically suggested all the time on a production server for performance reasons.

SQL Profiler

SQL Server includes a tool for tracking and viewing actions that are being performed against your server. SQL Profiler is broken down into two pieces. First there is SQL Trace, which is the server-side component used to track events in SQL Server. The second piece is SQL Profiler, which is the graphical tool for viewing the results of a trace file. SQL Profiler is the upgrade to the old SQL Trace utility, and, although the name has changed, the configuration is similar. The new version has been expanded to make it possible to capture more events.

SQL Trace

SQL Trace is the server-side component of the auditing mechanism. Auditing has been added into the same mechanism that was used in SQL Server 7.0 to provide performance information about SQL Server. Performance information and audit information are still returned, but the interface has been completely rebuilt in SQL Server 2000.

All SQL Server 7.0 extended stored procedures related to SQL Profiler have been replaced in SQL Server 2000. For information about the new stored procedures used for the security auditing process, see SQL Server Books Online for SQL Server 2000. Each time an auditable security event occurs inside the SQL Server relational or storage engine, the SQL Trace event engine is notified. If a trace is currently enabled and running that would capture the event that was generated, the event is written to the appropriate trace file.

SQL Trace is the process that captures events. As an administrator you should be comfortable with the SQL Profiler utility, which is the tool used to view the results of a SQL Trace. For more information on the stored procedures used by SQL Trace to capture events, refer to the SQL Server Books Online.

SQL Profiler Utility

The SQL Profiler utility is the graphical user interface utility that enables you to view the audit trace files and then perform selected actions on those files. You can search through the files, save the files to a table, and create and configure trace definitions using the user interface.

SQL Profiler is a client to SQL Trace; you do not need to have SQL Profiler running to perform a security audit. You can configure the audit information to be scheduled and viewed at a later time. The SQL Profiler utility has a "stop at" feature that is used to configure a time at which the trace should stop, allowing you to schedule the trace actions at various intervals. The SQL Profiler utility is helpful in monitoring and troubleshooting the security events of SQL Server 2000. This section identifies the log files that are used for auditing, and then the section moves on to a description of the options for using the SQL Profiler utility.

Audit Log Files

SQL Profiler system stored procedures support file rollover. The maximum file size for the audit log is fixed at 200 MB. When the audit log file reaches

200 MB, a new file is created and the old file handle is closed. If the directory fills up, if, for example, you run out of hard drive space, then the instance of Microsoft SQL Server stops. The system administrator then needs to either free up disk space for the audit log before restarting the instance of SQL Server or restart the instance of SQL Server without enabling auditing. SQL Server can be started with the -f switch to disable all auditing configuration. To start the SQL Server instance with the -f switch, perform the following steps:

1. Open the Services icon from the Administrative Tools program group.
2. Double-click on the MSSQLServer service.
3. If the service is started, click Stop to stop the service.
4. From the MSSQLService Properties dialog box, add the -f as a start parameter.
5. Restart the service.

The file rollover feature of the audit logs prevents the audit trace from failing because the audit log filled up. With file rollover, when a file fills up and a new file is started, the old file can be overwritten. When configured in this way, SQL Server will not shut down when the log fills up. When a configured audited event cannot be written to the log file, an entry is written in the Windows 2000 event viewer and the SQL Server error log.

NOTE It is strongly recommended that during SQL Server setup you create a new directory to contain your audit files. \mssql\audit is the suggested path. If you are running SQL Server on a named instance, the suggested path is MSSQL$Instance\audit. This directory is stored, by default, on the same drive as your system files. Through the SQL Profiler, you can choose an alternative directory for storing trace files. Because these files can get large in size, you will want to place them on a drive that has space available to accommodate the growth of the file. In most cases, you will not want SQL Server to fail because the audit information cannot be written to the log file.

Using the SQL Profiler Utility

SQL Profiler is a graphical SQL Server 2000 tool used to monitor (trace) selected SQL Server events and save the information to a table or file with a .TRC filename extension for later analysis. For example, you can monitor slowly executing stored procedures or events immediately preceding deadlocks. You can create traces and then replay them (in real time or step-by-step mode) on a test SQL Server computer to debug performance and coding problems.

In addition to monitoring performance-related issues, SQL Profiler is the primary tool that is built in with SQL Server to monitor security-related events. SQL Profiler is your primary auditing tool for following SQL Server events.

A *SQL Server event* is any action generated within the SQL Server engine. Events could include any of the following items:

SQL Server logins.   These logins include access from both Windows and SQL Server Authentication.

Transact-SQL statements.   Any Transact-SQL statement can be monitored. For security purposes you may want to view the users who are performing modification statements.

Stored procedures.   With stored procedures, you can monitor the user who is executing the procedure or the performance issues related to the execution of the procedure.

Errors.   SQL Profiler can monitor errors related to the execution of a statement in order to troubleshoot a failed Transact-SQL statement.

Security events.   These events can include the changing of passwords, adding of new logins, accessing of database objects, and many other security activities. You can use this category to track security configuration changes to your server.

For each event, you can choose to monitor selected information, including computer name, object affected (such as table name), username (both the database user and the Windows Account), the text of the Transact-SQL statement or stored procedure, and the time the event started and stopped. The information you choose to monitor is stored in a template with a .TDF filename extension that defines the information that will be captured into a file or table. The result of this capture of information is called a *trace*. Using the same information definitions over time is useful for detecting performance and usage trends.

SQL Profiler provides you with flexibility that is not offered through other SQL Server tools. When you are using Windows Authentication, you have the opportunity to grant a Windows group access to SQL Server. More information on group access to SQL Server can be found in Chapter 4, "Establishing Login Security." With most tools (Enterprise Manager and SQL Query Analyzer), the group name is all that you have access to.

If a user is performing an action against the server and the access to SQL Server was defined through a Windows group membership, you will not see the Windows username of the user performing the action. All users belonging to the Windows group are treated as a single SQL Server login and single database user. SQL Profiler is the only built-in SQL Server tool that effectively tracks the action back to the Windows Account that performed the action. If you use SQL Profiler for auditing, you have the flexibility of granting group access to SQL Server while maintaining a complete audit trail.

You should take care to avoid monitoring too many events, or you can affect SQL Server performance. The default maximum size of a trace file is 5 MB. By default, SQL Profiler creates a new trace file when the current trace file reaches the maximum size. The new trace filename is the original .TRC filename with a number appended to it. For example, if you create a .TRC file named NewTrace.TRC, the first file is NewTrace.TRC. After that file is filled to the 5 MB limit, the next file created is named NewTrace1.TRC. You can limit the trace size by limiting the type of events and data that are collected. For example, if you don't need to monitor events related to the locking of SQL Server, don't include locks as events to be monitored by SQL Profiler.

Filters can be used to limit the amount of data that is stored in your log files. Filters support key words such as like and not like, equals and not equals, and greater than and equal and less than, or equal should also be used to limit event data (such as by database, application, or user). For example, you may not want to monitor the events created by the SQL Profiler tool. You can add an application filter that prevents the capture of information from SQL Profiler. The process of adding a filter is described along with the other properties of a trace later in this section. The filter should appear configured in SQL Profiler as shown in Figure 14.3.

Events are grouped into event categories. Within each event category are event classes for capturing data about selected SQL Server events. Table 14.1 describes the event categories that you can monitor.

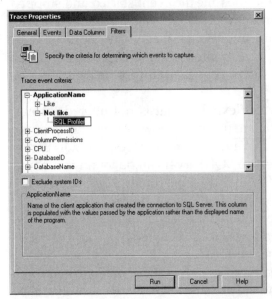

Figure 14.3 Filters control the amount of data that is captured by a SQL Server trace.

Table 14.1 Event Categories for SQL Profiler

EVENT CATEGORY	EVENT CLASSES	SUGGESTED USE
Cursors	Cursor creation, use, and deletion	Find out the types of cursors being used. Knowing this is beneficial in finding out if the cursor that SQL Server is using is consistent with the cursor that the application is requesting.
Database	Automatic growth and shrinkage events	Used to find out when databases are growing. Beneficial in determining appropriate growth and shrinkage parameters.
Errors and warnings	Error and warning events such as missing statistics	Used to find lengthy waits for resources and possible contention issues.
Locks	Locks acquired, canceled, escalated, and released	Useful for tracking locking issues. Specifically helpful for troubleshooting deadlocks.
Objects	Object creating, opening, closing, and deleting events	Useful for tracking the use of audits. Great security feature for tracking access to mission-critical database objects.
Performance	Query Optimizer showplan events	Used to track query execution and performance.
Scans	Table and index scan events	Used to track the types of scans being performed. These scans are beneficial in determining if indexes are being used appropriately.
Security Audit	Security audit events	Useful for tracking logins, logouts, security and permission changes, password changes, and backup or restore operations. This category is the key to auditing your current security configuration.
Server	Memory change events	Changes to server memory configuration.
Sessions	Length of time per user connection and amount of SQL Server processor time used by queries submitted using each connection	Connected users, database activity, and CPU time used for charging for usage and activity. This option should be used in conjunction with the security audit category to track the types of connections that are causing security violations.

(continues)

Table 14.1 Event Categories for SQL Profiler *(Continued)*

EVENT CATEGORY	EVENT CLASSES	SUGGESTED USE
Stored Procedures	Stored procedure execution information, including cache hits and misses, order of execution, when aged out of cache, and when recompiled	This feature is useful in tracking the performance and usage of stored procedures. Monitoring stored procedures can be a security benefit by helping determine how stored procedures are being executed.
Transactions	Transaction execution events	Transaction commits and rollbacks. Also useful in tracking distributed transactions.
TSQL	Execution of SQL Server statements and batch events	Accuracy of application results compared to expected results during application testing. This category can also be used to track events that take a long time to run, including the users who submit these queries.

With SQL Profiler, you can use the preconfigured trace definitions (called *templates*) either as is or as a basis for creating custom templates. These templates define the types of event information that SQL Profiler traces and captures. The following list of templates is a starting point for auditing security-related information. More templates are available, but their usage is limited more to performance, and these other templates don't provide the security information needed for the scope of this book.

- The *SQLProfilerStandard template* tracks general information regarding the execution of batches and stored procedures. These settings help in tracking connections and execution times.

- The *SQLProfilerTSQL template* tracks each Transact-SQL statement and the order in which it was executed. This template helps you pinpoint statements that are performing security violations.

- The *SQLProfilerTSQL_Replay template* tracks details about each Transact-SQL statement issued in sufficient detail to be used for replay in SQL Query Analyzer. Use this preconfigured template as a starting point for capturing data to replay for testing or security analysis.

■ The *SQLProfilerTSQL_SPs template* tracks details in execution order about each stored procedure that executes, including the Transact-SQL commands within each stored procedure. This template can help you track the details of the stored procedures being executed.

To create a trace based on one of these templates, perform the following steps:

1. Open the SQL Profiler tool.

2. From the File menu item, expand New and select Trace.

3. From the Connect to SQL Server dialogue box, enter your connection information and click OK.

4. The Trace Properties dialogue box should appear as shown in Figure 14.4.

5. Click the drop-down box under Template Name to select the template you would like to use.

6. Select the Events tab as shown in Figure 14.5. Use the Add button to configure any additional events you would like to monitor.

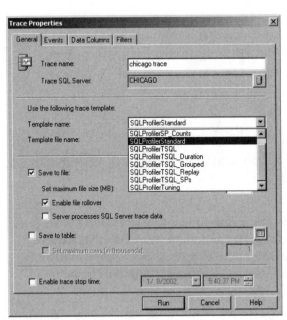

Figure 14.4   Use the Trace Properties dialogue box to select the template you would like to use as the basis for your trace.

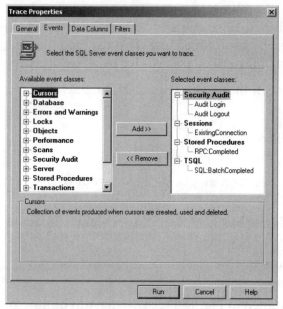

Figure 14.5 Event classes determine the actions that you will capture with your trace.

7. Select the Data Columns tab to view the columns that will be captured for each event. Use the Add button to add any additional columns you would like to capture.

8. Click the Filters tab to add any restrictions to the data you want to capture.

9. When the trace is configured, click Run to start the trace.

10. The SQL Profiler—Trace details window will appear as shown in Figure 14.6.

NOTE Trace details are complicated, and viewing the results may be time-consuming. Test this process and become comfortable with the utility before you need to view the security-specific information. You will be more efficient in tracking security-related audit events if you are familiar with the SQL Profiler utility.

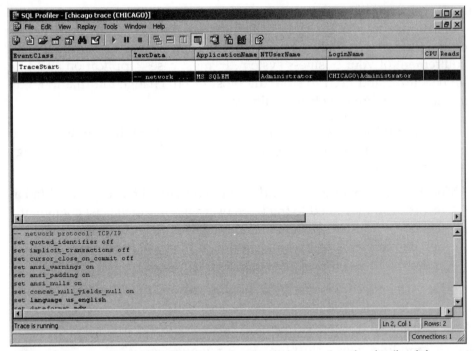

Figure 14.6 Use the SQL Profiler—Trace details window to view the details of the events that you choose to capture.

Application Auditing

In some cases auditing is required within an application. The SQL Profiler requires the trace (capture) of data on an ongoing basis. If your requirements are to be able to track the user who last added or changed a record in a table, then application auditing is for you. You will want to alter the schema of your database to include information about the user who performed the modification.

The most important step in application auditing is determining the level of detail that needs to be captured on each record. For instance, your application could take any one of the three layers of auditing. The more detailed the level of auditing, the more overhead you will have to create in the application. This overhead generally increases the complexity of maintaining the process. Use the more complicated options only when they are a requirement of your business system. In most cases, application auditing can be simple and used to store the most recent change information. Following are the three levels of auditing:

New record tracking.   You may only need to know the user who added a record to the table, which would make this level of auditing appropriate.

Modification tracking.   In addition to knowing the user who added a record, you may need to track the user who made the last change. If this is your desired level of auditing, you should determine how detailed this level of tracking should be. You will need to know the answers to the following two questions:

- After a record is modified, do you still need to know the user who added the record?

- When a record is modified, do you need to be able to track all modifications or just the most previous change?

Deletion tracking.   At this level, you need to determine if you want to track a record that has been deleted. If you want to track the deleted records, you also need to determine if you want to store the original new record tracking and modification tracking information.

The following sections describe the changes that need to occur within your database to support these levels of application auditing.

New Record Tracking

New record tracking is the easiest level of application auditing to implement. You will want to be able to track the user who performed the operation that added the new record. On the tables that you want to audit, you will need to add a column that stores the username of the user who created the record.

For the new column you need to create a default that uses the username() function. If the column is not supplied by the INSERT statement, then the username() function fills in the value. The username() function supplies the current username value. Defaults are applied only at insert time, so this process is an effective method of tracking the new record and will not change as users make modifications to the record. To add the username() function default to a table in your database, perform the following steps:

1. Open Enterprise Manager.
2. Click to expand your server group.
3. Click to expand the server that you want to alter.
4. Click to expand the Databases container.
5. Click to expand your database.
6. Double-click on the Tables container.
7. From the Details pane, right-click on the table you want to audit and select Design.
8. From the Design Table dialogue box, add a column that will be used for auditing (in our example the column is named Iusername), as shown in Figure 14.7. The Data Type should be a character type that allows for the current username to be added. More information on the character data types can be found in SQL Server Books Online.
9. Click on the column you created in step 8, and in the lower pane in the Default Value field type username().
10. Click the Save icon on the Toolbar to save the changes you have made.

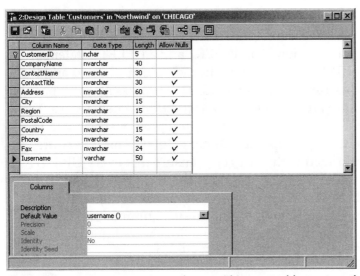

Figure 14.7 You can create a column within your table to store the username of a user who adds a record.

Modification Tracking

With modification tracking you first have to determine whether or not you need to track all changes that are made to the record. You also need to determine whether you want to store the name of the original creator of the record or just the name of the user who made the most current change. In this section the following three scenarios are described:

- The user who made the most recent modification is stored.
- The user who made the most recent modification is stored along with the original creator of the record.
- All modifications are stored.

The User Who Made the Most Recent Modification

This implementation is similar to new record tracking. You should implement this type of auditing when you need to track the user who performed the most recent modification, not just the creator of the record. When a new record is added, you want the user who added the record to be stored with the record. After a change is modified, you want to store only the user who made the most recent modification. Perform the following steps to maintain this level of auditing:

1. New record tracking has to be configured as described in the procedure in the preceding *New Record Tracking* section.

2. When a record is modified, you should perform one of the following actions within a transaction. The first option is to create a transaction that is a combination of an INSERT and a DELETE statement instead of an UPDATE statement. The old value is deleted and the new value is inserted as a new record. This process makes it possible for the username() function to work as it did for a new record. Your second option is to update the column you previously created for auditing whenever you update another column. This procedure should be performed with a trigger to ensure that every UPDATE statement includes the modification of the auditing column. The trigger should be set on the table and should be configured on UPDATE. The trigger should set the audit column to the current username by using the username() function. More information on triggers can be found in SQL Server Books Online.

The User Who Made the Most Recent Modification Is Stored with the Creator of the Record

In some cases it is useful to store the name of the user who originally created the record along with the user who performed the most recent update. In this case you need to perform the following steps to meet your auditing requirements:

- New record tracking has to be configured by following the procedure presented in the *New Record Tracking* section.

- A second column has to be created in the table for auditing purposes to hold the name of the user who most recently updated the column. Use your naming conventions to guarantee consistency throughout your database. The second column should also be configured with the username() function as the default. When a record is added, both columns should contain the username of the user who added the record.

- A trigger should be added to update the column you created in step 2 whenever the record is modified. The trigger should be set on the table and configured on the update action. Whenever an update occurs to any of the columns in the table, you want the trigger to update the newly added audit column. With these options set, you can maintain the name of the user who created the record in the first audit column you created and the name of the user who performed the most recent modification in the second audit column you created in step 2.

All Modifications Are Stored

In this scenario the process starts to get a little more complicated. This method of auditing should be configured only when the requirements of your system require a full audit trail of all of the modifications that are made to your database. As changes are made to the table in question, you will delete an old record and insert a new record into the original table. You will then take the deleted value and write it to your new auditing table. This is a very complete method of auditing, but it does not account for deletions. You should perform the following steps to make sure that you are able to keep track of all modifications that are made to the record:

1. New record tracking has to be configured on the table you want to audit. This feature should be configured as described by the procedure in the section *New Record Tracking*.

2. You also need to configure an additional column within your audited table to track the date and time that a record was added. Because every modification performed while you are in this mode of auditing deletes the old record and inserts a new record, the value of this column is always the date and time of the last modification. You should create a default for this column, similar to the username() default. In this case, however, you will want to use the GetDate() function. The GetDate() function returns the current date and time. This functions stores the date and time that the action occurred.

3. You then need to create an additional table to store the historical information needed to maintain the full audit trail. This table should have a column structure that is identical to that of the table that it is storing information for. The only difference should be the primary key. The primary key should be a composite of your existing unique identifier and the date and time column you created. This change to your primary key allows you to store the same column from your original table multiple times. Storing the column multiple times is necessary to track the entire life of the record. New record tracking should not be configured on your new table. It should receive both the username and the date and time columns from the original table.

4. You then need to write a trigger for the original table. The trigger should be assigned to the DELETE action. When a record is deleted from the original table, the trigger should take the values and insert them into the new audit table you created in step 3.

5. All modifications should be written as transactions. The transactions should be written as a combination of an INSERT and a DELETE instead of an UPDATE statement. When you modify a record, the old value is deleted from the table and written to the audit table by the trigger. The new value is inserted into your original table.

6. If you want to retrieve all of the iterations of a record, you will need to JOIN the original table with the auditing table to show all of the changes to the record.

Deletion Tracking

In many cases you will not need to keep track of deletions. You will need to evaluate your requirements to determine if a record has to be tracked after it has been deleted. In some databases data is not actually deleted when the user hits the Delete button in the application. The most common form of dealing with this issue is to create a history table. For instance, a customers table may require creating a customer history table to track customer records that otherwise would have been deleted. This concept could be applied to orders, inventory, employees, and many other items. To set up deletion tracking effectively, perform the following steps:

1. Create a history table that has the same table structure as the original table.

2. Create an additional column in the history table to track the user who performed the deletion. This column should be given a default that uses the username() function.

3. Create a trigger that is assigned to the original table. The trigger should be associated with the DELETE action. The trigger should take the record that was deleted and write it to the new history table. When the record is written, the username() function identifies the user who performed the deletion.

NOTE Triggers are advanced Transact-SQL statements and can be associated with the INSERT, DELETE, and UPDATE actions. When records are deleted or inserted, the values are temporarily stored in inserted and deleted tables in RAM on the server. When your trigger statements need to retrieve the values that were previously inserted in or deleted from the table, they should do so from these tables that are in RAM. Your statements will not always work right if you try to retrieve the values from the original table. By using these RAM tables, you will increase performance and guarantee accurate results. More information on inserted and deleted tables can be found in SQL Server Books Online.

Best Practices

- Use server auditing to audit the successful and failed login attempts when you suspect an unauthorized user is attempting to access your data.

- Only use C2-Mode auditing when your business system requires that you track all access to database objects.

- Use the SQL Profiler utility to track security configuration changes. Tracking these changes is useful for keeping a handle on changes to authentication modes and audit levels.

- Use the SQL Profiler utility to track Transact-SQL statements. This kind of tracking is beneficial in troubleshooting failed SQL statements. It is also helpful in tracking statements that are performing actions that are not authorized.

- Practice using the SQL Profiler utility. It can be a very complex tool. You will be more effective in tracking security violations to your system if you know how to take advantage of the SQL Profiler features.

- Use the SQL Profiler utility to track the Windows user account. SQL Profiler is the best tool for tracking an action back to the Windows account that performed the action. Most other SQL Server tools view all members of a group as the same login and database user. SQL Profiler allows you to retrieve information at both the Windows 2000 and SQL Server levels.

- Implement application auditing only at the level required by your business process. The more detailed your application auditing requirements are, the more complex the implementation of the solution will be.

- Use the username() and GetDate() functions to assist with application auditing.

- Use triggers to help maintain audit information that has to be stored across multiple tables.

REVIEW QUESTIONS

1. What is C2-Mode security?

2. What is a SQL Trace?

3. What are the SQL Profiler templates used for?

4. What templates are geared toward security auditing?

5. How can you limit the amount of information captured by SQL Profiler?

6. What is the purpose of the username() function?

Managing Internet Security

Whenever the Internet becomes involved, security becomes a concern. As the Internet has developed over the last couple of years, the functionality provided to the common Web user has continued to increase. SQL Server has grown in functionality over the same period of time, and inevitably there are organizations that want to view their data over a Web medium. There are also several Web-based applications that use SQL Server as a backend database product.

While organizations strive to make more data available on the Internet, they also have to address a whole new scope of security issues. The data has to be secure and possibly encrypted as it is transmitted, the database server needs to be protected from hackers who will try to expose the data, and firewalls and proxy servers add additional layers of filtering for which applications have to account.

As data has become more accessible with the growth of the Internet, the concern arises that your data will also be more accessible to millions of other users. Your organization will need to develop a security strategy that allows your data to be accessed over the Internet only by the users who need to see the data, while still providing as much functionality to the users as possible.

> **NOTE** This chapter focuses on interfacing with data via the public Internet. Most of the details provided apply equally to a private intranet.

This chapter addresses the Internet security concerns related to making SQL Server data available over the Internet. The first section of the chapter provides a detailed overview of the Internet integration features of SQL Server. The chapter then moves to a description of the options that are available for connecting to SQL Server over the Internet, including direct connections to SQL Server, connections made through Internet Information Server (IIS), and connections made through various Proxy Server and firewall configurations. This chapter then moves to the Web Assistant Wizard and other options for publishing SQL Server data over the Internet. Each section of this chapter addresses the security features of SQL Server 2000 that affect the data that is accessible over the Internet.

Overview of Internet Integration Features of SQL Server 2000

SQL Server 2000 has been upgraded from its predecessors with the Internet in mind. As making your information accessible via the Internet becomes easier, you will need to be aware of the security issues that may arise.

This section introduces the integration features of SQL Server and the Internet. It then identifies how SQL Server works in conjunction with other products to allow Internet access. This section then identifies the changes to the database engine of SQL Server to provide native support for XML.

Integration with Other Products

SQL Server 2000 works with other products to form a stable and secure data store for Internet and intranet networks. SQL Server 2000 works with Microsoft Windows 2000 Server and Microsoft Windows NT Server security and encryption facilities to implement secure data storage. SQL Server uses Windows Authentication, which depends on the integration with Windows 2000. The Windows 2000 Secure Sockets Layer (SSL) features can also be used to create secure, encrypted connections from the Internet to SQL Server. More information on SSL is found later in this chapter in the section titled *Connecting to SQL Server through a Web Server*.

- SQL Server 2000 forms a high-performance data storage service for Web applications running under Internet Information Server (IIS). The client browser can be used to connect to IIS, which authenticates the user, and IIS then connects to SQL Server to retrieve the data for the application interface. With this configuration the security model is a combination of SQL Server security and IIS security.

- SQL Server 2000 can be used with Application Center Server and Commerce Server to build and maintain large, sophisticated e-commerce Web sites. With this integration you can create Web stores that market products, accept credit cards, and guarantee encrypted connections. All of these items are security measures that Web users have come to expect from Internet-based applications. SQL Server is used as the database engine in this configuration, so the details of creating an e-commerce site are not included in this book. To learn more about using Application Center Server and Commerce Server to build and deploy e-commerce Web sites, refer to Microsoft's Web site at www.microsoft.com.

- Analysis Services includes features that support the functionality required in many Business to Business, or Business to Consumer Web applications. With Analysis Services you can analyze the data stored in SQL Server and build reports on the effectiveness of your Web site. Features such as distinct count and online analytical processing (OLAP) alerts allow you to perform activities such as analyzing Web site click-streams to evaluate the effectiveness of your Web interface.

- An integrated data mining engine supports data mining analysis of both relational databases and OLAP cubes. The data mining engine is extensible through OLE DB for data mining, allowing you to incorporate algorithms from Independent Software Vendors (ISVs) to support extended data mining features.

- English Query allows Web applications to support users of any skill level entering English language questions about data in either a relational database or an OLAP cube. English Query matches the question against a model of the database or cube and returns either a SQL or a multidimensional expression (MDX) query to retrieve the proper results.

SQL Server Engine Enhancements

The Microsoft SQL Server 2000 relational database engine includes native support for extensible markup language (XML), which is designed specifically for delivering content over the Internet, much like HTML.

With HTML you are limited to a set of predefined elements; after the data is displayed it loses all context. For example, if you display a report over the Web you may want to view your customers and the amount of money they spent last year. Even though the report is meaningful for you to look at, after it is displayed with HTML, all of the data is treated as the same type of text. There is no distinction between the currency data and the character data in the report.

XML allows you to define your own set of elements to maintain the structural integrity of your data as it is transferred from one location to another. This feature can be used to help facilitate the transfer of data over an unsecured medium such as the Internet. HTTP is a standard Internet protocol used to transfer files and data. The connections made over the HTTP protocol are generally made using port 80. With XML, SQL Server data can be passed over the Internet using port 80. This connection allows the data to be easily passed through secured environments, which include proxy servers and firewalls when necessary. The following set of options is available when you are integrating SQL Server with XML. More information on configuring XML support in SQL Server 2000 can be found in Appendix A, "XML for SQL Server 2000."

- Transact-SQL results can be returned as XML documents to Web or line of business applications using the OLE DB and Active Data Object (ADO) application programming interfaces (APIs), allowing for the easy retrieval of SQL Server data to a Web interface.

- You can define annotated external data representation (XDR) schemas that represent a logical view of the tables in your database. Web applications can then reference these schemas in XPath queries to build XML documents and populate data for the user. This process will create a view of your SQL Server database schema. XPath queries are defined in Appendix A, "XML for SQL Server 2000."

- The SQL Server 2000 includes a data-link library (DLL) that allows you to define virtual roots in Microsoft IIS associated with an instance of SQL Server 2000. Internet applications can then compose URL strings that reference a SQL Server 2000 virtual root and contain a Transact-SQL statement. The Transact-SQL statement is sent to the instance of SQL Server 2000 associated with the virtual root, and the result is returned as an XML document. Each virtual root has its own security settings, which are configured within IIS. You can control the level of authentication required and configure encryption options from within IIS.

- XML documents can be added to SQL Server 2000 databases. The OPENXML function can expose the data from an XML document in a rowset, which can be referenced by Transact-SQL statements, such as SELECT, INSERT, or UPDATE.

Connections to SQL Server from the Internet

You can connect to an instance of Microsoft SQL Server over the Internet using SQL Query Analyzer or a client application based on Open Database Connectivity (ODBC) or DB-Library.

To share data over the Internet, the client and server must be connected to the Internet. In addition, you must use TCP/IP or Multiprotocol Net-Libraries between the client and the server. More information about Net-Libraries can be found in Chapter 7, "Implementing Front-End Application Security." If you use the Multiprotocol Net-Library, you need to ensure that TCP/IP support is enabled.

This section breaks down your options for connecting to SQL Server over the Internet. The first part of the section discusses a direct connection to SQL Server. The section then describes the factors to consider when you connect to the Internet through a proxy server or firewall. Finally this section addresses connection issues when the browser first connects to IIS, and IIS connects to SQL Server to retrieve the data.

A Direct Connection to SQL Server

SQL Server supports direct connections to SQL Server over the Internet. A direct connection is one that doesn't involve an interface with a Web server to make the connection to SQL Server. In many cases the application will first make a connection to a Web server, which then connects to the SQL Server database. Applications can now also make a direct connection to SQL Server. The connection has to be made using TCP/IP sockets as the network library. A socket connection is made up of two parts: an Internet Protocol (IP) address associated with one or more network cards in a computer and a TCP port address specific to an instance of SQL Server.

Default instances of SQL Server use TCP port 1433. When you install multiple instances of SQL Server on a single machine, SQL Server assigns an alternate port number to each subsequent instance. These named instances dynamically assign an unused TCP port number the first time the instance is started. The named instance can also dynamically change its TCP port address on a subsequent startup if the original TCP port number is being used by another application. SQL Server only dynamically changes to an unused TCP port if the port it is currently listening on was dynamically selected; that is, if the port was statically selected (manually), SQL Server will display an error and continue to listen on other ports.

It is unlikely that another application would attempt to use port 1433, since that port is registered as a well-known address for SQL Server. You will need to know the IP address or hostname and the port number of your instance of SQL Server in order to connect to the server over the Internet. You can view the port number of your instance of SQL Server by performing the following steps:

1. Open your Server Network Utility from the Microsoft SQL Server program group.

2. From the General tab, highlight TCP/IP and click the Properties button. The dialogue box named Test—TCP/IP appears as shown in Figure 15.1.

3. You can change the port number that is displayed for your connection if you so choose.

To complete the connection the client must request a connection with the server using the TCP/IP Net-Library. The client can perform this connection by installing the SQL Server client tools or using another direct connection method, such as an Active Document from the browser, which provides the full usage of an OLE DB provider or ODBC driver. More information about connecting to SQL Server using OLE DB and ODBC can be found in Chapter 7, "Implementing Front-End Application Security." The following sections detail the differences when connecting via these methods.

Client Tools

When you install the client tools on the machine that is connecting to the server over the Internet, you need to configure the TCP/IP Net-Library settings. By default, the TCP/IP Net-Library is enabled, and it tries to make a connection over port 1433. If this is not the port you want to connect with, you need to modify the default setting in the Client Network Utility.

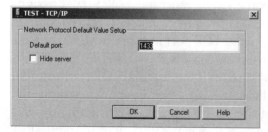

Figure 15.1 The Test—TCP/IP dialogue box is used to view and configure the port number assigned to your instance of SQL Server.

You may also need to connect to multiple instances of SQL Server. If this is the case, you need to configure aliases to each of the servers. The alias is a component of the Client Network Utility and is used to identify the connection properties (hostname and port number) for individual instances. When configuring aliases in the Client Network Utility, you have the option of allowing the utility to dynamically determine the port number. This option should be chosen to avoid having to update the configuration of the Client Network Utility when the server configuration changes. To configure an alias for a named SQL Server instance, perform the following steps:

1. Open the Client Network Utility from the Microsoft SQL Server program group.

2. Click the Alias tab as shown in Figure 15.2.

3. Click the Add button to display the Add Network Library Configuration dialogue box shown in Figure 15.3.

4. Type in a server alias to provide a friendly name for the server connection.

5. Click to select TCP/IP as the Network Library.

6. Type in the Server name. This is the hostname of the instance of SQL Server you are connecting to.

7. Choose your port configuration. Dynamically Determine Port is the default port setting.

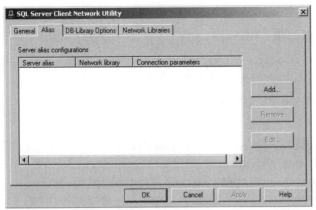

Figure 15.2 Use the SQL Server Client Network Utility to configure TCP/IP connection properties for each instance of SQL Server.

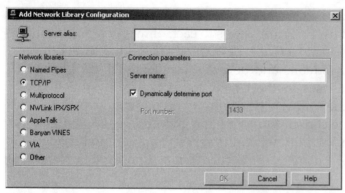

Figure 15.3 Supply the server hostname and port number for the connection to a SQL Server instance in the Add Network Library Configuration dialogue box.

From the client tools you also have the ability to configure an encrypted connection. The encryption supported by SQL Server depends on Secure Sockets Layer. To support this level of encryption you need to purchase and install a certificate on your SQL Server. You can use the same certificate for multiple instances of SQL Server.

VeriSign is the industry leader in selling and managing Internet certificates. For more information about purchasing and installing your certificate, refer to VeriSign's Web site at www.verisign.com. Once the certificate is installed, you can then enable protocol encryption for connections to your instance of SQL Server. If you want users to be able to establish an encrypted connection to an instance of SQL Server, you can do so by enabling encryption for the Multiprotocol Net-Library:

1. Open the Server Network Utility.

2. Under Enabled protocols, click Multiprotocol, and then click Properties to see the Test—Multiprotocol dialogue box shown in Figure 15.4.

3. Select the Enable Encryption checkbox.

NOTE When you plan to use encryption with a failover cluster configuration, you must install the server certificate, with the fully qualified Domain Name Service (DNS) name of the virtual server, on all nodes (servers) in the failover cluster. For example, if you have a two-node cluster, with nodes named Chicago.softouch.trn and NewYork.softouch.trn and a virtual SQL Server named "SQL1," you need to get a certificate for "SQL1.softouch.trn" and install the certificate on both nodes. You can then check the Force protocol encryption checkbox on the Server Network Utility to configure your failover cluster for encryption.

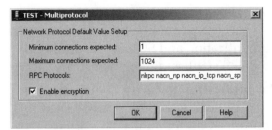

Figure 15.4 The Enable Encryption option configures your server to use Secure Sockets Layer encryption.

A Connection through OLE DB

Internet-based connections are also supported through the use of OLE DB. By default the browser does not support the use of OLE DB as a connection method. You will need to provide the basis for the connectivity through the application that you develop. Visual Basic supports a feature referred to as the *Active Document*, which allows you to simulate the Visual Basic environment through an ActiveX control. The control is downloaded and installed when you first connect to the application over the Internet. This control takes some initial overhead, but once it is installed you can use the OLE DB provider to connect to your data.

There are several other features that are supported by different development environments and that provide you with the ability to interact with your data via OLE DB or ODBC. For more information on these options, refer to the product documentation for the application that you have chosen to develop.

Inherently, applications that use a direct connection to SQL Server over the Internet have security concerns that need to be addressed. Once you allow a connection directly from the browser to SQL Server you have opened a door to SQL Server that all Internet users can try to use. If you prefer to have a direct connection between SQL Server and an Internet browser, you should consider the following security suggestions:

Implement SSL on your server.   You will want all connections to the server to be encrypted to protect your data as it is being passed along. The detailed configuration of SSL is described previously in this chapter in the section titled *A Direct Connection to SQL Server*.

Implement Windows Authentication instead of SQL Server Authentication.   With Windows Authentication you have control over passwords. You can configure a required length and a period of time within which the password must be changed. You also have the ability to lock out the account on a configured number of failed attempts. More details on Windows Authentication and SQL Server Authentication can be found in Chapter 4, "Establishing Login Security."

Implement auditing within the application to verify the usernames that are making all changes.   Application auditing can be used to track the users who have not properly secured the passwords for their Windows account. More information on auditing with SQL Server can be found in Chapter 14, "Creating an Audit Policy."

Create an instance of SQL Server just for the data that needs to be accessible from the Internet.   You may also want to install this instance on a separate machine. If the physical security of the machine is compromised, only your Internet data will be accessed.

Connections through Firewalls and Proxy Servers

When an application is created for use on the Internet, it is not always as easy as going from the client to the server. Organizations use firewalls and proxy servers to help secure their networks and isolate them from the Internet. This section describes the issues involved with making connections over these secured Internet mediums. The section first identifies the issues that arise when you connect to a SQL Server through a firewall, and then it discusses how you would connect to a SQL Server instance through a proxy server. This section also introduces the reverse-publishing feature that many proxy servers support to help secure SQL Server data.

Using a Firewall System with SQL Server

Many companies use a firewall system to isolate their networks from unplanned access from the Internet. A firewall can restrict Internet applications' access to your network by forwarding only requests targeted at specific IP addresses in the local network. Requests for all other network addresses are blocked by the firewall. You can allow Internet applications to access an instance of SQL Server in the local network by configuring the firewall to forward network requests that specify the network address of the instance of SQL Server.

To work effectively with a firewall, you must ensure that the instance of SQL Server always listens on the network address that the firewall is configured to forward. When using a named instance of SQL Server with a firewall, use the Server Network Utility to configure the named instance to listen on a specific TCP port. You must pick a TCP port that is not being used by another application running on the same computer or cluster. For a list of well-known ports registered for use by various applications, see www.ise.edu/in-notes/iana/assignments/port-numbers.

You should have the firewall administrator configure the firewall to forward the IP address and TCP port the instance of SQL Server is listening on (using either 1433 for a default instance or the TCP port you configured a named instance to listen on). Also configure the firewall to forward requests for UDP port 1434 on the same IP address. SQL Server 2000 uses UDP port 1434 to establish communications links from applications.

For example, consider a computer running one default instance and two named instances of SQL Server. The computer is configured such that the network addresses that the three instances listen on all have the same IP address. The default instance would listen on TCP port 1433, one named instance could be assigned TCP port 1434, and the other named instance could be assigned to TCP port 1954. You would then configure the firewall to forward network requests for UDP port 1434 and TCP ports 1433, 1434, and 1954 on to that IP address.

Connections to SQL Server through a Proxy Server

You can also connect to an instance of SQL Server through a proxy server. Proxy servers are stand-alone products that isolate your internal users from the Internet. The users send their Web requests to the proxy server, which then forwards the request to the Internet on behalf of the user. Proxy servers provide the following benefits to your organization:

- Internet data can be cached at the proxy server. After the proxy server retrieves a Web page on behalf of the user, that page can be stored on the Proxy server so that if another user requests the same page, the Proxy server can serve the request without going to the Internet, thus providing faster responses to requests and conserving your Internet resources.

- The proxy server can authenticate the user making the request of the Internet. With this feature you can control the users who have access to various Web applications and protocols.

- The proxy server can be used to reverse-publish data for you. More information on reverse-publishing can be found later in the next section, *Reverse Publishing with a Proxy Server*.

- The proxy server acts on behalf of the clients using a single external IP address. This feature enables your internal clients to use private IP addresses. The only real Internet IP address you need for Internet access is the IP address assigned to your proxy server.

- You can also use the proxy server in a similar fashion to a firewall. You can prevent unauthorized users from connecting to your private network. A proxy server keeps your sensitive data secure by controlling all the permissions and Internet users' access to the listening port. You can block access to restricted sites by ranges of IP addresses, domains, or individual users so you can ensure that your users are using their Internet permissions appropriately.

When you are a user behind the proxy server and you are trying to connect directly to a SQL Server over the Internet, you will be making the request to the SQL Server port number configured in your Client Network Utility. The proxy server administrator will have to allow that port to be connected to, and you will have to have permission to use the configured port for outgoing access. If you are not making a direct connection to SQL Server and have to go through a Web server first, your connection to the Web server will most likely be on a known port number that is already configured.

Reverse-Publishing with a Proxy Server

Reverse-publishing is a security feature included with many proxy server products. It allows you to store a server that needs to be accessed from the Internet behind the firewall without compromising the security of your network. An Internet client directs requests to the proxy server as though it were the server that is publishing data. The proxy server then accepts the request and passes the request on to the server that is behind the firewall. The proxy server is acting on behalf of the Internet client for the server access. By implementing reverse-publishing, you ensure that the Internet client never has direct access to the server that is publishing information to the Internet. You can use the proxy server to carry out the following security options:

- The proxy server can authenticate the Web user.

- The proxy server can perform packet filtering to make sure that only certain protocols are allowed in from the Internet.

- The proxy server can implement Secure Sockets Layer (SSL) to ensure that all data is encrypted as it is passed to and from the Internet. By using the proxy server for SSL, you can configure the certificate security in one location rather than having to configure SSL for each SQL Server instance.

For more information on configuring reverse-publishing, refer to the Internet Security and Acceleration (ISA) server documentation at Microsoft's Web site. The ISA server is Microsoft's new proxy server and firewall. The Web site is www.microsoft.com/ISAserver.

Connecting to SQL Server through a Web Server

Web browser clients, in most cases, do not directly access SQL Server databases. Rather, when a Web server receives a browser request requiring data access, it connects to a database on the browser's behalf, submits a query customized to that request, and constructs a response to the browser based on the query results. For Microsoft IIS, this server-side processing technology is implemented with Active Server Pages (ASP). Typically, ASP combines standard HTML and embedded script that executes on the Web server and sends the script's output in HTML to the browser. Since the ASP script executes on the server and responds in pure HTML, it works with any Web browser. Other Web servers have similar server-side technologies for accessing databases. Examples include Java servlets, Java Server Pages (JSP), and ColdFusion.

Web servers generally use one of three data access technologies to access SQL Server databases: OLE DB—Universal Data Access, ODBC (Open Database Connectivity), and JDBC (Java Database Connectivity). Since these data access technologies are low-level APIs that are difficult to learn, more programmer-friendly interfaces such as ADOs and Java SQL classes are available. Figure 15.5 illustrates how the pieces of data access fit together. This section first describes the process of using ADO for data access over OLE DB and ODBC and then describes the process of using JDBC to access SQL Server.

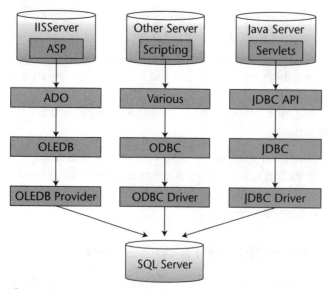

Figure 15.5 Connection methods are available to SQL Server from variety of Web servers.

Using Active Data Objects with Active Server Pages

When working with database servers such as SQL Server, your application needs to create a connection to the appropriate database. Using ADO, you can use the ADO Connection object to explicitly establish connections, or you can use the ADO Command or ADO Recordset object to make connections dynamically. When establishing the connection object, you need to identify the security credentials for the connection. You can either supply standard (SQL Server Authentication) security credentials, which require a username and password, or you can supply trusted connection (Windows Authentication) credentials, which use the Windows user account information for the connection credentials. After establishing the connection, your ASP application can issue the same sort of ADO commands that a standard Visual Basic (VB) application can perform. These commands include executing stored procedures; opening and scrolling a recordset; and inserting, updating, and deleting data.

As shown in Figure 15.5, ADO can use the OLE DB provider for either ODBC or SQL Server to connect with SQL Server. The OLE DB provider for ODBC lets you use the ADO object model with most existing ODBC drivers. While this provider can be used effectively with those data stores that do not have native OLE DB providers, it does not perform as well.

To connect with any database, a connection must supply its method of connecting (such as OLE DB, ODBC, and JBDC, and appropriate provider or driver), the location and name of the database, and a valid username and password. These elements typically comprise a connection's Connection-String property. For example, the following VBScript block illustrates the creation of an ADO Connection object, the setting of its ConnectionString property, and the opening of the connection. The following examples of code present the connection syntax for both a standard SQL Server connection and a trusted Windows Authentication connection. The lines of code that represent the security credentials used for the connection are in bold text.

```
'STANDARD SECURITY
dim cn
set cn = Server.CreateObject("ADODB.Connection") 'creates connection
object
cn.Provider = "SQLOLEDB"  'native SQL Server provider identifier
cn.ConnectionString =    "Data Source=ServerName;" & _
    "Initial Catalog=DatabaseName;" & _
    "User ID=UserName;Password=UserPassword;"
cn.Open
```

This example illustrates using standard SQL Server Authentication security since the username and password are supplied with the connection string. To use Windows authentication, or a trusted connection, the above VBScript block could be modified as follows:

```
'TRUSTED CONNECTION
dim cn
set cn = Server.CreateObject("ADODB.Connection") 'creates connection
object
cn.Provider = "SQLOLEDB"  ' native SQL Server provider identifier
cn.ConnectionString =    "Data Source=ServerName;" & _
    "Initial Catalog=DatabaseName;" & _
    "Integrated Security=SSPI;"
cn.Open
```

To create a SQL Server ADO Connection with the OLE DB provider for ODBC, you must conform to the connection requirements for an ODBC connection. This connection typically requires an ODBC Data Source Name (DSN), which identifies a specific ODBC driver and may contain all other information necessary to make a connection.

You can create a DSN in the "ODBC Data Source Administrator" program found in the Windows NT Control Panel or Data Sources in the

Administrative Tools menu in Windows 2000. Make sure to create a *system* DSN (not a *user* DSN) when using ASPs. The following VBScript code illustrates creating an ADO Connection object and connecting to a SQL Server database from an ASP page with the OLE DB provider for ODBC.

```
'STANDARD SECURITY
dim cn
set cn = Server.CreateObject("ADODB.Connection") 'creates connection
object
cn.ConnectionString =        "DSN=DSNName;" & _
    "Server=ServerName;" & _
    "Database=DatabaseName;" & _
    "Uid=UserName;Pwd=UserPassword;"
cn.Open
```

To use trusted connections, the above VBScript block could be modified as shown in the following example.

```
'TRUSTED CONNECTION
dim cn
set cn = Server.CreateObject("ADODB.Connection") 'creates connection
object
cn.ConnectionString =        "DSN=DSNName;" & _
    "Server=ServerName;" & _
    "Database=DatabaseName;" & _
    "TrustedConnections=yes;"
cn.Open
```

Using Java Database Connectivity to Access SQL Server

Java Database Connectivity (JDBC) is based on Microsoft's Open Database Connectivity (ODBC) interface, which has become an industry standard. However, since JDBC is a more recent database interface, not all database vendors have developed JDBC drivers. Therefore JDBC provides a JDBC-ODBC bridge that allows most databases to be accessed through their ODBC drivers until a native Java driver is released. Although the JDBC-ODBC bridge is adequate, it is recommended that the native database JDBC driver be used rather than going through another level of abstraction with ODBC. As of this writing Microsoft has yet to release a native JDBC driver for SQL Server.

The following code block is from a Java servlet making a connection to SQL Server via the JDBC-ODBC bridge. As when using the OLE DB provider for ODBC, using the JDBC-ODBC bridge requires a DSN.

```
String url ="jdbc:odbc:DSNName [,UserName][,UserPasswor]";
```

```
Class.forName("sun.jdbc.odbc.JdbcOdbcDriver");
Connection con = DriverManager.getConnection(url);
```

The username and password parameters reflected in this example are optional. If specified, they override any default username and password specified in the DSN. Additionally, these parameters would be left blank if Windows Authentication were specified in the DSN. If they are left blank, the Windows user account information is passed to the server.

Using the Web Assistant Wizard

The *Web Assistant Wizard* can be used to publish data on the Internet. It is relatively easy to use and should be considered an option when you are uncomfortable with the data access methods that have already been defined in this chapter. This section covers the purpose of the Wizard and then describes the security requirements for running the Wizard.

You can use the Web Assistant Wizard to generate standard HTML files from Microsoft SQL Server data. The Web Assistant Wizard generates HTML files by using Transact-SQL queries, stored procedures, and extended stored procedures. You can use the wizard to generate an HTML file on a one-time basis or as a regularly scheduled SQL Server task.

You can also update an HTML file using a trigger, but you should use this option with caution. If you use a trigger to update the HTML file, whenever you change the data in the table, the HTML file is regenerated, slowing down your system's performance.

With the Web Assistant Wizard, you can:

- Schedule a task to update a Web page automatically. For example, you can update a price list when a new item is added or a price is changed, thereby maintaining a dynamic inventory and price list for customers and sales staff.

- Publish and distribute management reports, including the latest sales statistics, resource allocations, or other SQL Server data.

- Publish server reports with information about who is accessing the server currently and which locks are being held by which users.

- Publish information outside SQL Server using extended stored procedures.

- Publish server jump lists using a table of favorite Web sites.

To run the Web Assistant Wizard, you must have the following set of permissions:

- CREATE PROCEDURE permissions in the selected database you wish to publish.
- SELECT permissions on columns you would like to make available.
- Permission to create files in the folder where you plan to store the HTML results. This is generally a location that is published to the Internet.

Best Practices

- Use a trusted connection to SQL Server whenever possible. If your application development environment supports trusted connections, you should use them. By using trusted connections you do not have to store hard-coded usernames and passwords.
- Implement Secure Sockets Layer (SSL) to encrypt data that is being disseminated over the Internet. Using SSL requires the purchase and installation of an Internet certificate.
- Configure SSL at either a proxy server that is performing reverse-publishing or on your Web server. If the clients first connect to the proxy server or Web server, the encryption can be enabled at this level of connection. The proxy server or Web server will then connect to SQL Server for the Web client. With this configuration you don't need to configure SSL on every instance of SQL Server.
- Whenever possible, use the native OLE DB provider and you will enjoy faster query response time.
- Use the Web Assistant Wizard to publish data only when you are unfamiliar with other data access technologies. The Wizard is easy to implement, but its use results in poor server performance and very little formatting flexibility.

REVIEW QUESTIONS

1. What is the difference between a direct connection and one that first goes through a Web server?

2. What is a native OLE DB provider?

3. What is the default port that SQL Server is listening on?

4. What is the purpose of the Web Assistant Wizard?

5. What is the difference between a trusted connection and a standard connection to SQL Server?

6. What is Java Database Connectivity (JDBC)?

XML for SQL Server 2000

Extensible Markup Language (XML) is a hypertext programming language used to describe the contents of a set of data and how the data should be output to a device or displayed on a Web page. With SQL Server 2000, you can execute Transact-SQL queries to return a result as XML rather than as a standard rowset. These queries can be executed directly or from within stored procedures. In addition, you can use the Transact-SQL to access data represented as an XML document.

This appendix introduces XML and its support in SQL Server. You will then be introduced to the options for configuring SQL Server support in Internet Information Server (IIS) to support both SQL Server virtual directories and XML. The appendix then introduces the process of accessing your data using HTTP. This appendix then goes into the details of using the FOR XML clause in a SELECT statement to retrieve data.

Introduction to XML and SQL Server

Both XML and Hypertext Markup Language (HTML) are derived from Standard Generalized Markup Language (SGML). SGML is a large, complex language that is difficult to use for publishing data on the Web. HTML is a simpler, specialized markup language that has a number of limitations when working with data on the Web.

Once the information is transferred to HTML, the data loses structure. Everything is stored as text. With HTML you have no equivalent to data typing, which makes it very limited when working with databases. You can not distinguish between text and other types of data so when you want to transfer the data from one location to another you can't maintain the data's original structure. XML is less complicated than SGML and more robust than HTML, so it is becoming an increasingly important language in the exchange of electronic data throughout the Web. XML allows you to maintain your data structure while the information is transferred to and from the Web.

In a relational database such as SQL Server, the result set of a SELECT statement is in the form of a table. Traditional client/server applications that execute a SELECT statement process the result by fetching one row or a block of rows at a time from the tabular result set and mapping the column values into program variables. The normal methods of data access are enhanced by the ability to support XML functionality for data retrieval and storage.

SQL Server2000 includes many features that support XML's functionality. The combination of these features makes SQL Server 2000 an XML-enabled database server. The following features in SQL Server 2000 support XML functionality:

- The ability to access SQL Server through the Hypertext Transport Protocol (HTTP). (See the *Accessing SQL Server Using HTTP* section later in this appendix for more information.)

- The ability to retrieve data by using the SELECT statement and the FOR XML clause.

- The ability to retrieve data using the Xpath query language.

- The ability to write XML data to SQL Server by using the OPENXML rowset provider.

- Support for XML-Data Reduced (XDR) schemas and the ability to specify XPath queries against these schemas.

- Enhancements to the SQL Server OLE DB (SQLOLEDB) provider that enable XML documents to be set as command text and to return result sets as a stream.

NOTE XML functionality is sophisticated and advanced. This appendix just scratches the surface of XML. For more information about using XML with SQL Server and other Microsoft products, refer to the XML Developer Center on the MSDN Web site located at http://msdn.microsoft.com/xml/default.asp.

Configuring SQL Server Support in Internet Information Server

Before accessing a SQL Server 2000 database via HTTP, you must set up an appropriate virtual directory. You can use the IIS Virtual Directory Management for SQL Server utility to define and register a new virtual directory, also known as the virtual root, on the computer running Microsoft Internet Information Services (IIS). This utility instructs IIS to create an association between the new virtual directory and an instance of Microsoft SQL Server. When you create the virtual root, you need to be able to supply the following items:

- The *name of the server* you want to publish in IIS.

- The *name of the virtual directory.* Queries will have to reference the server name and the virtual directory name to access the data.

- The *security method* you will use for the connection. You need to know whether you will use Windows Authentication or SQL Server Authentication.

- The *path* where the database files are stored.

- The *options* you want to support. You can configure the virtual root to support HTTP URL queries, template queries, XPATH queries, and POST operations. URL queries allow users to pass a query in the URL. Template queries allow users to execute queries stored in an XML template. XPATH queries allow users to execute XPATH queries over SQL views. XPATH allows you to create XML views of relational data and then query them. Post allows the user to post an XML template to the virtual directory.

When you are defining the security settings, you are configuring the account information that IIS will use when connecting to SQL Server. You have three options for security settings, which are as follows:

Use Windows Integrated Authentication.   This option is used to pass the current Windows username and password to SQL Server. If the user has not had to log on to Windows before this point, the user will be presented with a logon dialogue box. The account supplied by the user must be a valid Windows account and have access to the data being requested.

Use Basic Authentication (Clear Text) to SQL Server Account.   This option will also supply the user with a logon dialogue box. The user credentials will be passed to SQL Server in a clear text format. The account information supplied must be a valid SQL Server account. You can't pass Windows account information with this authentication option.

Always Log On As.   This option allows you to supply the username and password used to connect to SQL Server. This is beneficial if you do not want the user to log on. The user will access the information anonymously. The user is automatically using the account you supply. The Web user will then be limited to the permissions assigned to this account.

NOTE When using Always Log On As as your security option, you can supply either a Windows account or a SQL Server account. If you choose a Windows account, you can also choose to Enable Windows Account Synchronization. This allows you to sync the password of the account between IIS and Windows 2000. If the password changes in Windows, you do not have to change the setting in IIS. This setting is beneficial for keeping your account information in sync.

After you have made the decisions for all of the information you need to supply, you can now create the virtual directory. To create a new virtual root for your instance of SQL Server 2000, you should perform the following steps:

1. From the SQL Server program group, click Configure XML Support in IIS to open the IIS Virtual Directory Management for SQL Server utility as shown in Figure A.1.

2. Click to expand your server name.

3. Right-click the Web site where you want to create the virtual directory and select New Virtual Directory.

4. From the General tab of the New Virtual Directory Properties dialogue box, specify the name of the virtual directory and the path to your database files.

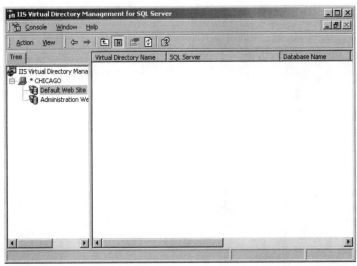

Figure A.1 Use the IIS Virtual Directory Management for SQL Server utility to configure HTTP support for SQL Server.

5. Click the Security tab to choose your authentication method as shown in Figure A.2.

6. Click the Data Source tab to define the server for the virtual directory.

7. Click the Settings tab to define the query options you want to support as shown in Figure A.3.

8. Click OK to create the virtual directory.

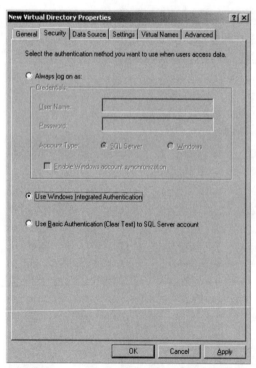

Figure A.2   From the Security tab of the IIS Virtual Directory Management for SQL Server utility, you configure the account information that IIS will use when connecting to SQL Server.

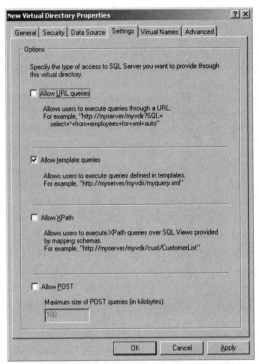

Figure A.3 From the New Virtual Directory Properties dialogue box, you can allow URL queries, template queries, and XPATH queries, after you have configured XML support for SQL Server.

Accessing SQL Server Using HTTP

You can access SQL Server 2000 using HTTP. The HTTP access to SQL Server allows you to access data through the following types of queries.

- Specify SQL queries directly in the URL. For example you could type the following in a URL request:

  ```
  http://Chicago/nwind?sql=SELECT+*+FROM+Customers+FOR+XML+AUTO&root=ro
  ot
  ```

- The FOR XML clause in this example returns the result as an XML document instead of as a standard rowset. The root parameter identifies the single top-level element. The FOR XML clause is covered in more detail in the next section *Using the FOR XML Clause to Retrieve Data.*

- Specify templates directly in the URL. Templates are valid XML documents containing one or more SQL statements. The templates allow you to put together data to form a valid XML document, which is not necessarily the case when queries are specified directly in the URL. For example, you could use the following to retrieve data using a template query:

```
http://Chicago/nwind?template=<ROOT+xmlns:sql="urn:schemas-microsoft-
com:xml-sql"><sql:query>SELECT+*+FROM+Customers+FOR+XML+AUTO</
sql:query></ROOT>
```

- Specify template files in the URL. Writing long SQL queries at the URL can be cumbersome. In addition, browsers may have limitations on the amount of text that can be entered in the URL. To avoid these problems, templates can be written and stored in a file. A template is a valid XML document containing one or more SQL statements and XPath queries. You can specify a template file directly in a URL, for example:

```
http://Chicago/nwind/TemplateVirtualName/templatefile.xml
```

- In this example, TemplateVirtualName is the virtual name of a template type that is created using the IIS Virtual Directory Management for SQL Server utility. Template files also enhance security by removing the details of database queries from the user. By storing the template file in the virtual root directory (or its subdirectories) where the database is registered, security can be enforced by removing the URL query-processing service on the virtual root and leaving only the SQL Server XML ISAPI to process the files and return the result set.

- Write XPath queries against the annotated XML-Data Reduced (XDR) schemas (also referred to as mapping schemas). Writing XPath queries against the mapping schemas is conceptually similar to creating views using the CREATE VIEW statement and writing SQL queries against them, for example:

```
http://Chicago/nwind/SchemaVirtualName/schemafile.xml/Customer
[@CustomerID="ALFKI"]
```

- In this example, SchemaVirtualName is the virtual name of a schema type that is created using the IIS Virtual Directory Management for SQL Server utility. Customer[@CustomerID="ALFKI"] is the XPath query executed against the schemafile.xml specified in the URL.

- Specify database objects directly in the URL. The database objects, such as tables and views, can be specified as part of the URL, and an XPath can be specified against the database object, for example:

```
http://Chicago/nwind/dbobjectVirtualName/XpathQuery
```

- In this example, dbobjectVirtualName is the virtual name of a dbobject type that is created using IIS Virtual Directory Management for SQL Server utility.

- Create XML Documents and Document Fragments. When you execute a template or a query with the root parameter, the result is a full XML document with a single top-level element. For example, the following URL executes a template. Following the example URL, an example template is provided with a description of its core components.

```
http://IISServer/VirtualRoot/TemplateVirutalName/MyTemplate.xml
```

This is a sample template file (MyTemplate.xml):

```
<ROOT xmlns:sql="urn:schemas-microsoft-com:xml-sql">
    <sql:query>
      SELECT  *
      FROM    Customers
      FOR XML AUTO
    </sql:query>
</ROOT>
```

The <ROOT> tag in the template provides the single top-level element for the resulting XML document. The queries can be specified directly in the URL. In this case, the <ROOT> parameter specifies the top-level element of the document returned:

```
http://Chicago/VirtualRoot?sql=SELECT * FROM Customers FOR XML
AUTO?root=root
```

If you write the same query without the <ROOT> parameter, an XML document fragment (an XML document without the single top-level element) is returned. This fragment has no header information. For example, this URL returns a document fragment:

```
http://Chicago/VirtualRoot?sql=SELECT * FROM Customers FOR XML AUTO
```

The byte-order mark identifying the document encoding is returned when you request an XML document. A *byte-order mark* is a standard sequence of bytes identifying the encoding type of the XML document. The XML parsers use this byte-order mark to determine the document encoding (such as Unicode). For example the byte-order mark Oxff,—0xfe identifies the document as Unicode. By default, the parser assumes the UTF-8 as the document encoding. The byte-order mark is not returned when you request an XML fragment, because the byte-order mark belongs to the XML document header, which is missing in the XML fragment.

Using the FOR XML Clause to Retrieve Data

You can execute SQL queries against existing relational databases to return a result as an XML document rather than as a standard rowset. To retrieve the data as an XML document, use the FOR XML clause. The following example uses the FOR XML clause to retrieve data from a database called Northwind:

```
USE Northwind
SELECT CustomerID, CompanyName
FROM Customers
ORDER BY CustomerID
FOR XML AUTO, ELEMENTS
```

The previous example uses the AUTO and ELEMENTS keywords. When retrieving data using the FOR XML clause, you will need to use the following syntax. The following sections outline the components of this syntax:

```
FOR XML {RAW | AUTO | EXPLICIT} [, XMLDATA] [, ELEMENTS][, BINARY
BASE64]
```

RAW, AUTO, and EXPLICIT Modes

The FOR XML clause must specify one of the following XML modes: RAW, AUTO, or EXPLICIT. The XML mode determines the shape of the XML result set. The XML mode is in effect only for the execution of the query for which it is set.

RAW Mode

RAW mode transforms each row in the query result set into an XML element. Each column value that is not NULL is mapped to an attribute of the XML element in which the attribute name is the same as the column name.

The BINARY BASE64 option (discussed further in the next section *Optional Keywords with FOR XML Clause*) must be specified in the query to return the binary data in base64-encoded format. In RAW mode, retrieving binary data without specifying the BINARY BASE64 option results in an error.

When an XML-Data schema (also discussed in the next section) is requested, the schema, declared as a namespace, appears at the beginning of the data. In the result, the schema namespace reference is repeated for every top-level element.

AUTO Mode

AUTO mode returns query results as nested XML elements. Each table in the FROM clause, from which at least one column is listed in the SELECT clause, is represented as an XML element. The columns listed in the SELECT clause are mapped to the appropriate attribute of the element. When the ELEMENTS option is specified (see the next section), the table columns are mapped to subelements instead of attributes. By default, AUTO mode maps the table columns to XML attributes.

A table name maps to the XML element name. A column name maps to an attribute name or a subelement of the table XML element name when the ELEMENTS option is specified in the query.

The hierarchy (nesting of the elements) in the result set is based on the order of tables identified by the columns that are specified in the SELECT clause; therefore, the order in which column names are specified in the SELECT clause is significant.

The tables are identified and nested in the order in which the column names are listed in the SELECT clause. The first, leftmost table identified forms the top element in the resulting XML document. The second leftmost table (identified by columns in the SELECT statement) forms a subelement within the top element (and so on).

If a column name listed in the SELECT clause is from a table that is already identified by a previously specified column in the SELECT clause, the column is added as an attribute (or as a subelement if the ELEMENTS option is specified) of the element already created instead of opening a new hierarchy (adding a new subelement for that table). This creates a single hierarchichal structure of elements and subelements rather than several hierarchies. For example, if you were retrieving the FirstName, LastName, and Address columns from the customers table, the customers table would be an XML element. Each of the columns (FirstName, LastName, and Address) retrieved from the table would be mapped to an attribute corresponding to its purpose. If the ELEMENTS option is used, then each of the columns retrieved would be a subelement of the customers table element.

EXPLICIT Mode

In EXPLICIT mode, the query writer controls the shape of the XML document returned by the execution of the query. The query must be written in a specific way so that the additional information about the expected nesting is explicitly specified as part of the query. When you specify EXPLICIT mode, you must assume the responsibility for ensuring that the generated XML is well-formed and valid (in the case of an XML-Data schema).

The BINARY BASE64 option must be specified in the query to return the binary data in base64-encoded format. In EXPLICIT mode (similar to RAW mode), retrieving binary data without specifying the BINARY BASE64 option results in an error.

Optional Keywords with FOR XML Clause

The following keywords can be used as optional components of the FOR XML clause. Each of these keywords helps control the way that the data is retrieved. The following list identifies each of the options:

The XMLDATA keyword specifies that an XML-Data schema should be returned.   The schema is added to the document as an inline schema. The primary purpose for specifying XMLDATA in a query is to receive XML data type information that can be used where data types are necessary (for example, when handling numeric expressions). Otherwise, everything in an XML document is a textual string. Generating an XML-Data schema is an overhead on the server, is likely to affect performance, and should be used only when data types are needed. If the database column from which values are retrieved is of the type sql_variant, there is no data type information in the XML-Data schema. If a given query designates different XML elements with the same name, XMLDATA might produce an invalid XML-Data schema. This will happen if element-name collisions and data type names are not resolved. (You might have two elements with the same name but different data types.)

The ELEMENTS option is used to return the requested columns as subelements.   Otherwise, they are mapped to XML attributes. This option is supported in AUTO mode only.

If the BINARY BASE64 option is specified, any binary data returned by the query is represented in base64-encoded format.   To retrieve binary data using RAW and EXPLICIT mode, you must specify this option. In AUTO mode, binary data is returned as a reference by default.

Best Practices

- Use Windows Authentication when setting up a virtual directory to allow Windows 2000 Active Directory to authenticate the user if you want the user to log on.

- If you want the user to access the data anonymously, define the account that IIS uses to connect to SQL Server. You should use a Windows Account, and you should also choose to Enable Windows Account Synchronization.

- Configure XML support only on the servers that need to be accessed via XML options. You should not configure XML support for servers that you don't want to be accessible to the users through HTTP.

- Use the FOR XML clause to retrieve data in XML format through a SELECT statement.

APPENDIX
B

Third-Party SQL Server Security Management Tools

SQL Server ships with most of the tools and features you need to effectively manage security. As with most products, several tools have been created to enhance your ability to view, manage, and report on the security of your SQL Servers. This appendix explains a couple of tools that you can use to help with your administration of SQL Server. Two types of tools are available to assist specifically with security administration: auditing tools and log analyzer utilities.

The *auditing tools* extend the built-in features for auditing. In addition to extra features, most of the auditing tools make the configuration and reporting of audit information easy and readable. SQL Server default auditing is functional, but in many cases it is not easy. An effective tool can save you valuable time in finding appropriate information about audited events.

Log analyzer tools are used to view and control the transaction log of a SQL Server database. As referenced in Chapter 13, "Managing Current Connections," by default you cannot view the data that is currently in your transaction log. A third-party tool can be used to view this current activity. The real benefit of these tools is found in the control you gain after the fact.

Most of the security options presented in this book assist you with preventing events from occurring. A good log analyzer can help you erase things that have already occurred. You can back out of changes and events that should not have been performed in the first place.

This appendix introduces a couple of third-party products you can use to manage the security of SQL Server. The first section describes the purpose and functionality of OmniAudit, an auditing tool released by Krell Technologies. The appendix then introduces the Log Explorer product released by Lumigent.

Omni Audit

OmniAudit allows you to automatically and transparently track changes to any column of any table in your Microsoft SQL Server 7.0 or 2000 databases. OmniAudit not only captures before and after values for each changed column, but also identifies the following information for you:

- The user who made the change
- The date and time a record was changed
- The computer that requested the modification to the table
- The application that performed the change

You have complete control over the tables and columns to audit. After you configure a table for auditing, OmniAudit automatically generates triggers to maintain an audit trail of all inserts, updates, and deletes made against that data. Even though auditing of this nature is available in SQL Server, you are required to create and manage the triggers as described in Chapter 14, "Creating an Audit Policy." This product can save you hours in configuring the auditing parameters.

This section describes the changes that are made to SQL Server by the OmniAudit software, discusses the steps you need to take to get started with the product, and then explains how to find more information.

OmniAudit and SQL Server

When you install OmniAudit, you should expect some changes to the dynamics of your SQL Server environment. OmniAudit tracks changes that are made to your system. To provide this feature, the program has to have a means of knowing when a change has been made to your tables and columns. Additionally, OmniAudit allows you to view the details of the modifications that have been made. This information has to be stored in

SQL Server to allow you to retrieve the information for reporting and analysis purposes. The two following modifications are made to the SQL Server architecture.

Triggers are added to the table you want to audit. The triggers are assigned to the actions you would like to audit. For instance, if you want to audit INSERT and DELETE operations, then OmniAudit adds triggers for INSERT and DELETE actions. As you add more tables and columns to be audited, OmniAudit adds an equivalent number of triggers to your tables. You should only configure the necessary amount of auditing. As triggers get added to your database, the performance of your modification statements will slow down.

NOTE Triggers are events that automatically execute every time a row in a given table is inserted, updated, or deleted. OmniAudit's triggers are specially built to examine the columns you've selected to audit in that table to determine if the data in that column has been changed.

Tables are added to store the audited information. The information that is stored about each record that is being audited is referred to as *Audit log data.* Audit log data is stored within tables created by Omni-Audit. These tables can be installed in the database being audited or in a different database on the same server. These tables can be queried via SQL Server or other data access tools. OmniAudit also provides a companion application—Audit Log Viewer—which makes it easy for you to sift through audit log records. You can filter and sort the audit log by audited table and audited column as well as date and time, user, application, and so forth. The following items are stored about each record that is audited:

- The user who made the change
- The date and time of the change
- The name of the application that was used to make the change
- The name of the computer the application was running on

Getting Started

OmniAudit is made up of two primary components: the Audit Manager and the Audit Log Viewer. The Audit Manager is used to configure your auditing requirements. The Audit Log Viewer is used to view the auditing data. It allows you to filter the data to easily find the information that you are looking for.

Installing the product on your system is a short process involving downloading approximately 6 MB of files. After the product is installed you are ready to start your auditing process. Before you start the configuration, you should know the following items:

- The database you want to audit.
- The tables or columns of the tables that you want to audit.
- The action you would like to audit. The product gives you the option to audit Inserts, Updates, and Deletes for a table.

The configuration of Auditing is broken down into several steps. You will be required to perform the following actions:

- Set up audit
- Build log tables
- Build triggers
- Purge log data (optional)
- Uninstall auditing (optional)

The first step is the Audit setup. At this phase you are configuring the system for auditing and you are choosing the tables, columns, and actions you want to audit. To perform the Audit setup, you should perform the following steps:

1. Open Audit Manager from the OmniAudit program group.
2. You are prompted with a connection dialogue box. Enter your connection information and click OK. The Audit Manager dialogue box appears as shown in Figure B.1.
3. From the database drop-down box, select the database you would like to audit.
4. Click Yes to create the Audit setup tables required to install auditing.
5. The Audit Setup dialogue box appears as shown in Figure B.2. Select the tables and actions you would like to audit.
6. You are now prepared to Build the Log Files. Leave the Audit Manager open to perform the additional required phases of the configuration.

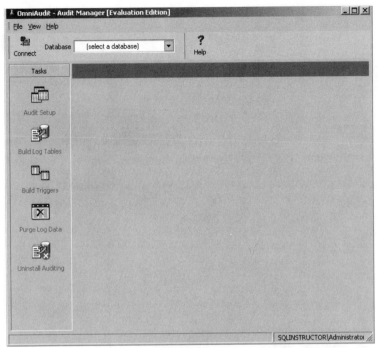

Figure B.1   Configure the database you would like to audit using the Audit Manager dialogue box.

The second required step is building the log tables. The log tables store the log information. These are the tables that you will interact with to view the audited events. To build the log tables, you should perform the following steps:

1. From Audit Manager, click the Build Log Tables button to bring up the Build Log Tables dialogue box as shown in Figure B.3.

2. Click the Build Audit Log Tables button.

3. Click OK after the Log Tables are successfully built.

4. Leave Audit Manager open to perform the final phase of the configuration.

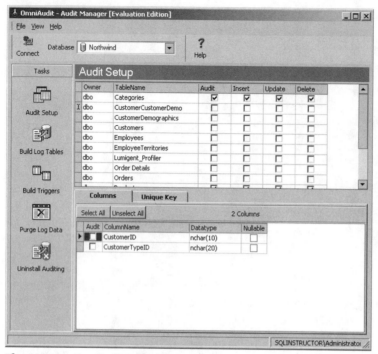

Figure B.2   Use Audit Setup in the Audit Manager dialogue box to configure the actions you would like to audit in each table of your database.

Finally, you need to build the triggers necessary to track the changes in the database. The syntax for creating the triggers is automatically created on the tables that you want to audit. To build the triggers, you should perform the following steps:

1. From Audit Manager, click the Build Triggers button.

2. Click OK to close the message box confirming that the triggers have been built.

After you have configured auditing, you can optionally purge the log data and uninstall auditing. You can use the Purge Log Data feature to help keep your Audit Log Tables small and manageable. The Uninstall Auditing feature is used to remove the settings you have configured.

The Audit Log Viewer tool is used to view the auditing information you have captured. The tool can be used to filter the data so that you can view the information that has been captured.

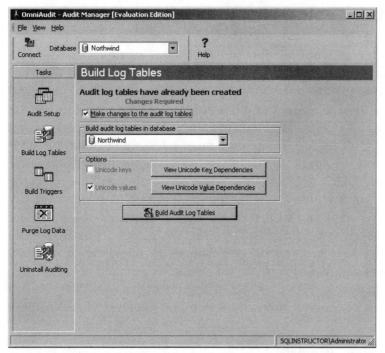

Figure B.3 Use Build Log Tables in the Audit Manager dialogue box to store details of each audited event.

More Information

OmniAudit is a completely server-side solution that requires no modifications to client software. As such, it works automatically for any client software used to change the contents of a table, including vendor tools such as Enterprise Manager and Query Analyzer, as well as all commercial or proprietary software that your databases are supporting.

OmniAudit was created by Krell Laboratories, which specializes in database development software for Microsoft SQL Server. You can find out more information about this product, download a free 30-day trial copy, and purchase a license to the software at Krell Labs Web site located at www.krell-software.com.

Lumigent Log Explorer

Log Explorer offers rich and flexible transaction browsing capabilities. By interpreting the database transaction log, where SQL Server records every operation that changes the database, Log Explorer gives you the historical information you need to figure out the problems and how to fix them.

Using Log Explorer's flexible filtering capabilities, you can review precisely the activity of interest, filtered by time, table, application, or other attributes. The row revision history feature lets you drill down on the data changes to a particular row over time. The row transaction history shows which operations made those changes. Log Explorer's virtual log capability lets you review current and historical log data together seamlessly, even for changes that occurred before Log Explorer was installed. Log Explorer's real-time monitoring lets you observe changes to the database as they occur. The data export facility lets you save selected changed data to a SQL Server table or to a file in HTML, XML, or text format, from which you can generate a variety of reports. You can use the Log Explorer to perform the following actions:

- Browse the transaction log
- Reconstruct past state
- Locate user and program activity
- Verify program behavior and identify program errors
- Trace program interactions, timing effects, and deadlock situations
- Correlate your application behavior with the actions of other system components

This tool can be helpful in finding past events and then reversing them without having to erase everything else that has occurred on the database.

Getting Started

Because the Log Explorer works primarily off the database transaction log, there is little modification within SQL Server. This product does not require alterations to the schema of the tables and databases you are viewing. After installation you will want to have the following information available to begin using the Log Explorer:

- The database log you would like to view.

- Whether you want to view the current log information or information from a log backup.

- If you select a log backup, you need to know the location where the log was backed up.

- If you are trying to restore a modification or a deleted object, you will need to have as much information as possible about the object that changed and the time that it most likely occurred.

To start using the Log Explorer, you should perform the following steps:

1. Open the Log Explorer from the Lumigent program group.

2. Enter your connection information for the server you want to monitor and click Connect. This opens the Lumigent Log Explorer dialogue box shown in Figure B.4.

3. Click the Attach Log File option.

4. Select the Database you want to view and whether you want to view the online log or a backup. Click Attach to attach the log.

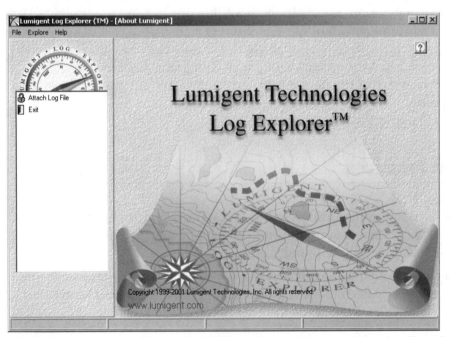

Figure B.4   The Lumigent Log Explorer allows you to attach an existing log file and view the current detail.

After you have attached a log file, you can use the functions of the utility to browse the data and make your changes. These functions can include the following items.

- Restore truncated or dropped tables
- Undo or redo user transactions
- Browse current log information
- Export the log records to SQL Server tables
- Execute a SQL Script

To get details on how to implement each of the previously mentioned functions, you should refer to the Help files that are shipped with the Log Explorer product.

More Information

The Log Explorer can be used as a stand-alone product or it can be an enterprisewide solution. You will need to evaluate the number of users that need to use the product and the number of servers that the users need to view.

You can get more information about this product at the Lumigent Web site, www.lumigent.com. Lumigent offers a free, 30-day trial copy of the Log Explorer as well as several testimonials of the product. Additionally, Lumigent has done an excellent job of citing case studies as examples of how their product can be used. The cost is low, and the first time you need the product to back out of changes or review application and user errors you will appreciate the product.

Best Practices

- Evaluate your auditing needs. If you need to enhance the auditing of your current system, you may want to consider an additional product to help with the process.
- Start evaluating a couple of log analyzer tools. They are invaluable when you need to reverse an action or recover a deleted object.

Answers to Review Questions

This appendix gathers all of the review questions at the end of each of the book's chapters in one place and provides answers for them. In some cases, your own answers may vary slightly from the answers provided in this appendix.

Chapter 1: Introducing SQL Server Security

1. Why is security critical to application design?

   A critical part of application design is determining the requirements of the system and users who will be accessing the database. The application design should include the following types of security concerns:

   - The required level of auditing.

   - The method in which users will connect to SQL Server (Windows Authentication versus SQL Server Authentication).

   - The permissions that users will require to the database objects.

- The types of statements that will be run to perform the work against SQL Server. The primary issue here is whether or not stored procedures will be used for data access and manipulation.

2. What are the advantages to Windows Authentication over SQL Server Authentication?

   - The user authentication process is encrypted.
   - Groups can be allowed access to SQL Server to simplify SQL Login management.
   - Users don't have to maintain multiple accounts. They use the same account for both SQL Server access and Windows domain access.

3. Why would you need to implement SQL logins?

   Logins are the objects that allow access to SQL Server. Without a valid login, a user cannot connect to SQL Server.

4. What is the purpose of a role?

   Roles are used to group database users. You can give a role permissions just as you would a user. Roles are an easy way to assign permissions to multiple users.

5. Who should own all database objects?

   The DBO.

6. What are the advantages of using stored procedures?

   Stored procedures increase performance, offer security, and supply a consistent application framework that can be used to standardize error messages and increase code reusability.

7. Why would you use an application role?

   Application roles can isolate one application from another. They are beneficial in restricting access for a database to an application instead of a specific user.

8. What are Data Transformation Services (DTS)?

   Data Transformation Services is the set of tools and services supplied with SQL Server that are used to transfer data.

9. What are the primary concerns of replication security?

   Replication security is controlled primarily through the configuration of the SQL Server Agent service account. If this is configured properly on all servers involved in replication, the administration of replication security should be minimal.

10. What is the SQL Profiler tool?

   SQL Profiler captures the events occurring within SQL Server. It can be very beneficial for auditing server activity and security access.

Chapter 2: Designing a Successful Security Model

1. Why do you need a test server?

   A test server should be implemented with a security model that is identical to that of the production server. The test server provides a layer between the development server and the production server. You will be able to test your applications for security concerns prior to deploying them to the production server. This increases the likelihood of a successful deployment to production.

2. Why is it important that the test and production server have a matching security configuration?

   If they have a matching security model, you will be able to resolve all security-related issues before the application is deployed to production.

3. What is the purpose of the Clustering service?

   The Clustering service is used to create a fault-tolerant data storage solution. If a server goes down, the Clustering service can failover and move the responsibilities for processing an application to another server.

4. As a DBA, why is it important to know the role of each database and application?

   Your troubleshooting skills will be enhanced if you know the purpose of the database and application. It is also helpful if you review the Transact-SQL statements that are used for access to your databases.

5. Why would you use multiple instances of SQL Server on a single server?

   Multiple instances of SQL Server can be used to isolate one application from another. Each instance of SQL Server has its own SQL Server and SQL Server Agent services. Each instance also has its own security model. You can deploy multiple applications on a single computer and isolate them as though they were installed on separate machines.

6. What is the difference between the Enterprise Edition of SQL Server and the Standard Edition of SQL Server?

   The Enterprise Edition of SQL Server provides the following security-related advantages over the Standard Edition of SQL Server:

   - Clustering services
   - Log shipping
   - Federated Database Servers (Distributed Partitioned Views)

7. Why is documentation of your security design so important?

   Documentition is esential to ensure that everyone who is using SQL Server understands the core of your security design. It will help ensure that applications that are purchased or created adhere to the current requirements.

Chapter 3: Exploring Initial Security Parameters

1. What is the purpose of the SQL Server Agent service?

   The SQL Server Agent service handles the SQL Server automation processes. The automation processes include jobs, operators, alerts, and e-mail integration for notification status of events.

2. What is a service account?

   A service account is a Windows account that a Windows service uses for its startup process. The account is also used as the security credentials for the service. For SQL Server you should have a service account for the SQL Server service and the SQL Server Agent service. In most cases, these two services use the same account.

3. Why should you use a domain user account for your service account?

By using a domain account for your service account, you can use the identical account for all servers that are running SQL Server.

4. What is the purpose of a server group in Enterprise Manager?

A server group organizes the servers you have registered in Enterprise Manager.

5. What permissions are required in order to install a SQL Server instance?

To install SQL Server you must be a member of the local administrators group.

6. Why would you want to create multiple instances of SQL Server on a single machine?

Multiple instances of SQL Server can be used to isolate one application from another. Each instance of SQL Server has its own SQL Server and SQL Server Agent services. Each instance also has its own security model. You can deploy multiple applications on a single computer and isolate them as though they have been installed on separate machines.

7. What is the purpose of the SQL Server service?

The SQL Server service handles all data interaction and query processing. If the SQL Server service is stopped, you do not have access to your SQL Server.

Chapter 4: Establishing Login Security

1. What are the advantages to Windows Authentication over SQL Authentication?
   - The user authentication process is encrypted.
   - Groups can be allowed access to SQL Server to simplify SQL Login management.
   - The users don't have to maintain multiple accounts. They use the same account for both SQL Server access and Windows domain access.

2. Why would you need to use SQL Authentication?

You need SQL Authentication if you do not require a login to the Windows domain or if a third-party vendor's application uses SQL Authentication.

3. What is the difference between Kerberos and Windows NT LAN Manager (NTLM)?

Kerberos is the authentication standard implemented with Windows 2000. It allows for mutual authentication and a more secure transmission of the authentication and authorization processes. Windows NT LAN Manager (NTLM) is supported for backward compatibility.

4. What is impersonation?

Impersonation is the process of SQL Server passing the security credentials of a user to another service or application on behalf of the user.

5. What levels of encryption are available with SQL Server 2000?

- Secure Sockets Layer (SSL) provides a network level of encryption.
- The WITH ENCRYPTION option provides an object level of encryption.

6. What is the difference between the public role and the guest account?

All database users are automatically members of the public role for that database. The guest account is used for individuals who have a server login but do not have a user account for a given database.

7. Why should you avoid the use of the SA account?

Each administrator should have an individual account to allow for auditing of the server administration functions. If all administrators use the SA account, you would not be able to track individual actions.

8. Under what circumstances should you create user-defined roles?

You should use database roles to group database users for the simplification of permissions management.

Chapter 5: Managing Object Security

1. What is the difference between implied and object permissions?

    An implied permission is one that is given because you're a member of a role that already has been given permission to perform an action. An object permission is one that is explicitly granted to an object in SQL Server.

2. Why is it best to avoid broken ownership chains?

    SQL Server has to check permissions every time the ownership chain is broken. This results in increased overhead for query processing and permission administration.

3. How can you create an object with the owner being the DBO?

    You can create an object owned by the DBO through one of two methods. The first option is through membership in the system administrator's role. When a member of the system administrator's role creates objects, the default ownership is DBO. The second option is through the db_owner database role. Members of this role can specify DBO as the owner during the CREATE statement.

4. If an object was created with an owner other than the DBO, how can it be changed?

    You can use the sp_changeobjectowner stored procedure to change the current object owner to the DBO.

5. What is the difference between a REVOKE and a DENY?

    REVOKE removes a previously assigned permission. DENY prevents the permission from being assigned.

6. Where are permissions stored in SQL Server?

    Object permissions are stored in their respective database. The sysprotects table is used to store the permissions for the objects of a database.

7. What is the WITH GRANT OPTION? When is it appropriate?

   The WITH GRANT OPTION allows the user who has been assigned a permission to give the permission to another user. It is rarely appropriate and should be used only in environments where permissions management is distributed to multiple users.

8. When should you use the AS option?

   The AS option should be used when you want to allow a user to assume an identity of another user or role.

Chapter 6: Designing Application Security

1. What are the benefits of using stored procedures?

   Stored procedures increase performance, provide a standard for your programming framework, and simplify security management.

2. When should you use views?

   Views are appropriate for restricting the data that is accessed by a user or group of users. They are especially useful in ad hoc query environments.

3. What are the differences between application roles and standard database roles?

   Application roles are invoked by an application. Standard database roles contain users and are tied back to the users' identity.

4. How do you invoke an application role?

   You invoke an application role by executing the sp_setapprole stored procedure.

5. Why is it important to use the ALTER statements?

   ALTER statements preserve the permissions of the object.

6. What are the methods of viewing the original syntax used to create a stored procedure?

   You can view the original syntax by either using Enterprise Manager or the sp_helptext stored procedure.

7. Why should all objects be owned by the DBO?

All objects should be owned by the DBO to prevent broken owner-ship chains. Using the DBO can help minimize permission management in SQL Server.

Chapter 7: Implementing Front-End Application Security

1. What additional security options can be supplied from the Server Network Library Utility?

Secure Sockets Layer (SSL) and the SQL Server port number for the server are configured through the Server Network Library Utility.

2. Why would you ever have to configure the NWLink IPX/SPX Net-Library?

You would configure the NWLink IPX/IPS Net-Library if you are in a Novell network that uses IPX/SPX as its network protocol. Keep in mind that in most cases Novell networks are also run over the TCP/IP network protocol, and this network library would not be necessary.

3. What is the advantage of using OLE DB rather than ODBC?

Using OLE DB rather than ODBC is beneficial when you have an ODBC driver and don't have an OLE DB provider for the data source you are connecting to. By using OLE DB rather than ODBC, you have the ability to use ADO as your data access method regardless of the driver used to access the data source.

Chapter 8: Understanding Microsoft's Enterprise Development Strategy

1. List the three logical services an application performs and briefly describe their roles in an application.

 - User services—The visual user interface responsible for collecting information from and presenting information to the user.

- Business services—Application logic that ensures the way an organization conducts business is properly abstracted in the application. These business rules are typically at the core of an application's purpose.

- Data services—Application logic responsible for data integrity and the storage and retrieval of data.

2. Briefly define tiers and services. Compare and contrast the roles of each in application development.

   The application services, reviewed in the preceding question, are the logical services an application provides that are conceptually placed in tiers, or layers. Both the services model and tiers are logical constructs to aid in the design of client/server applications. While services are units of work that may be combined in any manner, tiers permit the separation of one type of service from another, thus facilitating ease of maintenance and scalability.

3. Define the client/server architecture and discuss the considerations in choosing a two-tier or three-tier application model.

   Client/server applications represent the separation of application services from one another. Two-tier client/server applications typically separate the user interface from an underlying database. In three-tier architectures, all application services—user, business, and data—are conceptually separated into their respective tiers. While three-tier applications add an additional tier to your application, which increases complexity and can impede performance, they permit the conservation of scarce resources. For example, without a three-tier architecture you could not enable database connection pooling, which is typically the most significant constraint in the growth of two-tier applications.

4. Discuss the security issues inherent in multitier, distributed applications.

   Multitier, distributed applications are segmented by their very nature. The parts and pieces of the application are literally strewn across the enterprise landscape. The security issues seem endless. Where should security be implemented? Should security mechanisms be placed at the database or in the shared business components? Perhaps the client application should carry these mechanisms, or maybe they should be implemented throughout the application.

5. Describe how COM+ addresses these security issues.

   In COM+ applications, users are mapped to the application functionality they require through roles. Data security, on the other hand, involves authorizing the COM+ applications access to databases or other COM+ applications. Each COM+ application is assigned an identity or role that SQL Server or another COM+ application uses to authenticate the requester and, if appropriate, grant access.

6. Since connection pooling requires database logins to be identical, describe how you would implement a security model that would permit this feature.

   When configured to run as the interactive user, a COM+ application assumes the identity of the user invoking the component. If the particular COM component accesses SQL Server, each request will require a separate connection, since the user logins will be different. However, if the COM+ application is configured to execute under a specific identity, it will automatically initiate a system logon using that specified user account. This logon context, as with most logged-in users, may create objects, launch applications, and connect to databases. Since the user logins will always be identical, the connections to SQL Server can be pooled, thus conserving one of the most precious database resources.

Chapter 9: Introducing the SQL Server Agent Service

1. What is the purpose of the proxy account?

   The proxy account is used for the security context when a job is owned by a nonsysadmin and it contains steps that are either operating system commands or ActiveX scripts.

2. Why is job ownership important?

   Job ownership defines the security context of the job steps.

3. What is a multiserver job?

   Multiserver jobs are used to execute a job that has steps that affect multiple servers. They are also useful for consolidating job administration to a single server.

4. What is a MAPI profile and how is it created?

   The MAPI profile is the set of email services for a user. You can create a profile by using the Mail and Fax icon in the Windows Control Panel.

5. What is the difference between snapshot and transactional replication?

   Snapshot is a full copy of the data from one server to another. Transaction replication is an incremental or change-only copy of the data from one server to another.

6. What are the purposes of the Replication Agents?

   Replication Agents are similar to services. They act on behalf of the user or, in this case, SQL Server to perform an action. Agents only run when their service is required, so the ongoing overhead is less than a normal service.

Chapter 10: Managing Distributed Data Security

1. What is a linked server?

   A linked server provides the connection information for an external data source. A linked server allows for a single query or transaction to run against multiple servers.

2. Why should I consider the log-shipping feature?

   Log-shipping can be used to provide a fault-tolerant solution. Your data is automatically backed up on one server and then copied and restored on another.

3. What are the necessary steps for promoting a secondary server to a primary server when using log shipping?

   ■ Ensure that the secondary server has the database maintenance plan. If the secondary or destination server does not know about the process, it will not ship logs to anyone else.

   ■ Create a DTS package that transfers the logins from the current primary server to the secondary server.

- Perform the role change to set the current secondary server as the current primary server.

4. Which of the distributed database features depend on the Enterprise Edition of Microsoft's SQL Server 2000?

   - Log shipping

   - Federated Database Servers (distributed partitioned views)

5. What is horizontal partitioning?

   Horizontal partitioning is used to control the rows that are included in the data access. This is typically implemented with a WHERE clause that adds a criterion to limit the amount of data that satisfies the query.

6. What is the purpose of a distributed partitioned view?

   A distributed partitioned view treats databases from multiple servers as though they were one object. This is an effective way to scale a single point of user interaction across multiple servers. You can distribute your data across multiple servers while allowing the users to interact with a single point. This feature allows for databases to scale past the point of a single server.

7. How can Federated Database Servers slow down performance?

   Federated Database Servers take advantage of distributed partitioned views. The data that the view is accessing is distributed across multiple servers. Retrieval of data may have to come from multiple servers, which can be slower than accessing data from a single location.

8. How could Federated Database Servers be used to speed up query and application performance?

   If you have a very large amount of data, it may not be feasible to store it on a single server. For very large databases you may want to consider this feature to separate the processing of the queries for data access. The bottom line is that if you don't have a large amount of data, Federated Database Servers will most likely slow down performance. It is recommended that you only implement Federated Database Servers for very large databases.

Chapter 11: Managing Data Transformation Services

1. What are the core components of a DTS package?
   - Connections
   - Tasks
   - Workflow
   - Global variables

2. What are the management tools available to create and modify packages?
   - Import/Export Wizard
   - DTS Designer

3. What are the security concerns related to scheduling packages as SQL Server jobs?

   DTS packages are executed with the DTSRun command. This command is an operating system command, not a Transact-SQL command. You need to ensure that the job ownership is configured correctly so the DTSRun command can execute properly.

4. Where can packages be stored?
   - SQL Server (Local Repository in the MSDB database)
   - Meta Data Services
   - COM structured storage file
   - Visual Basic file

5. What is the advantage to storing packages as a Visual Basic file?

   When you store packages in a Visual Basic file, you can open the DTS package in Visual Basic and program against the package.

Chapter 12: Exploring Analysis Services Security

1. What are the core components of Analysis Server?

   The core components of Analysis Server are OLAP Services and Data mining.

2. What is the purpose of data mining?

   Data mining permits you to find relationships between the entities in your data that are not easily visible.

3. What is the difference between a data warehouse and OLAP?

   A data warehouse is the storage of summarized data that can be used for analysis purposes. OLAP is the extraction of data warehouse data to a multidimensional object that can be used to extend analysis and increase query performance.

4. Why should you use a star schema instead of a snowflake schema when designing your data warehouse?

   The star schema is a model where all dimension tables are implemented a single step away from the fact table, meaning that all dimension tables are directly related to the fact table. This decreases the number of necessary joins, which in turn increases query performance. The snowflake schema implements dimension tables that are related to other dimension tables and not always directly to the fact table. This model increases the number of joins necessary and decreases overall query performance.

5. Why is the grain of the fact table so important?

   The grain of the fact table defines the basic level of detail. Your OLAP analysis can reach a level deeper than the grain defined in the fact table.

6. What is a cube?

   A cube is a multidimensional data storage object that is used to analyze data in a summarized and aggregated fashion.

7. What are the differences between ROLAP and MOLAP?

   ROLAP stores all of the data and aggregations of a cube in a relational format within the underlying tables. MOLAP stores the data and aggregations of the cube in a multidimensional format.

8. Why should you consider partitions when designing a cube?

   Partitions can be used to store your cube in multiple places to facilitate faster retrieval of data. For example, most systems have historical data mixed in with the current or most used data. You could partition the historical data and store it as ROLAP to save drive space. You could take the most used data and store it as MOLAP to speed up access to the data.

9. At what levels can roles be defined in Analysis Server?

Cubes and Dimensions.

10. What are the advantages and disadvantages of dimension-level and cell-level security?

Cell-level security is much more granular and can be more complicated in determining the appropriate cell in which to set security. But because they are more granular you have a greater level of control.

Chapter 13: Managing Current Connections

1. What is the difference between the logical view and the physical view of the transaction log?

The logical view is the sequential view of the transactions that are written to SQL Server. Each transaction is first written to the log, and then the transactions are written to the physical file in a sequential fashion. The physical view is the operating system files that make up the transaction log, which are represented with an .LDF file extension.

2. What is the purpose of the checkpoint process?

The checkpoint process ensures that committed transactions are written from the transaction log file to the data files. The checkpoint process also keeps track of the transactions that have been written from the transaction log to the database files.

3. When does a checkpoint occur?

- Automatically
- Anytime the CHECKPOINT keyword is used
- At startup and shutdown of the SQL Server service
- Anytime schema changes are made to the database
- During the backup process

4. When is it appropriate to use the Bulk-Logged Recovery model?

   You should use the Bulk-Logged Recovery model when you are using the BCP utility or the BULK INSERT statement to load data into the database. The Bulk-Logged Recovery model helps to manage your transaction log size and speed up the data transformation process.

5. Why should you avoid the Simple Recovery model on a production server?

   The full transactional record is not kept in the transaction log. Transactions are overwritten (truncated) after they have been successfully written to the database files. You will not be able to back up the transaction log or use the transaction log for recovery purposes. You will have to rely solely on your last full or differential backup.

6. What are deadlocks? How can you help avoid them?

   A deadlock is when two processes collide, meaning that one action is waiting for the data that another action is already holding and vice versa. You can help to avoid deadlocks by accessing tables in the same order in every statement.

7. Give some examples of the information that can be viewed in the Current Activity window of Enterprise Manager.

   - Currently connected users
   - Current locks in use by system and user processes
   - The SQL statement of a given process
   - Processes that can be killed

Chapter 14: Creating an Audit Policy

1. What is C2-Mode security?

   The U.S. National Security Agency (NSA) created the C2 security rating as a standard to rate the security of a server. This standard evaluates all levels of software from the application to the operating system. SQL Server 2000 has been certified as C2-compliant. For your server to meet the C2-compliant security level, you must have C2-Mode auditing enabled.

2. What is a SQL Trace?

    A SQL Trace captures SQL events performed against the SQL Server. It is similar to a recorder. The trace results can be stored in either a file or a SQL Server table.

3. What are the SQL Profiler templates used for?

    Profiler templates are used to predefine some common events and columns that will be tracked and reported by a trace. The templates give you a starting point to work from.

4. What templates are geared toward security auditing?

    - The SQLProfilerStandard template tracks general information regarding the execution of batches and stored procedures. These settings help track connections and execution times.

    - The SQLProfilerTSQL template tracks all Transact-SQL statements and the order in which they were executed. This is beneficial in tracking statements that are performing security violations.

    - The SQLProfilerTSQL_Replay template tracks details about each Transact-SQL statement issued in sufficient detail to be used for replay in SQL Query Analyzer. Use this preconfigured template as a starting point for capturing data to replay for testing or security analysis.

5. How can you limit the amount of information captured by SQL Profiler?

    Filters can be used to limit the amount of data captured by SQL Server. You can use filters to limit data by application, database, user, or NTusername.

6. What is the purpose of the username() function?

    The function returns the current user who is performing an action. This function can be invaluable in storing auditing information in your tables. You can use this as a default value for a column in a table to build auditing information into your table schema.

Chapter 15: Managing Internet Security

1. What is the difference between a direct connection and one that first goes through a Web server?

   A direct connection is one that goes directly from the client machine to the SQL Server. A firewall must be configured to allow direct access to the server. A connection that goes through a Web server first connects to the Web server and executes a file or script that defines the connection information to the SQL Server. This extra layer often can slow the process down, but it can also simplify security management at the firewall and SQL Server level.

2. What is a native OLE DB provider?

   A native OLE DB provider is one that does not require an ODBC driver. The provider gives direct access to the data source. This is a very fast way to connect to the data.

3. What is the default port that SQL Server is listening on?

   1433 is the default port for the first instance of SQL Server installed on a machine.

4. What is the purpose of the Web Assistant Wizard?

   The Web Assistant Wizard generates HTML files from the results of a query. The wizard helps you take the results of a query and make them available on the Web.

5. What is the difference between a trusted connection and a standard connection to SQL Server?

   A trusted connection uses the current user's Windows login credentials for the connection to the server. A standard connection uses SQL Server authentication and requires a username and password.

6. What is Java Database Connectivity (JDBC)?

   Java Database Connectivity (JDBC) is based on the industry standard ODBC.

Index